50 Questions Executiv[es] Ask About Technology Projects

Is My Goldfish Happy, Sick Or Just Ugly?

A Practical Approach to Maximizing Value and Minimizing Risk On Technology Projects

Gary K. Dearing

DEDICATION

This book is dedicated to my family.

To my long-suffering wife and life companion Tammy who is a professor of Computer Science and Business and having worked with me on some projects can testify to my intensity and focus on project goals. She is an amazing intelligent woman who has more people skills than I could ever hope to have.

To our son Victor the highly talented up and coming computer game maker and aspiring technical director who is responsible for the lights dimming across mid-Ohio every time he starts working in our basement.

To our daughter Ashton, a talented competitive equestrian since age 6 who just received her MBA, is starting a promising career in The Business world, and who doesn't acknowledge it yet, but who definitely got The Project Manager gene from me and will someday be managing large projects.

They have all put up with my travels, long work hours, attempts to project manage our family, and listening to hours of conference calls from around the world. They are the reason I do this.

TABLE OF CONTENTS

ACKNOWLEDGMENTS

I would like to acknowledge a few of the many people that have had a great influence on my life and career.

Donald Rushing, my Boy Scout Master who many decades ago helped me to understand the value of accountability, planning, organization, and leadership.

Sid Hill, my college debate coach who taught me the value of research, thorough preparation, clear communications and negotiation skills.

Sgt Koucher, from Louisiana who failed during US Army basic training to turn me into an infantryman, but succeeded in teaching me what it meant to be an officer and a leader.

Jim Willburn, who introduced me to the world of rescuing runaway projects and taught me how projects really work and how to work with Executives to make them successful

Nagesh Sridharan of General Motors, the epitome of a business oriented technology Executive who taught me what makes large organizations work and how to deal with global initiatives

Jonathan Dove of Hewlett Packard, the most capable Technology Evangelist I have ever met. He can quickly understand what a company needs to become successful and then assemble a team of experts to successfully deliver it. He continues to teach me what it takes to make projects successful in the corporate environment.

I would also like to acknowledge Chris Starr, Andy Secrest, Brian Blust, Bryan Beske, Eugene Rider, Maj Gary Ross, Lowell Witter, Ralph Adams, and many other people who have helped me over the years

WHY YOU NEED THIS BOOK?

"No one can feel as helpless as the owner of a sick goldfish" - Frank McKinney Hubbard

ANOTHER PROJECT; ANOTHER LATE NIGHT

I am writing this introduction about 2:00AM on a Saturday night in the middle of a large project deployment. We have had many challenges during The Project and there were times when it looked like success would elude us. However, through hard work of a team of skilled and highly motivated people, we are going to be successful. There are many reasons for this success including good planning, good leadership, great Project Team with high morale, extensive testing, close attention to resolving project issues and risks, and a good strategy for dealing with post-deployment issues.

However, there is another factor that I believe has been integral to the success of this project, active Executive participation. We have had very active participation from both Business and Technical Executives throughout this project. They are continuously involved in The Project asking relevant questions in meetings and one-on-one discussions and provide assistance when required. They have allowed us the freedom to work without micro-management while ensuring we were making steady progress.

This level of active Executive participation is the exception rather than the rule in most Technology Projects. I believe that if Executives can be made comfortable in interacting with Project Teams, they will better engage with The Project Team to provide the oversight and assistance essential to project success. That thought is the catalyst behind this book. I believe we should assist Executives in forming questions to ask their Project Team and help them understand the importance of these questions. This will greatly increase the chances that a project will be successful.

I have been managing Technology Projects for over 30 years ranging from small 3 person Project Teams to very large 300 person teams. During much of this career, I have been assigned projects that were in some type of serious trouble. Many were well over budget, more had missed key dates, and quite a few resulted in systems that just didn't work as anticipated. Some of the worst had problems in all of these areas. I have been able to get quite a few of these projects back on track, while the best recommendation for others was to shut The Project down before any more time and money was wasted. A small number even ended up in litigation over performance of vendors. This book will provide Executives assistance in starting relevant conversations with The Project Team on important issues many project face. I can never cover all areas of concern with Technology Projects in a single book, but this is good start on the most relevant issues.

A PERVASIVE FEELING OF HELPLESSNESS

In discussing troubled projects with Boards of Directors, CEOs, Executives and Managers, one of the most common threads I encounter is how helpless these key Business Leaders feel in trying to oversee large Technology Projects. More than a few Executives have told me that they thought The Project was in trouble, but were assured by The Project Team (Business and Technical) that everything was on track right up to the day they announced massive cost/schedule over-runs. One very frustrated CEO of a large regional financial 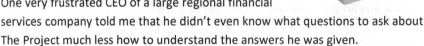 services company told me that he didn't even know what questions to ask about The Project much less how to understand the answers he was given.

2

That has stuck with me over the years and is another impetus for this book. Manufacturing Executives are usually comfortable going down on the shop floor and examining the machinery, financial Executives are very comfortable with financial statements and spreadsheet analysis, but neither has any idea how to manage a computer project or even to provide oversight to The Project. They desperately need and want to provide oversight, but feel helpless in understanding how to do so.

WHICH BRINGS US BACK TO THE SICK GOLDFISH METAPHOR

Frank McKinney Hubbard an American cartoonist in the early 1900s coined a phrase "no one can feel as helpless as the owner of a sick goldfish". I think applies nicely to the feelings of many Executives towards their Technology Projects.

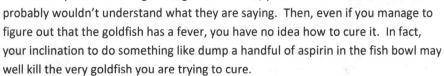

You cannot ask a goldfish what is wrong because you do not speak the "goldfish language" and even if you miraculously were able to get the goldfish to talk, you probably wouldn't understand what they are saying. Then, even if you manage to figure out that the goldfish has a fever, you have no idea how to cure it. In fact, your inclination to do something like dump a handful of aspirin in the fish bowl may well kill the very goldfish you are trying to cure.

So it is with Technology Projects. Technical personnel have their own very foreign language talking about routers, switches, Agile, The Cloud, foreign keys, LDAP, etc., etc. It is difficult for most Executives to discuss technology issues because they do not understand this esoteric lingo. To make matters worse, many technology personnel revel in the complexity and confusion and are reluctant to spend the time explaining things in a way that non-technical personnel can understand. They usually prefer to be left alone to make all the technical decisions out what they view as the prying eyes of the Executives.

Business and Project Management personnel on projects are sometimes little better in sharing information about The Project in a clear and forthright manner.

Once a project has been approved and funding has been provided Project Teams usually prefer to be left alone to make all decisions without involvement of the Executives that provided the funding and support. I understand this feeling because I have been there more than once myself. But leaving a project without what I call the "adult supervision" of an Executive is never a good idea except on the smallest of projects.

YOU NEED TO BE INVOLVED IN TECHNOLOGY PROJECTS

Involvement of Executives in Technology Projects should not be viewed as a distraction. Rather, one of the most basic responsibilities of Management is to protect company interests. If you find a need to slow a project down or change under-performing team members, you are just doing your job.
As an Executive, you are expected to keep the big picture in mind always looking out for the long and short-term health of The Business. A successful Technology Project can greatly improve company prospects and an un-successful one can literally shutter the doors.

This book will provide you the information you need to be able to better engage The Project Team on Technology Projects and by doing so dramatically increase the odds of a successful outcome. By providing you a range of relevant questions to ask yourself and The Project Team, you should be better prepared to perform your critical oversight function.

YOU DON'T WANT AN OBAMACARE WEBSITE LEVEL PROJECT NIGHTMARE

There is no clearer poster child for a failed Technology Project than the October 1, 2013 launch of the Affordable Care Act (also known as Obamacare) website named HealthCare.Gov. Ignoring the real and feigned emotions surrounding the law itself, as a Technology Project, it was an abject failure played out to a global audience.

Unless you are oblivious to the news (which is unlikely if you are reading this), the website that was launched with much fanfare quickly encountered devastating problems such as slow performance, a hard to use interface, incorrect/missing data, poor help desk training, poor code quality, lack of adequate testing, etc. The combination of these issues made the site fundamentally unusable for several months.

There have been volumes written about the failure, numerous congressional hearings have grilled everyone remotely involved in The Project, and there is as much disinformation as there is information about the system from people on both sides of the political spectrum pushing their agenda. Even determining how much was spent on The Project is open to disagreement with estimates running from $90M to $640M+.

In the end, the system was salvaged by assembling a team of people with deep expertise in the technologies being used, listening to their counsel, setting realistic timelines, and providing strong Executive support and oversight. These are the themes I carry through this book. While there were serious technology and
business missteps that the companies and individuals involved should be deeply ashamed of, I believe that fundamentally this was a failure of Executive oversight. There was inadequate contract oversight, failure of Executives to monitor status/progress, failure of Executives to understand and deal with issues and risks, and failure of the Executives to seek help when clearly help was required.

The most inexcusable failure in Executive oversight was deciding to deploy the system into production knowing that it had never been adequately tested and knowing that what little end to end testing had been done had to be aborted due to the system crashing under even small number of users. I see the decision by Government Executives to go forward with deployment in the face of this information as at the same time being indefensible and totally understandable given organizational dynamics. There was obviously a push from the top to implement the system on time or the proverbial heads would roll. The Executives who made the decision to deploy had not been involved with The Project on a deep enough level to understand the technology and risks, so they made a poor but politically expedient solution to go ahead with the deployment and deal with the consequences afterwards. Unfortunately they had so little understanding of the technology and the ramifications of what they were doing that they failed to predict the intensity of the failure.

It is easy to dismiss this as being the Federal Government where politics dictate everything. However, your business is probably little different than this, albeit on a smaller scale. I have seen strong-willed Business Executives direct Project Teams to deploy systems even in the face of significant defects and problems with predictable resulting failure. I strongly believe Executives always think they are looking out for the needs of the organization in the decisions they make. The problem is that since they do not understand Technology Projects, they don't know the questions to ask The Project Team, and subsequently do not get involved enough to make good decisions. The goal of the book is to address this by helping you as an Executive understand enough about key project issues to help The Project be successful and to make good project-related decisions.

WHY DO TECHNOLOGY PROJECTS FAIL?

"It's fine to celebrate success but it is more important to heed the lessons of failure" - Bill Gates

DEFINITION OF PROJECT FAILURE

There are numerous definitions of project failure many of which involve cost metrics like performance against budget, on-time delivery, achieving planned business benefits, etc. I believe that all of these are good indicators of project success/failure. However, I think it is most accurate to say that a project is a failure if the Stakeholders think it is a failure.

Many people look for absolute objective measures of success, but those are sometimes misleading and elusive. I have seen projects that were significantly over budget and/or deployed late, but were considered great successes because of high systems quality and usability.

Conversely, I have seen projects that were on-time and on-budget but were still deemed dismal failures due to functionality, performance and usability issues. This is why I think it most appropriate to define success/failure in terms of the perceptions of the Stakeholders. They are the people that authorized the investment of corporate resources for The Project. If they are satisfied with how that investment turned out then The Project is a success. If not, it is a failure.

PROJECT FAILURE STATISTICS

Gartner (formerly called the Gartner Group) is one of the world's leading information technology research and advisory companies. They are well-respect for their numerous studies of technology issues and provide their research and advisor services to most large companies. In 2012, they published a study looking at project success/ failure rates for projects using input from member organizations in five countries. The high level results are shown below which in summary shows that about one quarter of Technology Projects are considered failures with that number rising as project size increases.

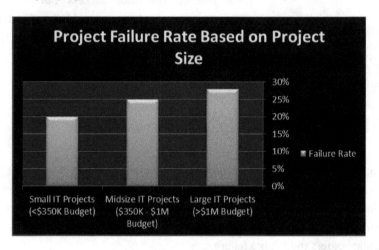

Source Gartner June 2012

EXAMPLES OF FAILED PROJECTS

The statistics above provide a sobering view of the chances of a project failure. The simple graphic however, does not begin to fully represent how bad a failure can be. There are so many major Technology Project failures that there is a section of the Calleam Consulting Ltd website dedicated to tracking them (**http://calleam.com/WTPF/?page_id=3**) called the "Catalogue of Catastrophe".

Here are some of the more significant Technology Project failures that are readily available on the Internet. The names of the involved consulting companies and software vendors have intentionally not been included since not surprisingly they dispute many of the "facts" in these project failures. It is worth noting however that several of these projects ended in litigation and or repayment of consulting fees paid to the vendors involved. If you are curious about the details of any of these projects, they are easy enough to find on the Internet.

Federal Bureau of Investigation Virtual File System- In the aftermath of the 9/11 attacks on the World Trade Center and the Pentagon, the FBI requested and was given $500M to replace aging information systems that prevented the Bureau from piecing together information that might have prevented this tragedy. It is hard to imagine a Technology Project of more importance and one which was under intense scrutiny throughout its lifecycle. Ultimately this project was deemed a total failure and was never implemented. There were a number of investigations as to the reason for this failure including Congressional Hearings. The consensus was that this expensive failure on a desperately needed project was more a failure of the FBI to manage The Project and the technology contractors than it was a failure of the contractor to build the system.

US Air Force Enterprise Resource Planning System 2005- Designated the Expeditionary Combat Support System, this project that was budgeted at $628M was cancelled after 7 years and expenditure of ~$1B due to failure to develop operational requirements, lack of a master schedule, strategy changes, and contractor performance.

New York City's CityTime Project 2011- A major new Payroll system for New York City was budgeted originally at $63M and grew to a reported $760M before being canceled due to massive cost overruns and indictment of contractor personnel on charges of kickbacks.

Avon Enterprise Resource Planning System 2012- System implementation was so bad that significant numbers of sales representatives left the company and Avon was required to write down approximately $100M in costs since the system was not able to be used as intended.

KMart IT Systems Modernization 2000- KMart launched a project to modernize major systems by linking sales, logistics, supply, and marketing systems so that they could better compete with their rival Wal-Mart. After 18 months and the expenditure of $130M of the proposed $1.4B budget, the company abandoned The Project, wrote off the costs and declared bankruptcy 4 months later.

Federal Aviation Administration Advanced Automation System 1996- This critical system designed to modernize the nation's air traffic control system was cancelled after numerous delays and cost overruns resulting the General Accounting Office determining that $1.5B of the $2.5B budget was completely wasted.

United Kingdom Stock Exchange Taurus System 1980's- This project is included just to show that technology failures are not limited to the United States and to show that this is not just a recent problem. This project was budgeted at 75M British pounds in the 1980's. After many years of work The Project was canceled due to scope creep and massive cost overruns. The system was never completed.

TOP TEN CAUSES OF PROJECT FAILURE

The Projects listed above failed for a variety of differing reasons. There are some themes that I have seen repeatedly in studying project failures. Below are my list of ten of the most common reasons for failure in alphabetic order.

1. **Boiling the Ocean-** The more ambitious a project is and the longer it is expected to take, the more likely it is to be a failure. Trying to do too much at one time is about as likely to be successful as you would be trying to "boil the ocean" at one time. Large projects should be broken into a series of discrete smaller efforts that can each be more effectively managed. Additionally dividing a large effort into a series of smaller efforts often has a side benefit of delivering at least some of the desired functionality to The Business much faster than if you have to wait until the entire project is complete.

2. **Commitment**- Many failures are caused by lack of user and/or Stakeholder engagement. There is often a lack of commitment manifesting itself in poor project participation, ambiguous sponsorship, and failure of Executives to engage to help resolve problems. Projects should listen to the wisdom of Yoda from Star Wars who spoke about commitment as "Try not. Do... or do not. There is no try." This is the type of commitment needed to have a successful project.

3. **Giving Up**- Quite a few projects never get completed simply because The Project Team and or the company loses the will to continue. Project can be long and hard endeavors that quickly lose their initial luster. Sometimes people get so tired of a project that at the next sign of trouble, they surrender and stop The Project. This is unfortunate, for if you can keep morale high and the team motivated, most of these projects could have been completed successfully.

4. **Leadership**- All but the smallest of projects need strong project leadership in order to be successful. However, complex projects too often are assigned Project Managers that do not have the experience and expertise to lead them through the complexity.

   There is a huge difference in Project Management and Project Leadership. Especially as projects become large and more complex, make sure that you put someone in charge that can lead The Project not just administer it.

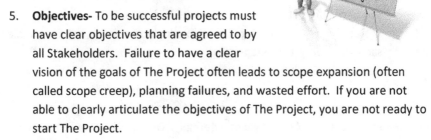

5. **Objectives**- To be successful projects must have clear objectives that are agreed to by all Stakeholders. Failure to have a clear vision of the goals of The Project often leads to scope expansion (often called scope creep), planning failures, and wasted effort. If you are not able to clearly articulate the objectives of The Project, you are not ready to start The Project.

6. **Organizational Politics and Intrigue**- A dark secret that most organizations don't like to discuss is that some Executives and organizational units thrive

on intense intra-company competition and political intrigue. While it is sometimes hard for people to understand and believe, it is not uncommon for internal and/or external groups within your company to be actively rooting for project failure.

Failure of **your** project could free up money and other resources for a project **they** are championing. It could also give their company a chance to sell more services to you, or may even facilitate their part of the organization getting more power and prestige. Be vigilant of efforts of people and organizations to subvert your project. I know some people will scoff at this notion, but I guarantee that in a few minutes of discussion, you will be able identify people that would not be displeased if your project were to fail.

7. **Project Management 101**- Projects are complex endeavors with lots of moving parts that must be managed. To accomplish this, there are basic Project Management functions that must be performed well including- scheduling, planning, resource management, risk and issue management, communications, estimating and reporting. If you are deficient in these basic areas, you are unlikely to have a successful project. This is analogous to a losing coach stating that they need to focus more on "blocking and tackling" after a loss or close game

8. .**Quality Issues-** Poor quality has a cascading impact from the point of defect until the end of The Project. In particular, business requirements that are poorly written, incomplete, incorrect, or suffer from other quality issues make it very unlikely that you will have a successful project. Quality needs to be built into The Project from the beginning. Set an expectation that it is not acceptable to sacrifice quality just to report a deliverable as complete.

9. **Resources-** Getting the right number and mix of personnel on a project is vital to project success. People are not interchangeable in most cases, so you need to fully define resource needs and then work to find those resources either internally or externally. One of the more common reasons for resource problems on projects occurs when an organization attempts to satisfy all Business Units by launching too many projects at the

same time. This usually results in resource conflicts and inefficiency as resources are shuffled between projects.

10. **Scope**- The first step in a project is to define the scope of what The Projects is intended to accomplish. It is important that business requirements that help define the scope be well written, accurate, and agreed to by all Stakeholders. After approval, the Requirements Document become the "contract" between The Business and IT groups for The Project and they should only be modified after the impact of the change is analyzed. Change of scope is a very common cause of cost overruns and late deployments.

The various questions in this book are designed to address each of these ten common areas of failure plus many more. By engaging your Project Team in open discussions on the various areas of concern the chances of your project ending up on the "Catalog of Catastrophe" list is greatly reduced.

EXECUTIVE ROLES IN TECHNOLOGY PROJECTS

"My role is to try to remove the impediments to entrepreneurs' chance to succeed. It's about improving The Business climate to give people a better chance of succeeding."- Jerry Moran, US Senator

AN EXECUTIVE NIGHTMARE

It is not uncommon for Executives to allocate a budget to a project, announce its launch, and then lose track of it until it either deploys successfully or it becomes a problem. This benign neglect is usually not due to lack of interest in The Project, but is more related to the thousands of other things Executives have to concern themselves with on a daily basis. Most of the Executives that I know are routinely faced with more work than they could ever accomplish, an email box filled with emails that cannot possibly all be read and responded to, and a business to run profitably.

Into the mix comes this Technology Project. It could be the installation of some new piece of hardware to solve a problem you didn't even know you had, or a new application system that somehow is going to make The Business more productive, or even just a project that just takes the data you already have and through some magic makes the entire company understand The Business better.

In any case, The Project is likely expensive, will take a long time, and will divert quite a few people from their normal jobs to support it. However, The Business

14

Managers and the geeks in IT are very excited about it so you push back on the budget size a few times like all Executives are supposed to do and then approve The Project amid claims of massive financial benefits when The Project is deployed. After you approve The Project, you get buried in the new product launches and new pricing discussions and forget about The Project except during monthly budget reviews.

Then one day, the CEO comes into your office and asks why the company's largest and most profitable customer is in their office complaining about late shipments, incorrect pricing on invoices, and problems ordering products on the company website. It is only then you recall the note you saw a few weeks ago announcing deployment of the system you approved over a year ago. You had almost forgotten about The Project except for periodically wondering what you were going to get for your multi-million dollar investment and now you were given the answer to that question directly from your boss.

What you need in situations like this is a basic understanding of how Technology Projects work and help in focusing on key project issue. These allow you to provide the management oversight that projects require. This book is designed to provide both that focus and overview of projects.

WHAT ARE KEY EXECUTIVE PROJECT ROLES

Before we explore these areas though, it is important to understand the various roles that an Executive is expected to perform on a project. The roles may vary somewhat based on project size and complexity, but the 8 key project roles in this chapter apply to most Technology Projects. These roles may all be assigned to one Executive or may be split across a number of Executives. You want to ensure that someone with Executive authority is involved in each of these key project areas. Also, you want to ensure that these roles are formalized in project organizational charts and project communications so that everyone is aware of who will be providing the Executive oversight.

BUDGET OVERSIGHT ROLE

Perhaps the most obvious role of Executives on projects is to manage the provision of financial resources to The Project Team. This is also a role that most Executives are very familiar and comfortable with. All Executives that are part of The Project should understand and support the initial project budget. The Budget Oversight Role of course does not end when The Project is approved. You will also want to ensure that at least one of the Executives involved in The Project is explicitly responsible to providing oversight of actual expenditures against the allocated budget.

The budget for a Technology Project should never be one single monolithic number. You want to ensure The Project Team divides the budget into categories (Software, Hardware, Consulting Services, Training, etc.) that are each separately budgeted and monitored. This budget granularity will give you greater insight into spending on The Project so that you can detect areas of concern much earlier than if you are just tracking against a single number. This is especially important on longer duration projects.

The related budget role on projects is dealing with inevitable cost variances. Costs may vary from the estimates because the scope of The Project has changed, because activities take longer than expected due to unexpected problems, or just because the original estimates were not very good. Regardless of the cause of the cost variances, the Executive in charge of the Budget Role will have to determine a course of action.

There are a number of chapters in this book having to do with budgets, costs, contingency, etc. that should be helpful in preventing and understanding budget problems.

STAFFING ROLE

Another valuable company resource that Executives will have to allocate to each Technology Project is internal staffing. All Technology Projects require at least some level of internal resources to accomplish and many require considerable internal personnel involvement. Executives in the involved areas will need to understand the resource requirements of The Project on their department and commit to supplying those resources.

Often projects require you to dedicate some of your most knowledgeable people that may already be overworked and who make a valuable day to day contribution to their Business Unit. If you are going to allocate these resources to The Project on a full or part time basis, there must be a plan for adjusting their current workload to accommodate their project involvement. Failure to provide needed internal personnel resources to a project is a common cause of projects not achieving time, cost, and functionality goals.

BUSINESS PRIORITY ROLE

Most business use some form of return on investment or value based process to determine if a project should be funded. However, it is not enough that a project have value to The Business in excess of its projected cost. To be successful, The Project needs to have sufficient priority to The Business to be a good use of resources. If The Project is not a sufficient business priority, it is unlikely to get The Business support, internal resources, and oversight it needs to be successful. The Executives on The Project need to agree that given the totality of everything else going on in the organization, this project is something worth pursuing. It is not enough for The Project to be important and worthwhile, it must be important enough to do **today**.

I am fond of using the term "straightening deck chairs on the Titanic". The White Star Line took great pride in the condition of the ship and undoubtedly had people dedicated to keeping the hundreds of deck chairs on the RMS Titanic in exact positions on the deck. This was important to the image that they portrayed to their passengers and a high priority on the ship. However at the point in time that the ship hit the iceberg and began to sink, there were obviously higher priorities to be considered than the condition of the deck chairs. Crew dedicated to straightening deck chairs presumably were re-directed to activities that were higher priority at that point in time.

This seems obvious, but is a mistake organizations make with Technology Projects. Regardless of how inefficient the warehouse system is, should you deploy a new upgrade at the same time you are launching a new project line? The Business Priority Role should focus on ensuring that at any point in time the organization is working on those projects that are most important to The Business currently. The converse side of deciding which projects are of sufficient priority to move forward is the need to make decisions on which projects and business activities will not be pursued.

One method of managing business priority that is used in many organizations is to have each Business Unit develop a prioritized list of all of The Projects they would like to work on in the coming year based on value to The Business, regulatory imperatives, operational needs etc. A cost/resource estimate is prepared for each project along with a projection of anticipated benefits is created to aid in the prioritization. Separately from the effort to agree on a priority list, the Company decides how much they intend to invest i

n Technology Projects in each of The Business Units. They then combine the two by drawing a line on The Project priority spreadsheet showing based on priority and available funding, which projects are to be funded. If The Project is above the line it gets funded. If The Project is below the line it does not get funded.

BUSINESS VALUE GUARDIAN ROLE

Technology Projects should only receive funding if their value to The Business exceeds the cost of The Project. I was working with one company where every year one of the managers proposed a project to automate the analysis of certain purchasing data. Currently, data for the analysis is assembled from a number of sources and manually entered into a spreadsheet each month resulting in trend graphs that were then distributed to various departments and managers.

While it was undeniable that the process could be improved through automation, doing so would be fairly expensive due to the need to accumulate data from several unique data sources into a common data repository and then create the necessary reports. To continue to do the task manually took one person less than half a day a month. Therefore even though The Project would have represented a business improvement, it would have taken many years to even begin to recoup the cost of automating the process so it was never funded.

One role of Executives is to make sure that only those projects that have value to The Business beyond their costs are funded. When you are evaluating The Business value of projects, keep in mind however that not all value is monetary and not all benefits can be easily quantified. I think that some companies spend too much effort trying to only fund projects that have monetary value that exceed monetary cost by a certain factor. There is also business value in improving customer experience on websites, satisfying legal requirements, improving system security, etc. The dollar benefit of these type of improvements are hard to define, but no less valuable to the company and its customers. The role of Executives is to judge the benefits of a project and decide which to pursue.

STEERING COMMITTEE MEMBER

All of the Executives involved in The Project plus others that are deemed beneficial to The Project should combine into a Steering Committee. Steering Committees as the name implies help guide The Project as it unfolds. They should meet once a month or so and perform a comprehensive review of The Project and its progress.

Understanding how difficult it is to coordinate the schedule of a number of very busy Executives, it is important to hold regular meetings and during those meetings focus on enabling project success.

When you are determining the composition of the Steering Committee make it clear to all potential members that if they become part of the Steering Committee they are making a time commitment to spend at least a modest amount of time on The Project each month. If they are unable to make the time commitment, there is really no value in having them serve on the Steering Committee regardless of their position in the company.

ISSUE RESOLUTION ROLE

Executives by the nature of their position, contacts, and personality usually have wide-ranging ability to cut through bureaucracy and get things done. When projects run into issues, The Project Team should attempt to resolve the issues themselves. However, if they are not successful in doing so in a reasonable amount of time, they should escalate the issues to the Executives for assistance.

Of course part of the role of an Executive is also to apply judgment as to the reasonableness of The Project Team's request. If you determine that the request is reasonable, then part of your role on The Project is to help resolve the issue.

However, if what they are asking is not reasonable in your opinion, you have a responsibility to stop the request from going forward. For example, if The Project Team wants to cancel production of paychecks this week to allow the Payroll Team to instead test the new system, you might urge them to seek another solution.

TEAM MOTIVATION ROLE

The Project Manager has primary responsibility for leading and motivating the team on a daily basis. However, one of the roles of Executives is to provide motivation and monitor morale for The Project Team. This is especially true when it comes to The Project leaders. Do not underestimate the value of an Executive showing up at a Project Meeting to tell people that they are doing a good job and helping people understand why their effort helps the company. Too often Executive focus on their legitimate and important role in pushing The Project Team to work faster and save money and neglect the importance of their motivational role

SOBER JUDGE ROLE

This is the role that The Project Team will like the least. A good Project Team usually gets very emotionally invested in The Project sometimes to the level that their judgment becomes clouded. They can begin to develop unrealistic expectations of their ability to fix problems and get The Project back on schedule. You want to be supportive of the team, provide all of the assistance you can and motivate them as much as is possible. However, you need to remain emotionally unattached to the results so that you can objectively understand where The Project is and what needs to be done.

Sometimes this means the deployment date needs to be changed, scope needs to be adjusted, key personnel need to be replaced or even The Project be canceled. The Executives need to be the "sober judge" that can remove all of the emotion from the decision and plot a course of action that is in the best interest of the company. In any case, this is a key role that the Executives on the Steering Committee must play when it is required.

HOW IS THIS BOOK ORGANIZED?

"Organizing is what you do before you do something, so that when you do it, it is not all mixed up". –
AA Milne (Winnie the Pooh)

GENERAL

The intent of this book is that it can be used both like a textbook and a reference book. If you read the book in from front to back like a textbook, it will give you a good overview of all major aspects of projects that are of special interests to Executives overseeing a Technology Project. As a reference book, you can scan the list of questions searching for areas of interest and concern.

SECTIONS

The book is divided into four sections each representing one of the key areas Executives should focus on. Within each of the four sections are a number of questions related to that area of interest.

At the beginning of each section is a list of the questions that will be addressed in this area for quick reference. Also, a complete list of all questions and their location in the book can be found in the Table of Contents

Major Book Sections

1. **Executive Oversight Questions-** This section of the book contains a series of questions that each Executive should ask themselves and the other Executives on The Project. These questions relate to why you are pursuing The Project, how important The Project is to you, project impacts, organizational impacts, etc.
2. **Business Questions-** This section of the book explore areas of importance to The Business side of the organization such as business requirements, customer impacts, sponsorship, data, process change, etc. The questions in this section are designed to help ensure that The Project is organized to maximize value to The Business and its customers while protecting The Business against unintended impacts.
3. **Project Management Questions-** Ensuring that The Project is well organized, staffed, and managed is one of the keys to project success. The questions in this section examine The Project management practices in a number of key areas.
4. **Technology Questions-** Explaining details of the wide variety of technologies in use today in an easy to understand way is far beyond the scope of this or any single book. The questions in this section deal not with the technical details, but rather focus on how technology is managed and planned for in a number of key areas to help you focus on specific technology areas.

23

QUESTION CHAPTERS

Each of the chapters covers a single question of importance to The Project. The chapters each have the same basic organization to make it easy to understand and find what you are looking for.

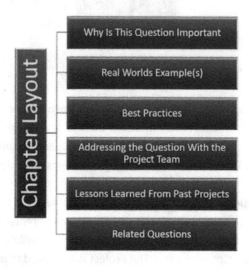

1. **Why is this question important?** - This section of each chapter explains why the question is important to project success. In many cases, this section contains a bulleted list showing various aspects of the question and areas that deserve special attention.

2. **Real World Example-** This area of each chapter presents a real example of where the principle described in this question was relevant to a project. These are examples from projects that either I or a close associate have been involved in. Some of the details have been slightly altered to make it difficult to identify the organizations involved, but the examples do represent how large projects unfold in the "real world".

Some of these examples are success stories representing how the concepts described in the chapter helped a project. Others represent a less successful outcome due to failures in the area under discussion. The intent of this book has always been to provide practical guidance. Looking at real world examples hopefully will drive home the importance of some of these areas of concern.

3. **Best Practices-** Projects can often be successful using any number of techniques or methodologies. However, in many areas, there are "best practices" that you should consider using. Your Project Team does not necessarily have to follow these best practices to be successful, but it is useful to understand these techniques. These lists of best practices are mine based on many years of working on projects and again represent a practical approach to managing projects.

4. **Addressing the question with The Project Team-** One of the complaints that I hear frequently from Managers and Executives is that they don't even know how to begin a discussion on issues related to Technology Projects. This potion of each chapter provides some thought starters that you can use to begin a dialog with your Project Office/Project Manager, Business Team, Information Technology Team, Steering Committee, etc. These are intended to be approaches to "break the ice" on various project related topics that you can use either in informal conversations and/or formal meetings. I have found that once you begin a dialog on a topic and show interest in it, it is much easier to engage the team.

5. **Lessons learned from past projects-** These are a bulleted list of suggestions based on my project experience and that of my friends and associates. Many of these represent what I think of as "places I have been lost in the past that I never want to get lost in again". It is not intended to be an all-encompassing list by any means. Rather, it is a list of important and practical suggestions that may be of help on your project.

6. **Related Questions-** The final section is a cross-reference to other chapters in the book that are related to this questions. They are included so you can refer to those chapters as needed

SECTION 1: WHAT EXECUTIVE OVERSIGHT QUESTIONS SHOULD YOU ASK?

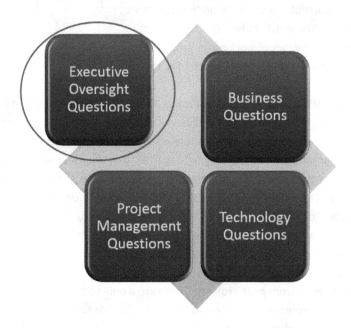

Much of this book focuses on things that you should discuss with your business, project management, and Technical Teams. However first you should focus on questions that you should ask yourself and your peers about The Project.

The Executive Team is responsible for protecting the interests of The Business as a whole and for ensuring that investments the company make in Technology Projects return value to The Business and are completed successfully. To accomplish this,

Section 1 Executive Oversight Questions

you must have a clear understand of how The Project fits into your business as a whole and reach a common agreement with the other Executives over its value to the organization.

This section focuses on the following questions you should address within the Executive Group.

1. Are The Project objectives clear to all?

2. How will the benefits of this project be achieved and verified?

3. What Is the impact if The Project fails?

4. How will I know if project status is being misrepresented?

5. Is there sufficient Executive oversight?

6. Are we ready to start this project?

7. What are key roles for project success?

8. Who would like this project to fail?

9. Am I sufficiently engaged in The Project?

10. What is the maximum amount of time and money I am prepared to invest in this project?

11. What will the post-deployment organization look like?

12. When should I ask for an outside review of he project?

t

1. ARE PROJECT OBJECTIVES CLEAR TO ALL?

"Objectives are not fate; they are direction. They are not commands; they are commitments. They do not determine the future; they are means to mobilize the resources and energies of The Business for the making of the future"- Peter Drucker

WHY IS THIS QUESTION IMPORTANT?

Objectives describe what a project is intended to accomplish. They put high level boundaries around The Project so that you understand what should be included within the scope of The Project and what is outside of the definition of The Project. By definition, a project should be considered closed when all of the objectives have been met.

Objectives should be concrete and specific, should be measurable, should be achievable, and should be realistically achievable. The Project objectives will be the basis for deriving the detailed requirements for The Project. An example of an objective might be to "Upgrade all Windows 2003 Servers to Windows 2012 by the end of June 2015 when Windows 2003 reaches official end of support life". Each project should have a small number of precise technical and/or business objectives defining what The Project is intended to accomplish.

The objectives are usually included in a document called Project Charter, Scope Statement, or even Project Brief depending on your organization. Regardless of the name, there should be a document formally approved by The Business and technical Stakeholders that includes The Project objectives.

It is important to have a common understanding of the final approved objectives of a project. Often during the conceptual discussion leading up to the approval and launch of a project, scope and objectives of project change significantly as budget, timing, benefits and other considerations are taken into account. What might start out as an objective to give every employee of the company a new iPad to access company information anywhere anytime might morph into providing iPads to just sales personnel in the outside sales organization. If an Executive only participated in the initial discussions but did not know the objectives had been refined, they may have an unrealistic view of what The Project will accomplish. Make sure that the final version of the objectives are documented and shared with all involved parties.

REAL WORLD EXAMPLE

A publishing company considered implementation of a new electronic publishing system that included automated creation of catalogs from a database. This was initially scheduled to be implemented prior to June of the following year. All of the key Executives supported and approved this objective and The Project was initiated. As estimates were received, it became obvious that project would require at least 6 months beyond the original date target to complete and would cost more than originally envisioned.

A few of the Executives got together and agreed to move forward anyway. However, there was never a formal Change Request created documenting this decision and not all involved parties were part of the decision process. As The Project progressed, the Executive in charge of catalog layout began to make organizational changes to support the new processes/systems. Over time this led to dismantling of the organization that previously had been responsible for manual layout of catalogs under the assumption that next year's catalog would use the new processes/systems.

By the time the disconnect was discovered, it was much later in the year than when manual catalog layout traditionally began and the catalog was not completed on time, cost more than usual to create, and resulted in significant internal company strife and finger pointing. Questions were also raised about the final cost of The Project with several Executives indicating that if they had understood what the real cost of The Project had become they would have insisted on a scope reduction to keep costs in line. All of this could have been avoided if a formal process of approving and changing project objectives had been in place and followed.

BEST PRACTICES

- Objectives should be clearly documented and formally approved by all Stakeholders in The Project.
- After approval, objectives should only be changed after the impact of those changes has been evaluated and the change has been approved by all Stakeholders.
- A good practice is to include the list of objectives in every project presentation so that all involved will be continually reminded of the approved project objectives.

ADDRESSING THE QUESTION WITH THE PROJECT TEAM

Project Manager - The Project Manager is responsible for ensuring that objectives are clearly defined and approved very early in The Project. To verify this, you can ask to see the approval documentation showing where the initial objectives were approved along the approvals for any subsequent changes.

Business Team- In discussions with The Business Team and the Stakeholders ask them what the objectives are so you can confirm that there is a shared sect of project objectives. You should also determine if there are people on The Business Team that understand the objectives but

30

don't agree with them. The reason for disagreement should be understood and taken into consideration even if there input cannot be incorporated into the current project.

 It is important that all people involved in The Project understand that even if they do not agree with the objectives, they will be expected to support them. Also ensure that the objectives have been cascaded to all Business Team members so that there is a common understanding of the official objectives of The Project.

Technical Team- It is not uncommon for the Technical Team to be so focused on the technology aspects of a project that they fail to take the time to understanding The Business objectives. Emphasize in your discussions with the Technical Lead, the importance of actively participating in discussions of objectives and the importance of cascading those objectives to all on The Project.

LESSONS LEARNED FROM PAST PROJECTS

- To prevent confusion, everyone of Project Team needs to understand both the technical and business objectives of The Project.
- Having one of the organization's senior Executives discuss The Project objectives and how it will help the organization with The Project Team is a great team motivator.
- As detailed scope and requirements are documented on a project, ensure that these are directly traceable to the approved project objectives. Any items that are identified that do not support the approved objectives should be eliminated from The Project or the objectives should be formally changed to encompass them. This is critical to ensure that The Project does not grow beyond its original purpose.
- Periodically, The Project Manager should ensure that the objectives are still valid and communicated to all on The Project Team.

31

Section 1 Executive Oversight Questions

- It is always a good idea to have an "elevator speech" version of The Project objectives handy so that you can succinctly explain your project to others. I was on one project where we were designing complex mathematical models to predict failure of critical components on US Navy Trident Submarines in order to establish maintenance cycle schedules. I always struggled with explaining this project to people until I heard our Program Director (who was an ex-Navy submarine Captain) describe it as "when the submarine goes down, we help make sure it can come back up". This made it easy to explain to my team how important our work was.

RELATED QUESTIONS

2. How will the benefits of this project be achieved and verified?

10. What is the maximum amount of time and money I am prepared to invest in this project?

15. Is there a holistic view of required business and technical changes?

19. Are all impacted Stakeholders actively involved in The Project?

20. Does The Business really support this project?

2. HOW WILL THE BENEFITS OF THIS PROJECT BE ACHIEVED AND VERIFIED?

"A benefit is estimated according to the mind of the giver". - Seneca

WHY IS THIS QUESTION IMPORTANT?

Projects should be authorized to proceed only if there is a clear benefit to the organization. These benefits can be quantitative such as cost saving or more qualitative in nature such as improving the customer experience.

For some projects like automating a manual invoicing process, The Business benefits are easy to articulate. For other projects like replacing old computer servers, they are more difficult to explain. But even technology centric projects have attached business benefits such as continuing to support business systems or perhaps decreasing maintenance costs. Sometimes the benefits may even address a mandatory legal or regulatory requirements or to satisfy an audit finding.

Regardless of the source, The Project should have clearly stated benefits to the organization that are understood by all. These benefits should be formally documented and approved by all Stakeholders. Additionally, the affected area of the organization must agree that if The Project successful implements the scope, the benefits are likely to be realized.

In many organizations, benefit estimates are the lies groups tell each other to get projects approved. There is often little basis to support the benefits estimate and little verification that the benefits were in fact achieved at the end of The Project.

A common method organizations use to justify projects is to state that we currently spend $50M per year making widgets and this project will increase efficiency by 2% so it will have benefits of $1M per year for the next 10 years or $10M in total benefits from a project cost of about$2.5M so benefits are 4 times the cost. Based on statements as simple as this, projects often get funded.

Total Cost Per Year Currently	$ 50,000,000
Times Percent Costs Will Be Reduced	2%
Cost Savings Per Year	$ 1,000,000
Times Expected Duration of Savings	10 Years
Total Project Savings	$10,000,000
Minus Project Cost	$2,500,000
Net Project Benefit	$7,500,000

Vague Benefit Calculation Example

This estimating example is flawed on many levels and should be actively challenged by the Executive Team. First, even if the organization spends $50M

34

Q2: How Will The Benefits Of This Project Be Achieved and Verified?

in costs, probably half or more are fixed costs that are likely unchangeable. Next the 2% estimate of improvement seems so small that it will often go unchallenged.

Failure to challenge project benefits is a mistake. You need to understand exactly **how** this savings will be realized. Will it be through personnel reduction, increased buying leverage, making better decisions because you have better information, etc.?

Instead, a better benefit statement might show that there are now 30 people processing invoices and after project deployment headcount will be reduced to 20 people starting in the year after deployment. This benefit can have real dollars assigned to it and most importantly achievement of the goal can be tracked after deployment to see if the organization actually realized The Projected benefits.

Number of Invoice Processors Currently	30
Number of Invoice Processors Post-Deployment	20
Net Headcount Reduction	10
Times Average Annual Savings Per Person	$100,000
Cost Savings Per Year	$1,000,000
Times Expected Duration of Savings	10 years
Total Savings From Project	$10,000,00
Minus Project Cost	$2,500,000
Net Project Benefit	$7,500,000

Better Benefit Calculation Example

This version of the estimate shows exactly **how** the savings will be achieved. Once you understand the thought behind the cost savings, it can be discussed and evaluated. It provides an opportunity for Managers and Executives to see the impact of The Project so that they can make an informed decision to approve it. Additionally, the proposed headcount savings provides a measurable way to judge whether The Project has met its goals or not. Especially for larger projects, it is important to spend time understanding exactly how the benefits are going to be achieved so that you can decide if The Project is justified.

Keep in mind that while every project should have a business benefit that does not necessarily mean that there is a fixed dollar benefit to every aspect of The Project. For instance while it is hard to assign a dollar value to making a system change mandated by financial accounting rule changes, there should be some perhaps non-quantifiable but nevertheless important benefit to keeping the CEO out of jail on a Sarbanes-Oxley or SEC violation.

REAL WORLD EXAMPLE

For years, the US Army had a program called Quick Return on Investment Program where with very minimal paperwork organizations could fairly easily get up to $50K in funding for small Technology Projects as long as your commander would sign off that The Project would have benefit of at least $150K in total over the next 3 years.

Under this program, I got funding for quite a few small projects over a 3 year period. Then the Army changed to program so that if you claimed $50K per year in benefits, there would immediately remove half of that ($25K) from your next year's budget and let you keep the other $25k per year in benefits for other uses. Predictably, the number of projects submitted across the command quickly dropped to almost none. It seems that if there was an impact of claiming benefits, groups were not nearly as willing to claim benefits of a project.

BEST PRACTICES

- Regardless of whether the benefit is tangible or intangible, it must be explainable. The Business and Technical Teams need to be able to articulate exactly what the benefits are and how The Project will help realize them.

Q2: How Will The Benefits Of This Project Be Achieved and Verified?

- Most organizations have sophisticated financial models used to evaluate investment decisions such as the decision to build a new plant or launch a new financial product. The processes are often formal and robust. However for various reasons such as lack of financial expertise within the IT organization, these process are often not applied to Technology Projects. You should consider using a formal financial modeling process to allow you to look at cost and benefit estimates over a period of time taking into account cost of money over time.

- Encourage people to be honest about benefits. While the industry trend is definitely towards identifying quantifiable benefits, sometime the intangible benefits are just as important. Many say that when Google changed to a very simple interface from your standard complex website, its usage soared making the company what it is today. The only stated benefit of the change was to "make the site easier to use" which is difficult to assign a hard dollar value. In many organizations today you would not be able to get funding for a project like that. Don't devalue the intangible benefits when deciding which projects to fund.

- Most organizations spend little effort on tracking project benefits after The Project has ended. Best practice is that you should track benefit achievement at least on larger projects. This will help you understand whether project benefits are being realistically forecast.

ADDRESSING THE QUESTION WITH THE PROJECT TEAM

Project Manager- The Project Manager should ensure that there is a robust process for estimating the value of project benefits for the organization. Ask The Project Manager to see documentation supporting the basis for the benefits being projected. Also ask to see the formal approval from the impacted Stakeholders indicating that they have reviewed and approved the estimated benefits.

Section 1 Executive Oversight Questions

Business Team- In discussions with The Business Team you should challenge the benefit estimates to gauge how comfortable The Business is with the estimates and how they were derived. The Business Leads/Stakeholders should be able to describe how they will verify the benefits are being achieved.

Information Technology Team- Ask the Technical Team if they are familiar with the benefits The Project has projected. They should be able to offer an opinion as to whether The Project deliverables are likely to help realize these benefits.

LESSONS LEARNED FROM PAST PROJECTS

- Benefits estimates should be challenged at least as strongly as cost estimates. If either are wrong you may make the wrong project decision.
- There is a trend in some companies to only fund projects that have a first year benefit of say 3 times The Project cost. This is basically a mandate to lie about your project benefits in order to get funding. Usually benefits do not even begin be realized until some period of time after deployment. To state that you will finish The Project and achieve massive benefits immediately in the first year happens only occasionally.
- I have seen Project Teams take the estimated cost and multiple by 3 or 4 to get the first year benefit estimate just so they can get The Project funded. In some cases, it even becomes a competition between Project Teams to see who can claim the biggest benefit estimate and capture funding. It is policies such as this which cause the illusion of projects having profound benefit to the organization when in reality the benefits may not be there. It is far better to have an honest estimate of the benefits.

Q2: How Will The Benefits Of This Project Be Achieved and Verified?

> If you want to be successful, you must
> respect one rule. NEVER LIE TO YOURSELF
>
> -Paulo Coelho

- It is not uncommon for the Technical Team to fail to take the time to understand The Business benefits claimed for a project. It is important to ensure that the system the Technical Team is building has the possibility of achieving the stated benefits.
- Likewise, even members of The Business Team are not always privy to the stated business benefits. It is important for everyone on The Project Team to have a good understand to ensure that benefits are achieved.
- If dollar benefits of a project are claimed, it is useful to have someone with financial background and organizational financial responsibilities be part of the approval process. Having someone like the Controller or Chief Financial Officer review the benefits is likely to improve the quality of the estimates and perhaps temper over enthusiastic benefits claims.

RELATED QUESTIONS

1. Are The Project objectives clear to all?

13. Does each documented requirement have real business value?

3. WHAT IS THE IMPACT IF THE PROJECT FAILS?

"Many of life's failures are people who did not realize how close they were to success when they gave up". - Thomas Edison

WHY IS THIS QUESTION IMPORTANT?

While every project should be important to your organization, the reality is that all projects are not of the same importance. Some projects are small in size and scope and the impact of failure is minimal other than lost time and money. Other projects are literally company killers. If The Project does not succeed, there is significant business disruption risk. Even though it is uncomfortable to discuss project failure with a Project Team, it is an important conversation since the answer to this question could impact the level of risk you are willing to tolerate, the amount of resources to dedicate to The Project, the amount of oversight required, etc.

Unless this is a technology-only project like a server replacement, this is a question best posed to The Business Team. A successful project may well move The Business forward significantly, while a failure could leave your organization in worse shape than it was before the start of The Project. To understand this, consider that for most projects, you are often diverting usually key personnel from their day to day work to spend time on The Project. This potentially creates a backlog of work caused by The Project so if The Project fails, you not only do not get the benefits of The Project, but also have a backlog of work to resolve. Additionally, you have probably spent significant amounts of money on The Project and may have chosen to defer other business initiatives.

Even more serious is when you believe a particular project is a "silver bullet". These are situations where The Project is seen as the only solution to a looming perhaps long-term business problem. We are not talking about situations where The Project will improve efficiency and save money. Rather we are talking about projects where if The Project fails we cannot bring our new $500M plant on-line for production or a project where we cannot sell any new mortgages after January 1st unless we have made these mandated system changes. Any project that is this important should be carefully monitored throughout its lifecycle.

It is important therefore to have a frank discussion with The Project Team about the impact of failure; the so called "worse-case scenario". This is sometimes an uncomfortable topic to broach with a Project Team that is fully engaged and focused on project success. However, it is a discussion that must occur and often results in concrete actions that make a project more likely to succeed.. It is important to emphasize to the team that you are not suggesting that The Project is going to fail, but rather than you want to understand what happens if it does fail.

REAL WORLD EXAMPLE

A large global manufacturing organization with plants around the world had a very aggressively timed project to consolidate systems world-wide into a single new data center. As part of this project, system hosting contracts with existing suppliers were given an end date when service would no longer be needed. When The Project began to fall behind schedule, a discussion was held as to the impact of being late (which in this case meant project failure).

The uncomfortable consensus was that given the criticality of the systems being migrated, project failure meant that the company would not be able to design, build, or sell a single unit of product after the date the existing hosting contracts expired and systems access was terminated. Just understanding this worse-case scenario brought additional resources to The Project, fostered faster decision making, and encouraged diverse teams to work together better to resolve issue resulting in a successful deployment.

BEST PRACTICES

- A written analysis of the impact of project failure should be prepared for all but the smallest of project. This analysis should be shared with both The Project Team and the Steering Committee/Stakeholders. Again, emphasize that you not assessing the chances of project failure, but rather are looking at the impact if it does fail.

- Failure can mean different things to different projects, so use the appropriate definition of failure in your analysis. In some cases, completion dates can be flexible while in others, the implementation date is unchangeable. Similarly, for some important projects, going over budget will upset the Stakeholders, but is not fatal to The Project. In other projects, the budget is absolute and exceeding the budget by any amount is considered a project failure. It is important to explore what a failure means in the context of the particulars of your project.

- Tailor project reporting, oversight, risk management, and resource to the impact of project failure to insure that potential failure points get the proper level of review and support.

ADDRESSING THE QUESTION WITH THE PROJECT TEAM

Project Manager- One of the key roles of The Project Manager is to identify and manage risk on projects. A conversation on the impact of project failure is a natural part of that role. You should discuss the impact of failure with The Project Manager and ensure that they are taking active on-going steps to identify and document risks in The Project Log and that they are taking appropriate steps to mitigate those risks.

Business Team- For most projects, discussion of The Business impacts of project failure is primarily a Business Team topic. You should foster an atmosphere where this discussion can take place in an open and honest way. The risk areas The Business Team identifies should be documented by The Project Manager and shared with all parties involved in The Project so that everyone understands the stakes involved.

Information Technology Team- If this is a technology only project, such as a server replacement, then the Technical Team should discuss the impact(s) if The Project is late or fails totally. As with The Business risks, contingency plans need to be discussed so that the team understands what is to be done if there is a complete or partial project failure.

Steering Committee- A key role of the Steering Committee is project oversight. Having a clear understanding of the impact of project failure is part of determining what level of project oversight is necessary. You should ensure that each member of the Steering Committee understands the impact of project failure.

LESSONS LEARNED FROM PAST PROJECTS

- It is difficult for some organizations to discuss the impact of project failure because they believe the mere fact you are discussing it indicates you think The Project is going to fail. That is absolutely not the case.
- The greater the impact if a project fails, the more closely you should monitor project risk, issues, and schedule.
- **Projects rarely fail all at once. They usually fail a little at a time and in post-mortem discussions, missed warning signs of the impending status are nearly always identified. Heed the warning signs, particularly if a project is struggling.**
- If a project is especially critical and you see that it is moving rapidly towards failure, do not delay considering radical changes such as new project leadership, scaled back scope, and addition of more resources. The longer

you delay implementing these type of changes to a project, the greater the risk that the remediation measures will not have time to have the desired impact on The Project.

- Sometimes the only way to lessen the impact of a project rapidly approaching failure is to kill The Project for now, regroup and re-launch The Project at a later date. This approach saves the money and resources that would have been spent on an unsuccessful deployment and gives the organization time to mitigate the impact of the failure.

- Time is one of the greatest enemies of projects. Examine The Project to identify any key dates that absolutely cannot be missed for solid business or technical reasons. An example for this might be changes for quarter end financial reporting. While many projects will not have these absolutely critical dates, any project that does should be carefully tracked.

RELATED QUESTIONS

8. Who would like this project to fail?

10. What is the maximum amount of time and money I am prepared to invest in this project?

17. Is the strategic impact of project timing being effectively managed?

4. HOW TO KNOW IF PROJECT STATUS IS BEING MISREPRESENTED?

"Honesty is the best policy"- Benjamin Franklin

WHY IS THIS QUESTION IMPORTANT?

One question that every Executive should ask is "how well can I trust the status being reported on The Project". It is an unfortunate reality that status reports can range from brutally honest to absolute works of fiction. It is important for you to understand ways in which status can be misrepresented and why this occurs. Misrepresentation of status often falls into a few broad categories.

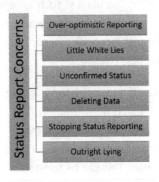

Section 1 Executive Oversight Questions

Over-optimistic Reporting- In this case, The Project Manager reports that The Project is having trouble, but the team is going to work the weekend and catch up. I have even seen teams report that they had missed every deadline for the last 6 months, but reported that they were still on-track for the deployment a few weeks away. A little probing into the details of this status usually reveals if the team has a plan to catch-up or just a hope that they can do so.

Little White Lies- These usually appear on status reports when teams are being pushed hard to meet deadlines. For example a tasks is due to be completed on a Friday which is also the day status reports are submitted.

The Project Manager will be told that the task is "nearly complete" or will be told that "we will finish it over the weekend". Based on this information, they will report the task is complete to avoid having to explain why it is late. Allowing this type of reporting puts all status reporting in doubt and must be actively discouraged

Unconfirmed Status- As project size and complexity grows, it may not be possible for The Project Manager to have personal direct knowledge of the status of all project tasks. This is especially true when The Project Team is geographically dispersed. In these cases, The Project Manager must rely on what others believe is the status of The Project.

Sometimes it is difficult to obtain updated status from all parts of The Project and The Project Manager has to "fill in the blanks" such as reporting an item as complete just because last week the developer said it was almost complete. Unless there is confirmation that a task has been closed, The Project Manager should not report that the task has been closed.

Deleting Data From Status Reports- If a task or issue is late or proving especially difficult to resolve, it is unfortunately not uncommon for The Project Team to just delete it from the status report. In this way, everything on the status report will be accurate, it will just be incomplete. This can be spotted by comparing statuses week to week to see if any items are just disappearing from the status.

Stopping Status Reporting Altogether- Sometimes when projects begin to experience problems, The Project Team will just stop reporting status. They will often use the excuse that they are so busy trying to execute The Project that they do not have time to do status reports that no one reads. This is especially dangerous since if the team is not creating weekly status reports, they likely are not monitoring status of all outstanding tasks as closely as they should.

Outright Lying- Some aspects of project execution are so technical and/or so difficult to independently verify that Project Teams are tempted to just lie about the status. This keeps the team from having to air their dirty laundry which may trigger review meetings. This goes far beyond the little white lies. The worst that I have seen of this was on a military project where data center operations were outsourced. The vendor reported the servers were installed and tested triggering a contractual payment when in fact they had not even been ordered yet.

The examples above could lead you to believe that you should not trust anything The Project Team reports on status. I find it hard to disagree with that totally given programs I have been called in to review, but would modify the statement and recommend that you do not "blindly" trust the status being reported.

Trust, But Verify

Ronald Reagan

I have always like things that Ronald Reagan said and did as US President. During arms control discussions in 1987 with former Soviet President Gorbachev, President Reagan invoked an old Russian adage that I am particularly fond of-- doveryai, no proveryai, "trust, but verify". I think this applies well to status reporting.

Section 1 Executive Oversight Questions

It is important though to understand why Project Teams sometime misrepresent the status of their projects. One of the biggest reasons why status gets misrepresented is often the reaction of an organization's to adverse project news. Many organizations have a "bad news gets you killed" environment where any bad news being reported results in The Project Team being threatened and The Project Manager being berated for being incompetent sometimes in front of their team.

If you allow an environment in the organization where honest status reporting is not valued, then you should not be surprised at lack of candor in status reporting.

REAL WORLD EXAMPLE

An extreme but true example of the outer boundary of project status misrepresentation comes from the last project I worked on as an employee of a large consulting company before I went independent. We were working on a very large very important project for the US Military. This project had very demanding requirements and involved creating technical solutions that had never been implemented before. I was The Project Manager on a portion of The Project with a development team of over 30 developers working very diligently trying to design and build a key portion of a complex system.

We had a major demonstration scheduled for November and by early January, I knew that we were going to miss that milestone by at least a year and diligently reported that to the Program Manager and Executive Team. Following this, in a series of meetings, the management team developed a formal strategy of misrepresenting project status where we would report on-time or slightly behind status until next year's budgets were approved in September, then announce the year's delay, apologies would be give, the Program Manager would be moved to a new Program, and The Project would move on.

These were fundamentally good honest intelligent people making decisions in an environment where honest reporting was not possible. However, I just could not participate in this process, so I shortly left The Project and have chosen to be an independent consultant in Program Management for the last 20+ years as a result.

BEST PRACTICES

- To be useful, status reporting needs to be done on a predictable cycle and must be mandatory. The status reporting cycle I prefer is every Friday so that you show what you have done this week and what you are going to do next week.

- The format of the status report is not as important on what it includes. It should include what you have done this week, what you are going to do in the next two weeks, the timing/status of major milestones/tasks, and a list of items The Project Team needs help to resolve.

  In addition to verbiage showing status, I strongly suggest that there be a section of the status report showing color coded status (green, yellow, red) for each of the following four areas- overall project, schedule, budget, and issues. This allows anyone to get a sense of project status at a glance.

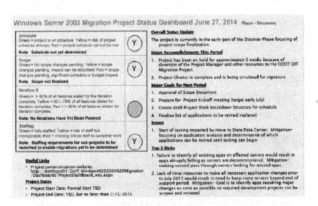

Sample Status Report Format

- Status reports should be easy to create and easy to read. Optimally, I like to keep the status reporting so simple it can be completed in 15-20 minutes per week. Any longer than that detracts The Project Manager from focusing on project execution and often results in a document so long that the management team does not bother reading it. Shoot for short, accurate, and concise versus long and verbose.

49

Section 1 Executive Oversight Questions

- The organization must have a culture that allows for honest status reporting. You should be concerned when problems/delays are reported and push for an achievable plan to resolve the problem. I am certainly not suggesting that you do not hold people accountable for deadlines, but rather to focus on how to resolve the problem.

ADDRESSING THE QUESTION WITH THE PROJECT TEAM

Project Manager- You should set clear expectations with The Project Manager that you expect clear, honest, complete, and timely status reporting on a weekly basis. Also provide The Project Manager a sense of comfort that status reporting will be used to help resolve issues and prevent small problems from become bigger problems rather than as a tool to beat up The Project Team. Asking The Project Manager occasional questions about items on the status report shows that you are at least scanning the status each week and have interest in reporting accuracy.

Business Team- Status reporting on Technology Projects is often done by The Project Manager and Technical Team sometimes with little Business Team participation. In discussions with The Business Team, emphasize that they are also responsible for accurate reporting and that business related status also needs to be candidly discussed in the status reports. Encourage The Business Team to take a few minutes each week to read the published status report so that they will understand what is being reported and able to question status as needed.

Technical Team - The Technical Team sometimes tends to complain that they are too busy doing the work to report status. However, if you don't understand the true status of a project you cannot properly manage and control it. Emphasize that status reporting has been streamlined to take as little time as possible but that it is not optional. Also encourage the Technical Team to review the status weekly to ensure that it is accurate and to understand where all parts of The Projects are from a status perspective.

Steering Committee-The Steering Committee should be included on the weekly project status distribution and should be encourage to ask questions about any item that they do not understand and do not agree with. However, it is important to emphasize with the Executives on the Steering Committee not to over-react to any single item on a status report and kill the messenger who reported the status.

LESSONS LEARNED FROM PAST PROJECTS

- If you use the weekly status report as a hammer to beat up The Project Team they are quickly going to get tired of the beatings and stop giving you the hammer. This is not dishonesty, it is human nature.
- Used correctly, honest status reporting on a troubled project can help focus attention on the areas where assistance is needed and get The Project back on track.
- If you see a series of status reports on a number of different projects and all show green every week, I can almost

Don't Shoot The Messenger. You Might Miss the Message

Unknown

guarantee that at least some of them are misrepresenting project status. This is especially true on large projects with critical timeframes. Several of what I consider my most successful projects where filled with issues, resource challenges, technical hurdles, etc. As a result, they showed an honest status of yellow for much of The Project. However, this focused attention where it was needed and The Project deployed successfully on schedule.

Section 1 Executive Oversight Questions

- Status is a reflection of the situation not just the people on The Project. Make sure that you have created the culture that nurtures reporting honesty. Just because a Project Manager reports a project as red does not automatically mean they are a bad Project Manager. Often it shows you have an experienced Project Manager that understands the status of their project and if working to resolve the problem areas.

- A red flag on status reporting is when a project begins to create two sets of status reports for The Project, one for The Project Team and one for people outside of The Project. Teams may tell themselves that this is because there are some things The Business or Executives would not be interested in or wouldn't understand. Generally this is done to "spin" the status and obscure the real issues.

- Another huge red flag is when The Project Manager on a regular basis cannot provide status on key items. Occasionally, any Project Manager may need to get an absolutely current update from the people doing the work, but in general, The Project Manager should nearly always know the status of the critical items on The Project any time that you ask.

- There should be a section in the status report where teams can report items they need assistance on. One way to encourage candid reporting and integrity in the reporting process is for you to ensure that the Executive Team understands what The Project Team needs help with and provides that help as expeditiously as possible. It is a huge morale booster for The Project Team when they come to believe that the Executive Team can and will provide help on the items where help has been requested..

- Continual material misrepresentation of the status of a project is a warning sign that you should consider replacing The Project Manager. Either they do not have control of The Project enough to report the status or they know the correct status and have made a conscious decision to misrepresent the status. Either is a strong indication that a new leader is needed.

RELATED QUESTIONS

5. Is there sufficient Executive oversight?

9. Am I sufficiently engaged in The Project?

12. When should I ask for an outside review of The Project?

25. How well are project costs being tracked?

5. IS THERE SUFFICIENT EXECUTIVE OVERSIGHT?

"Whenever you do a thing, act as if all the world were watching"- Thomas Jefferson

WHY IS THIS QUESTION IMPORTANT?

In some organizations, once a project is approved for funding, there is little involvement of Senior Executives beyond a status meeting every month or so. For many routine projects, this is sufficient. However, as the size and risk of a project grows, so does the need for increased Executive oversight. However, size alone is not the sole indication that increased oversight is warranted. Any project that has the potential to have a material impact (positive or negative) on the organization should be considered as a candidate for increased Executive oversight.

During the approval process, each project should be evaluated to determine how much Executive oversight is warranted and who will be assigned to provide this oversight. As The Project progresses, the level of oversight should be reviewed if project conditions change. Understand that Executive have only a finite amount of time to spend on any project. There is a balancing act between expecting Executives to actively engage in projects and not having sufficient Executive oversight.

REAL WORLD EXAMPLE

A regional financial services company approved a significant change to their insurance quoting system to accommodate entry into new lines of business and improve their ability to react to changes in policy terms and conditions across insurance lines. It was a very important project to the company which was rapidly expanding into new lines of business and new markets. After The Project was approved and a Project Team empowered, the Executives moved their focus to other priorities.

Unfortunately, from the very beginning, The Project did not go well. The software vendor selected to develop the system struggled with understanding The Business requirements and had difficulties in integrating these new requirements into the existing system Also because of poor system design, there were significant system performance problems.

To address these issues, The Project Team agreed to scale back business requirements and diverted funds approved for later phases of software development into purchase of more powerful hardware. This was all dutifully if not very clearly documented in project status reports. Purchase orders were presented to Executives where there were quickly signed without any indication from The Project Team that this was a deviation from the original concept and The Project proceeded with nearly no oversight for over a year.

As deployment neared, it became clear that the software that had been developed did not support the Corporate Business Goals and Company Vision and could not be deployed. There was much finger pointing with some Project Team members leaving the company to pursue other opportunities. The whole matter was deemed an IT failure. To a point, this assessment of The Project as an IT failure was correct.

However, it was even more a failure of the Executives to perform their oversight function. When interviewed, nearly all of the Executive team admitted to getting the status reports but rarely if ever reading them. They signed purchase orders as they were presented never asking questions about whether this purchase was in the original budget or not. If they had reservations about The Project, they never raised those with IT management or The Project Team. Executive involvement in this critical project, which significantly delayed their entry into new lines of business, was practically non-existent after The Project funding was approved.

BEST PRACTICES

- There should be a Steering Committee for any large or high risk/impact projects. The Steering Committee should meet periodically to review project progress, set direction, and provide assistance to The Project as needed.
- There should be one Executive on each large or high risk/impact project specifically tasked to provide routine oversight and to report back to the Steering Committee on The Project.
- The most effective Executive oversight I can recall on a large project was also the most simple. A couple of times a week and on the weekends if we were working, the Senior Vice President for Manufacturing spent 10-15 minutes walking through The Project Team area just chatting with people and asking how things were going. It was an atmosphere that was much more conducive to honest and open discussions than being called to the Executive offices in the tower to stand at attention and report progress.

☑ Do it routinely
☑ Do it impartially M
☑ Do it on your own B
☑ Listen to everyone W
☑ Don't criticize A
☑ Build rapport

This practice has been called Management By Wandering Around (or Management By Walking About) – MBWA for short. William Hewlett and David Packard, founders of Hewlett Packard (HP), used this approach in their company.

- Executive oversight must include both Business IT Executives. Business Executives will probably not understand the technology enough to provide detailed oversight and likewise IT Executives will not have the detailed understanding of The Business issues to provide oversight in that area.
- Executive oversight should be clearly indicated on The Project Organizational Chart so that there is no question who (by name) is responsible for providing oversight.

ADDRESSING THE QUESTION WITH THE PROJECT TEAM

Project Manager- Ask to see The Project organization chart which should show the Steering Committee and Executive oversight. The Project Manager should be able to discuss what assistance The Project needs from the Executive team and how they will report status to Executives. Set the expectation with The Project Manager that you are relying on them to do whatever it takes to get the attention of the Executives if direction changes or issues arise.

Business Team- In discussions with The Business Team, you should discuss who supports Business's interests at the Executive Level. Get their view on whether that involvement is sufficient given the size and importance of The Project. Emphasize the need for The Business Team to be candid but not overly pessimistic with their Executive Sponsors about status on The Project.

Information Technology Team- As with The Business Team, you should ask the IT Team if they believe the Technical Team is being adequately represented in discussions at the Executive level. You should also discuss with the Technical Team which areas of The Project the might need

Executive assistance. Set the expectation that are to do whatever is required to ensure issues are escalated in a timely manner.

LESSONS LEARNED FROM PAST PROJECTS

- There is a significant difference between an Executive benignly neglecting a project and their wanting to be involved in every detail as a micro-manager. Understand however, that neither of these is conducive to a successful project.
- The Steering Committee should discuss their role on each particular project based on the level of size and level of risk/impact. The amount of oversight required varies based on the characteristics of The Project.
- Important status should be given to the Executives overseeing The Project in person. Putting a critical issue in an email that goes to 20 people or burying it in a weekly status is not dealing with the issue, it is merely covering for yourself if things go wrong. Anything important should be communicated directly to the appropriate Executives.
- If you have an Executive that has not been involved with Technical Projects of similar size and scope to the current project it is often useful to spend time "training" them in how to provide oversight. This could be from another Executive that has been through similar projects or from an outside coach. Do not assume that all Executives

---

It is much, much worse to receive bad news through the written word than by somebody simply telling you.

Lemony Snicket

---

will automatically understand their role in often complex Technical Projects.
- If the Steering Committee creates an adversarial atmosphere where all they do is beat up The Project Team and continually push for

faster/cheaper work, they should not be surprised when the team begins to hide status from them. Very few Project Managers will provide candid reporting if they get beat up with it at each meeting. This is no different from how Executives report their status up the line to their bosses and is just human nature.

- The key to good oversight it to create an atmosphere where problems can be openly discussed with a view of finding a path forward. The Steering Committee needs to be seen as a group that will help solve problems and remove barriers.

- Be practical about expectations of available time that can be spent on Executive oversight. The organization's Executive's days are nearly always full of meetings, activities, and responsibilities outside of The Project. It is important to provide well written, brief status to the Executives if you have any expectations that they will review the material.

RELATED QUESTIONS

8. Who would like this project to fail?

9. Am I sufficiently engaged in The Project?

20. Does The Business really support this project?

6. ARE WE READY TO START THIS PROJECT?

"To be prepared is half the victory"- Miguel de Cervantes

WHY IS THIS QUESTION IMPORTANT?

Starting a project is similar to starting a ride on a huge scary roller coaster. Once it leaves the platform, the die is fundamentally cast as to how the ride is going to proceed. There is often little chance of safely getting off the roller coaster until it gets back to the station and the best you can do is hold on and hope for the best. Hopefully, if you want to go 10 miles on a roller coaster, you will take 10 trips on a 1 mile roller coaster instead of 1 trip on a 10 mile roller coaster to lessen risk, but that is a different discussion focusing on dividing a large project into discrete smaller segments with checkpoints where you can stop or change direction.

But back to the roller coaster metaphor. While little can be done once the roller coaster starts, there is a considerable range of prudent things you can do before getting on the roller coaster. You can research the record of the roller coaster team and the people that lead that team, you can ask questions about safety and operations, you can ask to see the inspection certificates, you can make sure that you have appropriate clothing, make sure everyone is tall enough to be on the roller coaster, and most importantly make sure you don't eat three chili cheese dogs from the food cart while in line.

60

In the real world, you should never allow a project to start if you are not comfortable that The Project is prepared to be successful. There are 5 major project components that should be in place prior to approving a project to move forward.

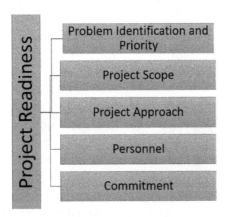

Problem Identification and Priority- There must be a clear statement of what problem The Project is intended to solve and the anticipated business benefits of successful project completion. This problem statement needs to be agreed to by all Stakeholders to make sure that you are not launching a project to address a problem that does not exist.

This seems common sense, but often Project Teams and mid-level sponsors have trouble articulating exactly what problem The Project is intended to solve. I have seen numerous projects to create new reports (often at considerable cost) where The Business sponsor could not articulate how that report would help The Business, who would use the report, nor how The Business is being harmed by not having the report currently. Sometimes the real motivation is as simple as I have some developers assigned to my business area and I am going to keep them busy doing something so that I don't lose them to another Business Unit. Challenge the team as to why this project is important.

61

Section 1 Executive Oversight Questions

In addition to ensuring that The Project is working on a valid business problem, you want to make sure that you are putting your resources towards the most important business problem. You don't want to put significant amounts of time, effort, and resources into solving a problem that has $10K per year in business benefits when the same team/resources could have resolved a problem that would result in $1M in benefits per year.

Look at projects across The Business to make sure that projects you choose to launch have the greatest value to The Business as a whole. Organizations often assign IT resources to individual Business Units in such a way that a low priority project in one Business Unit might get resourced when a project with much greater benefits in another area does not get funded this year. Look across the entire organization when determining how project resources will be allocated.

Project Scope- Once you determine that there is in fact a valid business problem of sufficient priority to be solved, you need to ensure that the team has documented the boundaries of The Project. This will help ensure that The Project addresses the stated problem and that it does not get overly ambitious straying into areas outside the approved scope. Like Bills in the US Congress, Business and Technical Teams like to load up projects with items that do not directly contribute to the resolution of the stated problem. Conversely, you want to ensure that the scope statement adequately covers the problem area. In any case, the scope statement should be written and approved by all Stakeholders.

Approach- After scope is determined, the team should be able to articulate at least a high level approach to solving the problem. It is unrealistic at the beginning of a project to expect all questions to be answered, but there needs to be some understanding of how The Project will proceed with major milestones, deliverables, etc. I like to see a good bit of detail on activities that will take place in the first few weeks/months of a project and am OK with much less details for activities taking place later in the timeline.

Personnel- You can have the best approach to solving a problem and yet not be successful if you are not able to properly staff The Project with appropriate technical and business personnel. The Project Team needs to have a good concept for acquiring the right resources as they are needed. This could be a combination of internal and external resources, but should concentrate not just on putting generic "bodies in a chair", instead insuring assigned resources have the requisite knowledge and skill.

Properly staffing projects is the subject of another chapter in this book, but one area that needs particular attention at the beginning of The Project is availability of knowledgeable business resources. Most business organizations periodically examine organizational efficiency and align staffing levels to the minimum number of people required to get the work done.

Along comes a project that needs to divert key business personnel away from their day to day work to participate in project activities such as requirements gathering, data review, Project Meetings, reviewing prototypes, testing, etc. Before a project is allowed to go forward, you need to ensure that The Business has identified by name who will be assigned to support The Project and how the regular work of these resources will be managed. Knowledge of how The Business works today is something that you cannot outsource.

Commitment- The last major component that should be in place before you launch a project is ensuring that all involved areas of the company have at least some level of commitment to project success. This means that Executives in each impacted area support the need, scope, approach, funding, personnel, etc. and that they commit to providing some of their time to perform the critical oversight function. If the only level of commitment your organization offers a project is to provide funding, the likelihood of success is greatly lessened.

REAL WORLD EXAMPLE

-A State Agency received bad publicity because they had trouble quickly providing documents when requested. The Legislature quickly passed a bill requiring electronic scanning and storage of documents and a project was launched intending to use standard of the shelf hardware and software to address this legislative mandate. Within a year The Project was determined to be a total failure, was cancelled, and significant finger pointing began in earnest. It turns out, The Project failed because it was never properly formulated.

The root cause reason why documents could not be provided as requested turned out to be a problem in how the agency indexed the document not how the documents were stored. So the mandated approach did not address the real problem. Additionally, managers in the agency did not see any value in electronic imaging and so did not dedicate knowledgeable agency personnel to help on The Project. As a result the IT Group brought in an outside vendor who assembled a solution with off the shelf components and quickly tried to implement it.

Since the various departments/locations in the agency did not actively support or participate in The Project, it was only at implementation that it was discovered that there were physical limitations in office spaces that kept scanning equipment from being installed in several key locations. Additionally, it was found that State personnel classification rules and union intervention kept existing clerks from being used to scan documents.

In the few offices where significant amounts of documents were able to be scanned into the new system, chaos resulted when it was discovered that the out of the box document indexing/search features not only did not resolve the original problem, but also did not allow documents to be easily located in numerous key ways that had previously been successfully used to find documents.

Eventually, the agency reverted to the original document storage processes with the addition of an enhanced indexing capability while the imaging solution was shelved and the equipment given to another agency. This is an example of a project that was allowed to launch without consensus on problem, scope approach or resources and which did not have the commitment of the Stakeholders. It is not enough for top management to mandate a project, it has to be correctly launched if it is going to be successful.

BEST PRACTICES

- The formal project document must be sufficiently detailed to define what The Project will and will not include and what business benefit can be expected upon completion.
- There should be a formal document prepared documenting the purpose of The Project. This should be approved prior to any project being launched. The exact format of this document (which I have seen called Project Charter, Project Scope Statement, and even Project License) is not as important as that it covers the five items listed above- problem identification and priority, scope, approach, resources, and commitment.

ADDRESSING THE QUESTION WITH THE PROJECT TEAM

Project Manager- Usually The Project Manager takes the lead in creating The Project Definition Document. You want to ensure that they take into account the needs of all of The Project Stakeholders and that all involved parties are included in creating and reviewing the document.

Business Team- In discussions with The Business Team, you should ensure that they have given sufficient consideration to the exact business problem being solved and that they are convinced that this is the highest priority business problem that needs to be addressed. You should also discuss where the necessary business resources to support The Project will come from and how the current jobs of these resources will be accomplished across the timespan of The Project.

Information Technology Team - The Technical Team usually has at least a high level technical solution in mind before projects begin. You should explore how well they understand The Business problem and ask them to explain how the proposed technical solution addresses this business problem. Also explore with the Technical Team areas that they believe business resources will be needed and ensure The Business is prepared to supply that level of support.

> Most people fail, not because of lack of
> desire, but because of lack of commitment
>
> Vince Lombardi

LESSONS LEARNED FROM PAST PROJECTS

- Projects that are mandated by the upper levels of an organization or by outside entities seem most likely to skip the critical project definition formality. This is a mistake, because projects forced upon an organization are likely to suffer from lack of agreement on problem/scope, approach agreement, and often lack of commitment from management. The documentation process will ensure that the mandate is understood by all.
- Smaller projects also tend to want to skip this project definition formality using the logic that the process takes too long. If a project is small and relatively simple, then so should The Project Definition Document. It is a mistake to allow projects to proceed without this agreement regardless of how small it is.
- Some Project Teams try to avoid creating a Project Definition Document merely because they feel The Project will never get formal approval if people understand which problem they are trying to solve. However, that is the purpose of the document. Some percentage of projects that a Business or Technical Team would like to pursue will be killed in this process because they lack value, personnel, priority, commitment, etc. This is exactly why you want to go through the process.
- One process that a Vice President that I worked with used very effectively on projects was to assemble all the Stakeholders in a room at one time and review The Project Definition Document.

66

At the end, the VP would individually poll each of the Stakeholders asking them if they support The Project moving forward. This put each area "on the record" as supporting The Project.

- Keep in mind the message from the Matthew Broderick movie War Games that sometimes "the only way to win is not to play the game". Do not be reluctant to turn down projects or to send Project Teams back to work on the concept before it is approved. Not all projects deserve to be funded.

- The Project Definition Document has value after The Project launch since it should be the basis for defining the parameters of The Project through the life cycle and should be the yardstick used to measure project success.

- If the scope or direction of The Project change, you should have The Project Team go back and update The Project Definition Document and have all Stakeholders approve the change. This helps ensure that the revised project still have value in the eyes of the Stakeholders.

RELATED QUESTIONS

1. Are The Project objectives clear to all?

7. What are key roles for project success?

26. Are The Project risks understood?

7. WHAT ARE THE KEY ROLES FOR PROJECT SUCCESS?

"Never doubt that a small group of thoughtful, committed citizens can change the world; indeed, it's the only thing that ever has."- Margaret Mead

WHY IS THIS QUESTION IMPORTANT?

While project success requires the effort of all members of The Project Team, there are a few roles on every project that are critical to project success. You should give careful consideration to the people that perform these roles. Additionally, you should monitor the performance of these leaders providing mentoring and guidance as needed. The key project roles are:

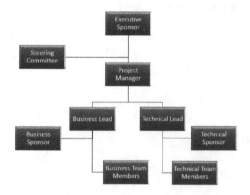

Executive Sponsor- This is the organization's Executive charged with overall responsibility for The Project. They could also be The Business Sponsor or the Technical Sponsor based on the size and complexity of The Project and your organization.

This person will be the ultimate decision-maker on The Project focused on ensure The Project achieves its stated benefits. It is important that this role be formally designated in organization charts, etc. and be endorsed by Senior Leadership.

Steering Committee - The Steering Committee is a group of Executives/Senior Managers that represent all involved parties in The Project. This group should include people that represent both technical and business interests on The Project. They will meeting periodically (once a month is the usual cadence) to get a high level status update, help with issue resolution, review budget and timeline, and provide guidance to The Project Team.

Traditional members of the Steering Committee include the Executive Sponsor, Business Sponsor, Technical Sponsor and other business Executives from affected Business Units. The Project Manager generally creates and presents The Project status information at these meetings and leads the discussion but is not considered a formal part of the Steering Committee.

Project Manager- This is the person that has been selected to lead your project. You are going to entrust them will the use of company financial and personnel resources and rely on them to successfully deliver The Project and achieve the desired business benefits. You want to carefully consider who you put in this position of trust. There are three key skills areas that you should consider when selecting a Project Manager.

1). Basic Skills- There is a core set of skills that a Project Manager needs such as planning, scheduling, estimating, risk/issues management, reporting, etc. You will want to ensure that your Project Manager possesses these basic skills. One good measure of project management basics skills is the Program Management Institute (PMI) Project Management Professional (PMP)

certification program. Attaining this certification requires a combination of classroom training and some practical experience in project management plus successful completion of a certification test.

However, PMP certification is not the only measure of mastery of project management basics. Project Managers who have completed a number of real world projects successfully also will have a good grounding in The Project management basics, but additionally will have practical experience in the application of these principles which is at least as valuable as passing a certification test.

I am a supporter of the PMP certification process, but am more than a little troubled by the growth of organizations offering "boot camps" and similar programs that in a weekend or two will teach what you need to know for the test and help you fill out the paperwork to get the certification with little to no real experience in project management. You want to insure that your selected Project Manager has at least some real world experience in successfully delivering projects. This is especially true as project size and complexity increases.

2). Leadership Skills- In addition to a solid grounding in basic project management skills, you want to ensure that your Project Manager is a leader. They need to be able to earn the respect of The Project Team and

---

You don't manage people, you manage things. You lead people

Commodore Grace Hoper

---

the sponsors, organize the work, drive the team to success, and resolve issues as they are encountered. As The Project gets larger, longer, and more complex, leadership skills become ever more important. Unfortunately, while the basics of leadership can be taught in a classroom, leadership skills cannot be measured by a certification test so the PMP certification by itself is not a good measure of leadership skills.

For that, you will want to explore the background of The Project Manager candidate to see if they have been successful in delivering projects of a similar size and complexity to your project. This is also an area where reference checks can be invaluable in understanding ability to lead a Project Team.

3). Domain Knowledge- There is no doubt that having some knowledge of The Business area subject/domain is a valuable trait for a Project Manager. However, I intentionally listed it as the last of the three traits. A good Project Manager with deep experience and strong leadership skills can deliver a project in a business area they know very little about initially. Remember that you are not engaging The Project Manager to be The Business or technical subject matter expert. You are engaging them to lead The Project.

One of my most interesting projects given my near total background in business-oriented Technology Projects was the accelerated build-out of a manufacturing facility. While I knew very little about building a factory at the beginning of The Project, my project management skills coupled with the manufacturing skills of the plant team resulted in a successful project. Focus more on leadership and basic project management skills and most successful Project Managers will quickly learn what they need to know about The Business domain.

Business Sponsor- Unless The Project is strictly technical in nature, it should have a Business Sponsor. The Business Sponsor is responsible for providing the definitive guidance on what the system is intended to do and what benefits are anticipated. They will help ensure that promised business resources are available  and will work to resolve issues as they arise. If The Project is large and/or complex, it may have multiple Business Sponsors each representing one of The Business Units affect by The Project. In general, The Business Sponsor(s) are not involved in The

Section 1 Executive Oversight Questions

Project on a day to day basis, but rather provide Executive Oversight and support as needed.

Technical Sponsor- All Technology Projects need a Technical Sponsor. Depending on the size of the organization and The Project, this could be the Chief Information Officer (CIO) of the company or their designee. In any case, it should be someone authorized to make decisions in technical areas related to The Project. The Technical Sponsor will be responsible for reviewing/approving technical documents, resolving technical issues escalated by The Project Team, and ensuring that required technical personnel are available as planned.

Technical Lead - The Technical Lead is responsible for the day to day management of the technical resources on The Project. They are generally on The Project full-time. This must be someone with sufficient stature in the organization to be able to speak with authority on behalf of the IT group. They need to have a solid technical background and be able to make technical decisions for the group while understanding when those decisions should be escalated to the Technical Sponsor.

Business Lead - The Business Lead is the person on The Project who represents Business interests on The Project on a day by day basis. They coordinate with The Business Sponsor and other business managers/Executives as needed to address business related questions/issues as they arise during The Project. They should also proactively ensure that promised business resources are available as needed. In general, they are the central focal point for all business activities on The Project. This is a role that not only requires deep knowledge of how The Business operates, but also requires a person that has sufficient stature in the company to be in a position to speak for The Business on The Project.

REAL WORLD EXAMPLE

A large manufacturing company began a process of redefining how capacity management would be addressed inside their extensive and complex supply chain. For approximately 6 months a large team of people met to define requirements for new processes and systems. Nearly all of the mid-level managers in the potentially impacted areas participated in multi-hour meetings twice a week resulting in a set of high level requirements. The Executive Sponsor was invited to all of the meetings and attended a few minutes of most meetings but gave the message that the team had the expertise and understanding of the problems needed to define the new processes without their help.

At the end of the process there was an extensive review process to refine and finalize the requirements documents so that it could be used for the next step in The Project which was to review commercially available software packages that might be used as the basis for the new system. However, when it was time for the Executive Sponsor to sign the document, they were reluctant to do so. No specific deficiencies in the document were cited, but there were repeated requests for more people to review the document before they would

---

Procrastination is the thief of time-

Edward Young

---

sign it or pronouncements more time was needed to review.

In the end, this consumed almost two months of time, delaying the solution selection component of The Project and causing The Project overall to lose momentum that it struggled to regain. Deliverable approvers need to either be sufficiently involved in The Project to participate in the decisions or assign people they trust to do so.

BEST PRACTICES

- A project organizational chart should be developed prior to The Project being formally approved outlining how The Project will be organized. Included in this organizational chart should be the key project roles with named resources assigned.

Section 1 Executive Oversight Questions

- Depending on their time availability and project size, a single person could fill more than one of the key project roles.
- The Project organizational chart should be shared widely both within The Project and with related organizational units/projects. It should be updated as necessary when personnel or roles changes during The Project.
- The organization should establish decision making limits for each of these roles to remove confusion over the level at which decisions should be made. This is especially true in areas such as budget commitments, negotiating contracts, deciding technical direction, designing new business processes, approving requirements, etc. Failure to define decision making limits can easily lead to time delays and impact project morale.

An example of this might be a Business Lead that believed they had the authority to agree to Requirements Documents discovering well after development has begun that The Business Sponsor wanted to approval the Requirements. This is likely to stop or delay development work and be costly to the organization. Discovering additional approvals are required adversely affects team and project leader morale as they have to revisit decisions that they believed had already been made.

ADDRESSING THE QUESTION WITH THE PROJECT TEAM

Project Manager- Roles and responsibilities for The Project Manager should be clearly defined and communicated. Set the expectation with The Project Manager that they are to take the lead in The Project and to provide honest, forthcoming project status. Also emphasize that you expect them to escalate project issues in a timely manner.

Business Team- Discuss with The Business Lead and Business Executive their responsibilities. Also facilitate a conversation to clearly define decision making limits emphasizing the need for quick informed decisions on business issues.

74

Information Technology Team- Facilitate the same discussion with the Technical Lead and Technical Sponsor over roles, responsibilities, and decision making limits.

Steering Committee- Ensure that all of the Executives on the Steering Committee understand the time commitment expected of them and the importance of the oversight function. Review and gain consensus on decision making limits especially on financial items so that it is clear which decisions they expect to be involved in and which decisions they merely want to be informed about.

LESSONS LEARNED FROM PAST PROJECTS

- Most Executives do not have the time to be involved in the detailed meetings where business or technical issues are discussed and detailed decisions made. This is not an issue as long at the Executives have people that they trust in the meetings representing their interests. Where it becomes a problem is when the Executive wants to understand the material in detail before approving it yet does not have the time to do so. It can literally take weeks of effort for a number of people to go through and explain discussions/decisions that unfolded perhaps over a number of months.

  At the beginning of complex discussions like requirements documentation, The Project Manager or Business Lead should meet with all the people who will have to approve the document and understand their approval expectations. If the approver expects to review the document in detail, then they must be pulled into the discussions as they occur at least during the final stages of document review. I have seen several cases where a whole team of people burning several thousands of dollars in budget each day has to sit idly while an Executive tries to find the time to review a large complex document.

- If you find that someone does not have the time, skill and/or interest to fill their assigned role on The Project, a change should be made to replace them with someone better situated to fill that role. This is especially true when people are overcommitted on time and literally are unable to participate regardless of how much they would like to. It is not fair to either the person or The Project to leave someone in a role that they are not able to perform.

- Decentralize decision making to the lowest level possible to facilitate fast decisions. You put people on The Project because you trust their judgment so show that trust by empowering them to make appropriate decisions. If you require all decisions to be made at the top of the organizational chart, you are adding significant cost and time to The Project.

RELATED QUESTIONS

5. Is there sufficient Executive oversight?

21. Who is really speaking for The Business on The Project?

8. WHO WOULD LIKE THIS PROJECT TO FAIL?

"Integrity is the lifeblood of democracy, deceit is a poison in its veins."- Edward Kennedy

WHY IS THIS QUESTION IMPORTANT?

On the surface, this seems like an odd question since everyone should have the best interests of the company in mind and should be working hard to make all projects successful. However, by giving this question some consideration you will gain insight into behaviors on The Project. I can honestly say on most of the larger projects I have been involved with, there has been at least one person or organization that had a vested interest in at least partial project failure.

Once you have identified the people/ groups that fall into this category and understand their motivations you can work to ensure they do not adversely impact The Project. Examples of potential groups that may try and influence project success include:

Section 1 Executive Oversight Questions

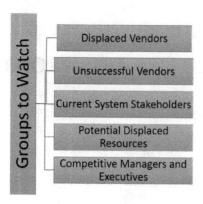

Groups to Watch
- Displaced Vendors
- Unsuccessful Vendors
- Current System Stakeholders
- Potential Displaced Resources
- Competitive Managers and Executives

- **Displaced Vendors-** Sometimes, a project replaces one brand of hardware or software with another or brings in a new group of developers/consultants to replace or supplement vendor personnel already in place at your organization. When this occurs, it makes sense that the displaced vendor and their personnel currently working within your organization will not be pleased. It is not uncommon for the incumbent vendor to reduce service levels, pull key people out of the organization to start new projects, withhold information that would help the new vendor, and create discord in The Project Team by emphasizing issues the new vendor is having.

- **Unsuccessful Vendors-** You probably think that once a vendor selection has been made, you can ignore the unsuccessful vendors. While that is often the case, it is not always true, especially if this is a large high dollar sales opportunity. During the competition for a contract, vendors usually develop one-on-one relationships with key managers and decision makers within your organization. It is not uncommon for Sales Representatives/Customer Managers from the loosing vendors to continue to meet with managers within an organization in an  attempt to overturn the decision and gather information about any missteps the winning vendor may make.

- **Current System Stakeholders-** Even the most out of date systems tend to have champions at some level of an organization. It could be a user that doesn't want to have to learn new processes and new systems. You may even have people who are perceived as the "expert" in a legacy system and wonder about loss of status when the new system is installed. These people may not embrace the idea of a new system to help the company and thus may limit their cooperation/participation in The Project activities.

- **Potential Displaced Resources** - If one of the goals/results of your project is to reduce personnel, then an all absorbing discussion in the organization will become speculation on who is going to lose their job. It would be difficult for most people to enthusiastically support a project that if successful will result in their losing their job. Some organizations try to deal with this by not announcing who is going to be downsized until late in The Project. This however, just drives the conversation underground as people waste time speculating over who is going to get fired. This can have a chilling effect on project productivity.

- **Competitive Managers/Executives**- Some organizations are highly competitive at the manager/Executive level even to the point of people being more interested in their personal career and advancement of their Business Unit over the best interest of the company as a whole. This is especially true if approval of a project draws funding and/or personnel away from their area of responsibility. In these cases, it is not uncommon to have Executives be slow in providing knowledge and personnel support to projects.

These are a few examples of reasons not everyone may be pushing for project success. This lack of support can manifest itself as subtly as not responding to requests for information/support all the way to actively plotting to make a project fail. This is a topic that most business would deny ever occurs and refuses to talk about openly, but most Executives could identify situations where it has occurred in their organization.

Section 1 Executive Oversight Questions

REAL WORLD EXAMPLE

- A major State Agency embarked on an ambitious plan to replace an internally developed mainframe transaction processing system with an "off the shelf" package that had been successfully implemented in a number of other states. This new system ran on much less expensive midrange servers and overall represented a significant cost savings to the State. However, the new technology and new selected vendor were perceived as a direct threat to the State Data Center employees and entrenched legacy mainframe vendor. As a result, several attempts were made to delay The Project and have contracts cancelled.

Ultimately the Agency had to build and operate a new computer facility for the system since they were not allowed to house the equipment in the State Data Center where every other major system in the State was hosted. This failure to support The Project significantly increased cost to implement the new system and delayed system deployment by a number of months. It also saddled the Agency with recurring costs to staff and operate the computer facility going forward.

REAL WORLD EXAMPLE TWO

I was brought in to clean up the mess on a large system development project at a major chemical company. This multi-year project also included a planned IT reorganization that everyone believed would include a major downsizing. No one from the Management team ever explained the general reorganization process and certainly did not discuss plans for individual employees. Predictably the discussion of who was going to be laid off became all-consuming and created a toxic work environment where eventually an employee decided to sabotage a critical system.

This senior employee with a family, mortgage, and other financial obligations began to believe that they would be laid off at the end of The Project (which it turns out ironically was not the plan). Since The Project extended for over a year, they had time to delete all versions of the source code for a portion of a critical international taxation system from the production system, the code library and the backup storage over a period of months.

Towards the end of The Project, this was discovered and the employee feigned ignorance even in the face of computer logs and offered to re-write the systems on a contract basis for a fee. Upon threat of legal action, they eventually provide a copy of the source code that they had moved to their home and lost their job.

BEST PRACTICES

- Asking "who wants this to fail" is an impolite question at best to ask in an open meeting with a large number of people. However, this question should be given serious consideration either in the counsel of your own thoughts or in private conversations with a small number of people. Doing so will help you understand the group dynamics and potentially head off issues.
- If The Project involves replacement of technology vendors, have an open and frank discussion with these soon to be displaced vendors as soon as the decision is made. You should lay out your expectations for how work will be wound down, expectations of cooperation with incoming vendors, and expectations on knowledge transfer. Final payment to the incumbent vendors should be made contingent on the smooth transfer or responsibilities.
- If The Project involves downsizing or radically changing employee jobs, it is recommended that you have a general discussion with all potentially affected organizational units as early as possible. You can then have more focused discussions with individual employees as the personal impact on them is known. You should also consider if any steps are necessary to control access to information or data.
- Personnel involved with vendor selection and their Executive managers should be informed once the sourcing decision has been made there should be no additional discussions with unsuccessful vendors.

ADDRESSING THE QUESTION WITH THE PROJECT TEAM

Project Manager- Ask The Project Manager to be vigilante in guarding against attempts to derail The Project. Instruct them to immediately report any effort to slow or stop The Project and any cases where people/groups are not participating as agreed.

Business Team- Ensure that The Business Team understands the expectation that they will actively work to further The Project and that attempts to impede project progress will not be tolerated

Information Technology Team- Caution the Technical Team about having continued contact with unsuccessful bidders after purchasing decisions have been made. Also ask them to pay attention to the activities of incumbent vendors who will be displaced at the end of The Project.

LESSONS LEARNED FROM PAST PROJECTS

- Human Resource departments may well advise that you shouldn't say anything to employees that may be impacted by a project until all final employee disposition decisions have been made and approved. However, you cannot stifle hallway discussion and speculation. Tell potentially impacted people as much as you can as early as you can.
- If any of the Stakeholders/Executives try and delay or derail The Project you should first explore whether their concerns are valid. If they are not, then you should remind them of their obligation to support the approved organization decision. Sometimes a good frank discussion with detractors will make a big difference in establishing project cooperation.
- If The Project involves major contract changes for an existing vendor, the Legal Department should review the relevant contract(s) to identify termination clauses so that you can negotiate the contract changes required.

> Old age and treachery will always beat youth
> and exuberance. –
>
> David Mamet

- Do not underestimate the ingenuity, tenacity, and cunning displayed by long-time employees in finding innovative ways to scuttle projects that they are against. Even if they do not stop The Project, their tactics (which usually in their minds are well meaning) could cause deadlines to be missed and increase the cost of The Project.
- If you identify people who will be severely impacted by The Project, it is prudent to keep an eye on their activities and what they have access to. In situations like this, it is not uncommon to have salespeople download customer and contact lists, engineers create copies of designs they have worked on, etc. In general, you want to believe that your employees are honest ethical people (and most are). However, living under the cloud of maybe losing your job can make people act in an uncharacteristic manner.
- Assemble potentially affected people (or even better talk to them one on one) to discuss retraining possibilities, potential re-assignment within the company, etc. This is the right thing to do for your employees and it will help morale.
- If you have personnel (employee or vendor) in the organization now that are critical to project success, but who will be released at the end of The Project, it is unlikely that they will stay until the end. One way to mitigate this is to negotiate a "Stay Bonus" with key resources. This would provide extra compensation to them at the end of The Project if they stay until the end. It is often money very well spent.
- If people do begin to leave the organization due to uncertainty about the future it is likely to be your better talent. Mediocre and poor performers usually stay until the end and sometimes keep their jobs just because all of your best people left. This is not a good staffing dynamic.

RELATED QUESTIONS

3. What Is the impact if The Project fails?

20. Does The Business really support this project?

21. Who is really speaking for The Business on The Project?

9. AM I SUFFICIENTLY ENGAGED IN THE PROJECT?

 "Oh, You forget your pencil, show up late, and don't pay attention? Tell me again why I should give you an A?" Willy Wonka

WHY IS THIS QUESTION IMPORTANT?

Most of the rest of the questions in this book are aimed at The Project Team, but this questions is one that each Executive should ask themselves. If you want to help ensure project success, it is not enough to just give The Project Team a generous budget, attend a meeting every few weeks, and tell yourself that you have an open door where the team can come if they need assistance.

I have seen Executives get intimately involved with manufacturing details like where the logo should go on a product that will be eventually hidden inside a structure never to be seen again. Yet that same Executive couldn't tell you what the system they are spending millions of dollars on even looks like and what it will do for the organization.

Many will argue that details are what you pay the IT leaders and consultants to take care of, and to a great extent, that is true. However a key part of being an Executive is understanding enough about everything in your span of control at a sufficient level to ask probing relevant questions and to make informed decisions. That should be the goal of your engagement on Technology Projects.

If you get too deep in the details, you honestly will get in the way of the team of experts, but having no involvement is even worse. You especially need high level understanding and involvement in at least the following 7 key areas

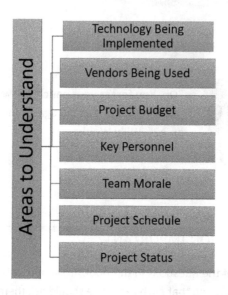

Technology Being Implemented- Many business oriented Executives intentionally shy away from even trying to understand the technology being implemented. Often IT people speak in "technobabble" that is impossible for the lay person to understand. However, you should understand whether the technology being implemented is cutting edge/experimental, mainstream, or already outdated. If multiple technologies are being integrated together, you should understand whether this has been done before and how much effort will it take to integrate the technologies.

You should also have a one page pictorial view of how the new technology components will be integrated together and then integrated into the remainder of your system architecture. The pictorial view is not only important to help you understand the way the system is architected at the high level, but also provides a tool that can also be used within the team. A dirty secret of IT is that IT is so specialized and diverse that on a project, it is not uncommon that no one will know how all the technology works and will fit together, but few would admit to that lack of understanding in front of their peers.

Vendors Being Used- It is important that you understand what vendors will be involved with providing goods and services to The Project, when they will be engaged, and approximately how much you expect to spend with each. You should also understand at least at a high level the contractual and payment terms for each of the major vendors. This will help in managing vendor relationships and in approving purchase orders and payments.

Project Budget- The Project budget should not be a single number that The Project Team can spend as they wish. Rather it should outline expected spending levels in broad areas with the understanding that the team must not only stay within the total budget target, but cannot exceed the budget in any of the individual spending areas without approval. I have had many Executives complain on big projects that I seem to be in their office every day asking them to sign a purchase order for something that they don't understand and don't know how it fits into the overall budget. You should be involved enough in The Project to understand the major categories of planned expenses so you will be able to ask informed questions when approvals are requested.

Key Personnel- It is important that you be involved enough with The Project to know the key personnel on The Project personally. This should include both employees and vendor personnel. If you are going to entrust The Project Team with large sums of money and the ability to positively or negatively impact the future of the company, you should spend some time getting to know those who are leading it. As with most business relationship building, the best way to accomplish this is outside of the normal work environment through drinks after work, team outings, and/or one on one discussions. The intent of this is to get to know the key leaders as people including their backgrounds and role on The Project. This will also make it easier for them to approach you with issues they need assistance with.

87

Team Morale- You should be involved enough with The Project to understand when team morale changes. Few things can derail a project faster than poor morale. Whether poor morale is a result of poor leadership, overwork, or other issues, you should be involved enough in The Project to judge the morale level of both The Project leadership and the rank and file members so that you can take appropriate action if needed.

Project Schedule- It is likely that your Project Manager will maintain a very detailed Project Schedule with hundreds or even thousands of tasks in a hard to understand Project Management tool such as MS Project. It is not important that you understand all aspects of this schedule. However, it is important that you have a one page high level pictorial view of the major activities/milestones in The Project and when they are scheduled to occur. This will allows you and The Project Team to have a quick reference showing where The Project is against the approved schedule.

Project Status- One exercise that I was taught as a young second lieutenant in the US Army was to always know the status of your platoon. Senior officers would at random come up and ask me how many people I had fit for duty and what they were doing at that particular moment. You should expect this type of instant accountability from your Project Manager. They should know key dates, issues, etc. at all times.

However, you should always be ready **yourself** to answer general questions about high level project status such as what are we working on now, when is it due to be completed, and what problems are we having. If you cannot answer those questions, then perhaps you need to read the weekly status reports more closely, talk more often to your Project Manager, and in general become more involved in The Project.

REAL WORLD EXAMPLE

- I was once consulted on a project review on a data warehousing project that had missed several delivery dates. Senior Leadership had lost confidence in The Project Manager and was considering replacing them. In the course of the review, it quickly became obvious that none of the key Executives had been sufficiently involved in The Project to effectively perform their Executive Oversight function.

This was not a project failure that was sudden and hard to foresee. Rather, it was a situation a number of months in the making. It had been well reported in both weekly status reports, monthly program reviews, and quite a few candid emails from The Project Manager to the Executives. It quickly became obvious to me that while The Project Manager had some communications  issues, they were overall effective in performing their required functions. Issues were being raised correctly including repeated requests for assistance in getting business participation and with other resource and contractual issues.

The Executive Team on the other hand, admittedly never read any of the status information, only attended the occasional Program Meeting where they often reviewed emails instead of actively participating in the discussion. They also admitted to rarely opening emails from The Project Team. My recommendation was to retain The Project Manager, but increase participation from the Executive team including designating one Executive as being the lead on project oversight.

Mentoring was put in place for both The Project Manager and the Executives for a period of time to help them better understand their respective roles and to build a bridge of trust and communications. As a result, The Project was brought back on track and able to slowly get back on schedule with a successful deployment reasonably near the original deployment date.

BEST PRACTICES

- Designate one of the Executive Stakeholders on The Project as having primary responsibility for providing Executive oversight and for reporting back to the Leadership Team. If no one has time to fill this function consider whether this project is important enough to warrant being launched. If it is, then some provision for Executive oversight is required.

- Schedule a short 10-15 minute meeting with The Project Manager on a weekly basis to review status and identify areas where assistance is needed. This can be either in person or on the phone. If you do not make time for this meeting on a regular basis, you are sending a message to The Project Manager that you have more important things to work on than The Project.

- At least scan the weekly project status report on a weekly basis focusing on status against near term milestones, issues, risks, and requests to assistance. If the status report is well organized, this should only take a few minutes. If you cannot quickly glean this information from the status report, consider working with The Project Manager to simplify it.

- Spend at least a few minutes each week walking through The Project area if it is local or talking to key project leaders to get a sense of The Project and the morale of its participants.

ADDRESSING THE QUESTION WITH THE PROJECT TEAM

Project Manager- Establish a one on one relationship with The Project Manager so that you understand what drives them and what their strengths and weakness are. This will set the stage for candid communication and will help create an environment where assistance can be requested. Set the expectation with The Project Manager that you expect them to not be shy about letting you know if they feel your participation is not adequate.

Business Team- In discussions with The Business Team, you should keep an eye on project morale and be open to suggestions about improvements and how to deal with issues. Even if you do not implement all suggestions, it is important to the team that they believe you are listening to their concerns and input.

Information Technology Team- Take the time to get to know at least the key members of the technology team. Making the team comfortable in talking with you makes it much more likely they will be candid in reporting issues or requesting assistance.

LESSONS LEARNED FROM PAST PROJECTS

- One very effective Executive on a project I was involved with always carried a folder with him anywhere he went during the day. This folder contained high level information about nearly every aspect of the work in his area of control including our project. For our project, he always had a one page technical drawing of the architecture, a one page depiction of The Project timeline, the most  current status report, and the high level project budget with expenditures to date. In hallway discussion, meetings, etc. he was always able to quickly see the status of not only our project, but similar information about everything else in his span of control.

- It is a mistake for an Executive to try and act like they fully understand complex technology issues. Your team will immediately sense your lack of knowledge and honestly will make fun of you behind your back. What is appropriate to even the most technologically naïve Executive is that you try to understand at a high level the fundamental problems they are trying to solve.

  Often the problems they are struggling with turn out to be contractual, personnel, money, or time issues and rarely entirely technology problems. If they are having trouble getting technology to work, it is often solved by bringing in some outside help, pushing the vendor to be responsive, or arranging for some training. These are all things that you can assist the team with.

- Money is often tight within companies and on projects. However, considering the long hours usually worked on project (a fair amount of which is uncompensated on most projects), a great way to show involvement and help morale are periodic after hours team building events at a local restaurant/bar (depending on your corporate rules/guidelines) and bringing in food for the team when working late at night or on weekends.

RELATED QUESTIONS

5. Is there sufficient Executive oversight?

10. What is the maximum amount of time and money I am prepared to invest in this project?

10. WHAT IS THE MAXIMUM AMOUNT OF TIME AND MONEY I AM PREPARED TO INVEST IN THIS PROJECT?

"Sometimes your best investments are the ones you don't make."- Donald Trump

WHY IS THIS QUESTION IMPORTANT?

As project size and complexity increases, so do the odds that it cannot be completed within the originally estimated time frame and budget. While this is sometimes the result of poor estimating technique, it is more often the result of uncertainty, scope changes and the compounding effect of small delays across the duration of a project. It is only at the end of The Project that you will truly know how long a project took and how much it cost. The question then becomes if you had known the real project cost and duration would you have approved it in the first place.

This is a question that the Leadership Team should ask themselves prior to approving a project, especially large and complex projects. It the answer is that based on The Business benefits anticipated, I would fund The Project even if it took 25% longer than the estimate and cost 25% more, you should probably go forward with most projects. However if, your answer is that if the actual cost of The Project exceeded the cost estimate at all, I would not approve The Project, then you should study The Project more closely before approving it.

> There is no such thing as absolute value in this world. You can only estimate what a thing is worth to you."- Charles Dudley Warner

This discussion does not mean that you announce to the world that you are OK with a 25% overrun. This is one of the few things I would suggest you not share with The Project Team. You want to keep steady reasonable pressure on The Project Team to deliver The Project on time and on budget. However, this discussion is intended to understand how important The Project is to the organization and how you should go forward if problems are encountered. It is a measure of your tolerance to schedule and cost variance.

REAL WORLD EXAMPLE

I was once asked to look at estimates for a large financial services project. The benefits of The Project while quantifiable were not overwhelming. The Project Team had developed an estimate that was probably 20% above what the Leadership Team was willing to invest in The Project. At the urging of the Executives, The Project Team went back and removed all cost/schedule contingency, slashed end user training, and significantly scaled back the power of the hardware to be purchased. This brought the cost close to the budget target established by the Executive Team. I was asked to do a review of the numbers before a final decision was made.

10. What is the Maximum Amount of Time and Money I am Prepared to Invest in this Project?

After spending some time with The Project Team and reviewing the basis for estimate, my recommendation to the Leadership Team was to not approve The Project in its current form. By scaling back hardware and training the risk of incurring additional costs to make The Project fully deployable was greatly increased and removing the contingency left no buffer against problems that might crop up. Given the more than one year duration of The Project, it seemed highly unlikely for The Project to be delivered within the downsized budget.

After the reality of this sank in, I worked with the Leadership and Project Teams to break the scope of The Project into multiple releases that while slightly increasing the total investment, achieved some business benefits earlier than originally anticipated and spread the cost out over a longer period which satisfied the Leadership Team concern. This led to a successful project in the mind of all involved.

BEST PRACTICES

- Before you approve any project, it is helpful to ask yourself whether you would approve The Project if it cost 20%, 50%, or even 100% more than anticipated or took longer to complete. The answer to this question may help you decide whether to approve The Project or not. For large projects with considerable duration, risk and cost, this should be an open discussion with the Leadership Team.
- The inclination of people reviewing budgets is to remove any explicit contingency from the budget. This is usually a mistake. What is prudent however, is to place strict controls over the use of the contingency funds so that they can only be used with explicit justification and approval. This will keep the funding in the budget but not make it easy to spend.

ADDRESSING THE QUESTION WITH THE PROJECT TEAM

Project Manager- Discuss with The Project Manger how much time and cost contingency is in the estimate and the types of things they might anticipate   using the contingency for. Also discuss how contingency will be managed. Contingency is like a savings account. You want to have some money in it, but make it a hard to spend so it will only be spent on important things and then only through a formal approval process.

It is also a good idea to have a discussion with The Project Manager about risk. You want to understand what items The Project Manager sees as risky in The Project Schedule/budget. Understanding this will usually help you gauge the likelihood of The Project exceeding the cost and time estimates.

Business Team- Ask The Business Team if they know of additional things that need to be done but which are not included in the approved scope/ budget/ schedule. An example of this might be that the company will need to bring in temporary help in the Payroll Group to backfill for payroll personnel assigned to The Project. Information like this will help you understand how complete the estimates are.

Information Technology Team- Have the same discussion with the Technical Team to understand if there are items that they feel are critical to project success that are not in the current cost and time estimates or if there are items that they feel may cost more than currently estimated.

LESSONS LEARNED FROM PAST PROJECTS

- The more you push to lower project time and cost estimates, the more likely The Project is to exceed those estimates when The Project is completed.. The exception to this is when you ask The Project Team to reduce cost and time by reducing the scope of The Project.
- For large multi-year projects, especially complex Enterprise Resource Planning (ERP), retail systems, manufacturing systems, a good rule of

10. What is the Maximum Amount of Time and Money I am Prepared to Invest in this Project?

thumb is to ask yourself the question- **"would I approve this project if it cost twice as much and/or took twice as long as the estimate"**.

If the answer is clearly yes, move forward immediately. If the answer is no or maybe, you should take a closer look before approving The Project.

What if the short path becomes the long path?

- There are a number of commercial estimating tools on the market. Having used a few of these, they are very helpful for novice estimators, but are no more accurate than the manual estimate of an experienced Project Manager. Make sure that the person/group preparing the time and cost estimates are up to the task.
- If you don't have personnel in your company with deep experience in estimating costs/timeline for large projects, you should strongly consider engaging an outside expert to help create/review the estimate. This will usually help you avoid unpleasant surprises as The Project progresses and will help identify the areas of greatest uncertainty and risk.

RELATED QUESTIONS

20. Does The Business really support this project?

25. How well are project costs being tracked?

27. How were project estimates determined?

11. WHAT WILL THE POST-DEPLOYMENT ORGANIZATION LOOK LIKE?

"The world hates change, but it is the only thing that has brought progress."- Charles Kettering

WHY IS THIS QUESTION IMPORTANT?

Most Technology Projects have little if any impact on your business or IT organizational structure. If that is the case for your Project, then you can skip this chapter. However, some projects either intentionally or as a by-product can have a significant impact on the organizational structure. This could include changes to required mix of personnel, changes in reporting structures, creation of new departments and/or elimination of existing departments.

As soon as it becomes apparent that The Project will necessitate even moderate organizational change, you should begin to plan for it. There are several aspects of the post-deployment organization that you will want to consider.

Q11: What Will the Post-Deployment Organization Look Like?

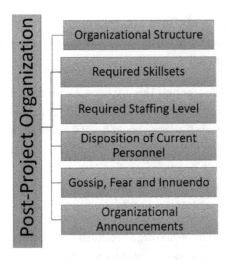

Organizational Structure- The first step in understanding the post-deployment organization changes is to determine the impact on the organizational chart. You should spend time understanding what organization units will be added/changed/eliminated after the conclusion of The Project and will want to identify who is proposed to lead each of the restructured organizational units. This is an important decision that can have profound Human Resources impact especially among your current managers/Executives.

Required Skillsets- You also need to identify the skillsets necessary to support the post-deployment changes. New customer service software might change the role of your call center personnel from merely recording customer complaints to resolving 90% of all complaints while the customer is on the phone. This new role may require re-training and skills development. If The Project necessitates skillset changes in the IT department you should ensure that steps are taken to prepare the IT workforce to be ready to provide necessary support.

Required Staffing Level- If one of The Project's stated business benefits is to achieve cost saving through staff reduction, early in The Project you need to determine exactly where and when these reductions will take place. In some cases, you may need to consider transferring personnel between organizational units to reflect changes in workload and department responsibilities. In any case you need to consider needed headcount changes if any needed to cover the post-deployment period.

Disposition of Current Personnel- This is where the HR decisions become uncomfortable and personal for many people. Once you understand what the go forward organizational structure should be, the required staffing levels, and the required skillsets, you need to map current employees into this structure. Since you are dealing with people's lives and careers you want to approach this fairly and in compliance with all applicable rules and laws. Your HR and Legal Departments should be an integral part of this process.

Gossip, Fear and Innuendo- While organizational change begins as boxes on an organizational chart, it eventually translate into people's lives, careers and families. Do not delude yourself into believing that you can keep discussions of organizational changes isolated to top managers behind closed doors. In most projects that involve significant future organizational change, it can become the all-consuming topic of discussion among the potentially involved groups. It is important that you understand this will occur and that you try to address the issues as candidly as possible given the situation.

Organizational Announcements- Perhaps one of the most critical aspects of changing the organizational structure is deciding how and when this information will be communicated to the organization. If the change is relatively small involving just a very few people, then the issue could be handled relatively easy and perhaps even privately.

If on the other hand, the change is extensive involving layoffs, union personnel, multiple physical locations, plant/office closures, etc. then you want to plan how it will be communicated very carefully and with the participation of the HR and Legal Departments to avoid future problems. This includes both communications within the company and externally.

REAL WORLD EXAMPLE

A major company embarked on a project that included a fundamental re-structuring of the Corporate IT department. This was a stated objective from the beginning of The Project. Over an 8-12 moth period, Corporate Management would fly in and talk to some managers but not others about the new structure. At employee "all hands" meetings, the Executives would deny that any organization discussion were taking place even though that was clearly not the case. Productivity and morale on The Project and in the IT organization in general decreased significantly resulting in poor deliverables and missed deadlines.

By the end of the process, many of the most talented people had long ago left the company and Management was forced to fill lead positions in the new organizational structure with second tier talent. The irony is that it eventually came out that Corporate Executives had decided not to interview a number of key personnel because they had already selected them to fill key roles in the new structure. The employees on the other hand assumed that since they were not interviewed they had no future in the organization. If someone had let these key resources know this, the company would have retained a number of very talented resources.

BEST PRACTICES

- If a Technology Project is likely to involve more than nominal organizational/personnel change, appoint an Executive to lead the organizational transformation effort supported by a team of Executives/Managers from all affected areas plus HR and Legal.
- To the extent possible, minimize the amount of time between when you begin to consider organizational changes and when you announce them publically to lessen the amount time for fear and gossip to take hold.

Section 1 Executive Oversight Questions

- Ensure all required HR, Legal, Union, and Executive reviews are completed and the change is formally approved before announcing it.
- If the organizational change includes personnel leaving the company, ensure that you have support resources readily and immediately available to discuss issues such as timing, transition support, benefits continuity, and severance pay.
- If you have key personnel that are needed to support the current organizational structure but who will not be part of the new structure, consider providing "Stay Bonuses" to compensate them for remaining as long as they are needed.

ADDRESSING THE QUESTION WITH THE PROJECT TEAM

Project Manager- Organizational structure changes are generally (but not always) handled outside of The Project Team Structure. However, you should discuss with The Project Manager when in The Project Schedule the organizational decisions need to be made and request that tasks/milestone related to organizational change be added to the schedule.

Business Team- While The Business Lead may be involved in organizational structure meetings, in general, The Business Team is only involved when the results of the change are announced.

Information Technology Team- Exactly the same as The Business Team

Steering Committee- As soon as the need for organizational change is identified, the Steering Committee should be made aware of this and begin to discuss how to proceed. The Steering Committee should determine who is to lead the change effort and how results/progress are to be reported.

Human Resources- HR should be engaged in The Project as soon as the need for organizational changes have been identified. They should assign a sufficiently senior person to the process to ensure that all applicable corporate rules and government laws are followed. You should heed their guidance on all HR aspects of the change process.

Legal Department- Unless the HR Department is staffed with personnel competent to render legal advice, you should engage the Corporate Legal Department to assist in the organizational change process. As with the HR process, you should carefully consider all advice and direction that they provide.

LESSONS LEARNED FROM PAST PROJECTS

- It is impossible to keep employees from knowing discussions on organizational changes are occurring. Also, regardless of direction to keep discussions confidential, results will slowly trickle out to the organization with little regard as to whether the information is accurate or not.
- If you reach a point where everyone is questioning whether they will have a job after deployment or not, it will be your best employees that will leave not your worst. If there are people that you feel are important to be retained in the new environment, then to the extent HR/Legal will allow, you should give private assurances about their future. Even a chance comment over drinks at happy hour can go a long way towards easing the fear
- HR and Legal have to be heartless and pragmatic when it comes to organizational changes. However keep in mind that these are real people and you should try very hard to treat them how you would like to be treated.
- If you have talented and dedicated employees that because of the organizational changes are no longer needed in their current organization, think outside of the box and consider what they might be able to accomplish in another part of the company with some training.

RELATED QUESTIONS

2. How will the benefits of this project be achieved and verified?

15. Is there a holistic view of required business and technical changes?

12. SHOULD I ASK FOR AN OUTSIDE REVIEW OF THE PROJECT?

"Objectivity – 1. Based on observable phenomena; empirical: objective facts. 2. Uninfluenced by emotions or personal prejudices" American Heritage Dictionary of the English Dictionary

WHY IS THIS QUESTION IMPORTANT?

Success of large Technology Projects depends to a large part on the dedication of The Project Team. This team often works long hours in a stressful environment striving hard to be successful. Unfortunately, this dedication and drive clouds their objectivity.

Project Teams become so invested in project success that they cannot step back and objectively see what it will take to make The Project successful and to understand the true status of a project. I have led Project Teams myself where we think that if we can just work a few extra weekends and have some luck, we can get back on track.

In situations like these, it is often helpful to bring an outside perspective to The Project from someone who has not been actively involved. In the case of large complex risky projects, this moves from being a helpful idea to being a critical need. The outside perspective does not have the emotional baggage that people on The Project Team have from their long work on The Project and can provide an objective assessment of The Project.

Section 1 Executive Oversight Questions

An outside review is not appropriate for all projects. Such reviews can temporarily hurt morale on The Project Team, disrupt The Project for a period of time as the evaluation is being conducted, and incur costs that must be absorbed by The Project budget. However, when a review is justified, you should not hesitate to do so. On troubled projects, an outside review is nearly always money well spent.

Here are some indicators that a project would benefit from an outside review

- The Project has significantly missed key milestone/ deliverable dates in the last few months.
- The Project is currently overdue on a considerable number of tasks/activities.
- The Project Manager regularly changes due dates on tasks and milestones
- The Project stops issuing status reports or issues vague status
- There is significant turnover in project staff due to morale problems
- Staffing is significantly above or below that originally projected
- Key Stakeholders are getting numerous complaints from their participants on The Project
- Vendors on The Project are requesting significant contract changes because of project delays or scope changes
- You no longer trust that The Project Team is giving you accurate status

For several years, I worked as part of a team that specialized in independent project evaluations. Most of these reviews were initiated by very Senior Leadership or even by the Company Board of Directors. The primary issue that drove most companies to engage our group came down the trust. Senior Leadership reached a point where they no longer trusted the assurance of The Project Team and no longer trusted their ability to deliver the intended business value within the timeframes and budgets approved.

Trust?
Years to earn, seconds to break.

Results of outside reviews I have been involved in have run the continuum from determining that The Project Team was doing an adequate job with only minor changes needed to determination that The Project should be immediately terminated and a new Project Team/concept be considered. The most extreme cases resulted in litigation with vendors to recoup payments made for work determined not to meet standards.

An outside project review should be a tightly focused examination of key project components. It is best done quickly and efficiently so as not to disrupt the on-going process any more than is necessary. Key areas that should be covered in The Project review include:

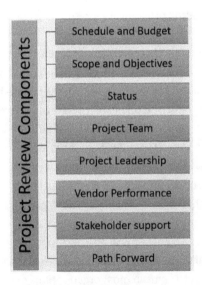

- **Schedule and Budget**- The review team should compare the earliest Project Schedules and budget documents to the current schedule/budget to understand how these have changed over time. The purpose of this analysis is to develop an informed opinion on current schedule and budget reliability.

Section 1 Executive Oversight Questions

- **Scope and Objectives**- The current Project Scope and objectives should be examined to see if they are still in alignment with the original scope. A determination should be made as to whether The Project is likely to deliver the scope and meet these objectives. In particular, the review should look at whether The Project is likely to achieve the planned business benefits.

- **Status**- The accuracy of status reporting should be carefully examined. On a spot check basis, the review team should talk directly to the personnel accomplishing the work to ensure that current status is objectively understood. Key to this is to review status from the perspective of both The Project leadership, but also with the rank and file people doing the work.

- **Project Team**- The review should look at how the well the team functions as a group, morale, turnover, decision-making processes, and team member experience, etc. Rancor within a Project Team can have a devastating effect on project success. Recommendations on staffing levels, replacement of ineffective personnel, team organizational structure, operating procedures, etc should all be included in the review process.

- **Project Leadership**- The review team should spend time with each of the key leaders on The Project to develop an informed opinion as to their capabilities and effectiveness. Removing someone from a key leadership position should never be taken lightly as it has an impact both on The Project and the person. However, sometimes, the best thing for both The Project and the person involved is to make a change.

- **Vendor Performance**- If The Project involves participation from vendors, their contractual performance should be examined to see if the organization is getting what they are paying for. Most vendors are highly ethical and perform beyond the contractual minimums, but that is not always the case. The Project Teams in most organizations may have only worked on a large project once or twice.  In these cases, The Project Team may not have the skill and experience to face off against an experienced delivery manager from a large vendor who is compensated on their ability to expand contracts. The review team should include someone with expertise in evaluating vendor contractual performance to level this playing field.

- **Stakeholder Support**- Each Stakeholder on The Project should be interviewed as part of the review to determine their level of support of The Project and their views on where The Project should go. Concerns raised by the Stakeholders should be investigated by the review team and included in the review findings. Understanding current Stakeholder support is a key to finding a path forward.

- **Path Forward**- It is usually not difficult to find a number of minor or not so minor things that have not gone as planned even on successful projects. The value of an outside review is not to point fingers, but rather to get an objective experienced view of The Project. This should include an evaluation of which project issues are important and recommendations of how The Project should proceed..The go forward recommendation must be specific in detail and must be practically implementable within the organization. In the end, this recommendation is the key review deliverable and it must be brutally candid and detailed.

REAL WORLD EXAMPLE

A regional financial services company had a large strategic project to replace major systems. The Project had missed several key deliverable dates, had a major deployment scheduled about 2 months in the future which was not deemed achievable, and the prime vendor had requested a senior level meeting to "review the contract". Based on this and a general feeling of unease about the status of The Project, the CEO asked for an outside review of The Projects.

This review showed issues with The Business providing access to required people, ineffective vendor oversight, poor morale with in The Project, and no real vision on how The Project could be delivered on time.

Our team recommended shuffling of The Project management to better align skills and interests with duties, implementation of a Project Management

Office (PMO) with a significant increase in project management rigor, assistance in negotiating with and managing the prime vendor, and a strategic re-alignment of the deployment date to increase the chance of a successful launch while moving to a time window that better aligned with business cycles. These relatively minor and inexpensive changes resulted in a successful deployment albeit a few months later than originally planned. However this was preferable to the original path which was likely to have resulted in deployment of software that did not work correctly prematurely just to trigger payment of fees to the prime vendor.

BEST PRACTICES

- To be successful, an outside review must be sanctioned by Senior Leadership. This must include a clear and public message to all involved with The Project that empowers the review team to talk to anyone on The Project, to review any documentation requested, and to ask any question deemed relevant. This empowerment by the top Executive is critical to keeping The Project Team from refusing to participate in the review.
- You should engage a person or group to perform The Project review based on the skillset of the individuals that will be onsite preforming the review not just the reputation of the company. It does not add any value to your Project if you engage a company that has done hundreds of similar reviews in the past, yet the review team they are providing are all recent college graduates with no experience.
- Project reviews are best done by highly experienced personnel with deep experience and the force of personality to ask what I call the "impolite questions".
- The review itself should be short in duration to minimize disruption, but of sufficient duration to cover the needed areas. In general, I like to review

Better to get hurt by the truth than comforted with a lie. –

Khaled Hosseini

as much project documentation as possible before coming onsite then concluding the review in a maximum of 2 to 3 weeks on on-site work. With time to review results and create the report, it is often possible to complete the review in less than a month.

- Results of the review should be first communicated to the Senior Leadership team that requested the review and then with The Project Team. Addressing the recommendations with The Project Team first usually results in immediate efforts to spin and discredit the report results. This distracts from the facts and the recommendations. You should report first to the people that requested the review and then allocate as much time as needed to review and discuss with The Project Team.

ADDRESSING THE QUESTION WITH THE PROJECT TEAM

Project Manager- Telling The Project Manager that you are going to bring in an outside person/group to review The Project is not necessarily an easy conversation. It is human nature for The Project Manager to get defensive and argue that the review is not necessary since they already know what The Project problems are.

Stress to The Project Manager that the goal is the help The Project be successful overall and that they will have an opportunity to provide their insight and thoughts to the review team. In the end though, stress that the review is going to happen and that you expect cooperation and openness.

Business Team- The Business Team needs to understand the need to be candid with the review team about status and direction of The Project. They also need to understand the goal of improving The Project.

Technical Team- As with The Business Team, stress to the Technical Team that they need to be candid in providing information and insight and that the Review Team is representing Upper Management and cooperation is expected.

LESSONS LEARNED FROM PAST PROJECTS

- Project Teams on troubled projects often argue that they are too busy to participate in an outside review. They will use this excuse to decline meeting appointments and refuse to participate in discussions. A clear communication issued directly by a key Executive will help prevent this. However, one other key is to have a senior Administrative Assistant who is well known throughout the organizations made available to assist in scheduling appointments, finding meeting rooms, and coercing people to participate in meetings. Their participation adds instant credibility to the review team.

- You should insist that the review team adopt a "two source" approach to determining facts. The accuracy of any key information that will lead to a recommendation for change must be validated by a second source. These sources could be documentation or interview, but it is important to get two sources for all findings to ensure help insure the accuracy of the facts that drive the recommendations.

- Project problems are like medical problems. Once they begin to manifest themselves, they rarely resolve themselves. Delaying addressing project problems usual makes things worse and more expensive to resolve. If you think you are having significant problems, don't delay too long triggering a review. The longer the wait, the more money you will have spent on The Project and the less time will be left to make required corrections.

- A rule of thumb is that if you have had more than one or two hallway conversations worried about not knowing the real status of The Project or if it has been openly discussed in meetings, it is probably time to bring in someone to do a review. At the best, it will confirm that everything is on track, but also will discover problems if they exists

- You are hiring the review team to give informed opinions based on The Project situation. Be prepared that not everyone will agree with these opinions especially in areas where they have a vested interest. In some cases, you are literally telling people that "your baby is ugly" and the reaction to that is pretty predictable.

- A tendency when an organization decides to do an external review is to use the company that performs your outside audits or to engage a large consulting firm to perform the review. Be careful that you are getting experienced personnel and recommendations that are not biased by plans to sell you extensive assistance in "fixing" the problems. It is not uncommon for large consulting company to provide recommendations that include engaging a large team from their Company to implement the recommendations.

Consider instead using a truly independent review team that is not in the core business of selling project resources, but rather in The Business of making unbiased project recommendations. If you do decide to use a large consulting company for the review, consider reaching an understanding with them that they will not be engaged for any follow-on remediation work and see if they are still interested in doing the review. If the review is not truly independent and unbiased, it cannot be trusted.

RELATED QUESTIONS

3. What Is the impact if The Project fails?

4. How will I know if project status is being misrepresented?

37. How is project morale?

SECTION 2: WHAT BUSINESS RELATED QUESTIONS SHOULD YOU ASK?

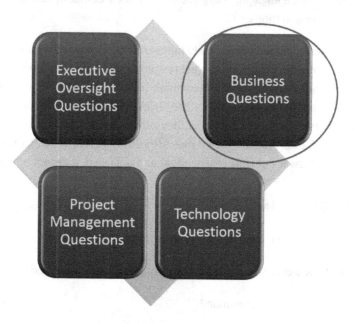

One key theme that I emphasize continually with Project Teams is that every Technology Project exists only to provide some business benefit. If you cannot identify The Business benefit of The Project (either quantitatively or qualitatively) then The Project should not go forward.

Even the most technical of projects such as replacing a network router should have an identifiable business benefit such as improving user response time, increasing system uptime, reducing maintenance cost, etc.

This section of the book focuses on the questions that Executives should ask to ensure that The Business needs and benefits are clearly understood and are being addressed in The Project.

13. Does each documented requirement have real business value?

14. Is the cost of unwillingness to change business processes understood?

15. Is there a holistic view of required business and technical changes?

16. Is there a strategy for statutory record retention?

17. Is the strategic impact of project timing being effectively managed?

18. Is the tactical deployment plan acceptable to The Business?

19. Are all impacted Stakeholders actively involved in The Project?

20. Does The Business really support this project?

21. Who is really speaking for The Business on The Project?

22. Are customer and Supplier impacts of The Project understood?

23. Are project business requirements well documented?

24. Are external access requirements understood?

13. DOES <u>EACH</u> DOCUMENTED REQUIREMENT HAVE REAL BUSINESS VALUE?

"Those who buy unnecessary things all the time, will have to sell all the necessary things in the end to pay for them"- Benjamin Franklin

WHY IS THIS QUESTION IMPORTANT?

I am continually amazed and dismayed about how many laws passed in the United States have provisions that have nothing to do with the stated intent of the law. For example in a 2102 Social Security Bill passed by Congress, there was a provision preventing the Environmental Protection Agency from applying pollution standards to industrial boilers. In 2009, a provision expanding the definition of hate crimes was added to a must pass Defense Appropriation bill.

These types of provisions are added to important legislations because they would likely not be able to gain approval on their own merits. They are often inserted into large proposed Bills at the last minute by someone with power and political savvy. When the bill goes to the president, there are only two choices- approve the legislation in total or reject it in total.

Q13: Does <u>Each</u> Documented Requirement Have Real Business Value?

You may be asking yourself what this has to do with Technology Projects. It turns out that requirements documents are not unlike bills in congress in that they may contain items that would not stand on their own merits either because of their cost, their limited benefits, or even their have nothing to do with the stated purpose of The Project.

Once Business and IT managers discover that there is a project starting up that has Executive support, overall business value, and most importantly funding, there is a natural tendency to try and add scope items to that project to further the agendas of their parts of the organization. The larger the Technology Project, the more likely it is to have unnecessary and/or unrelated components. Identifying and eliminating these unnecessary items can result in significantly lower project costs and more importantly, shorten Project Schedules.

It is important to keep in mind that unlike the US Government, organizations have another option than to just approve everything or approve nothing. That option is to look at the requirements one at a time and only approve those items that have direct business value. This approach is proven to significantly lower project costs usually without having significant impact on The Business objectives of The Project.

REQUIREMENTS GATHERING

To understand this, you have to understand how requirements are usually elicited from users. Often a number of people are brought together in a conference room to determine what the requirements for a project will be. Alternatively, a Business Analyst will sit one on one with a business user and ask then what they think the system needs to be able to do. In either case, notes are taken documenting the "requirements" and then there are usually a couple of rounds of reviewing the verbiage of the requirements followed by an approval. This approval is often by a manager that was not involved in the requirements session and probably has not had the time to read and fully understand the Requirements Document.

Section 2: Business Related Questions

So much time is spent working on the exact wording of each requirement, often no one questions whether the requirement is really necessary, whether its value to The Business justifies its cost, and whether it is within the scope of The Project. A perfect example of this is the definition of reports (which is covered in a separate chapter elsewhere). I have seen numerous projects where over half of the reports developed at considerable time and expense are never or rarely used. Likewise I have seen literally millions of dollars spent on complex automated workflow processes that in the end save one or two people a few hours a month of work.

Do not assume that just because The Project has overall business benefit that each individual component of it also has benefits that justify their cost. Make sure that in one last pass before requirements are finalized, each is examined individually for value to The Business and necessity. Doing so will likely reduce both cost and The Project timeline.

REAL WORLD EXAMPLE

I was part of a very large global program for a manufacturing company with design, procurement, and manufacturing operations literally around the world. A multi-year project was launched to make small but fundamental changes in systems that would allow greater flexibility in moving design, procurement, and manufacturing processes quickly between regions/countries. This project had tremendous financial benefits and was a top Corporate priority.

Originally about 45 projects over a 2 year period were identified and quickly funded for immediate launch. These projects progressed well towards completion/ deployment when it was announced that about 60 additional projects had been identified as being required for the program to be a success. Since these were all part of this key corporate initiative, they were quickly approved with only cursory review and fully funded.

Q13: Does <u>Each</u> Documented Requirement Have Real Business Value?

The next year, more projects were identified as being needed, etc. until the 2 year project became a nearly 4 year project and costs had more than doubled.

Later analysis showed that much of the work in the later projects had very little to do with the original objective, but were added because this program was fully funded and others were not being funded. Business and IT Leaders added projects to the overall program and dramatically inflated the scope of projects to include items that they had previously been unsuccessfully in getting funded. One system that only needed a small database changes and small changes to two interfaces to support the global initiative was found to be scoped out with a new simulation tool and data warehouse for reporting.

REAL WORLD EXAMPLE TWO

When it is time to buy a new car, you begin to notice ads for the car you want showing the Manufacturer's Suggested Retail Price (MSRP) is say around $30K. At this price point, the vehicle contains everything that you need in a good looking basic vehicle to commute to work each day. So you go to the dealership and look at cars suddenly noticing that all of the cars are as much as $10K or so above the based MSRP because they have upgraded wheels, sun roofs, special paint, trim packages, etc.

While these features do make the car look a little better, you question whether these upgrades are worth paying extra for, so you opt for the basic car and achieve all of your original goals at a reasonable price. You don't want to pay for features that have little or no value to your organization.

BEST PRACTICES
- Just because The Project as a whole has value do not assume that every facet of it is required.
- Ensure that each requirement documented is reviewed from the perspective of cost justification
- Keep in mind however, that one aspect of business value is future cost to maintain the system so if there are requirements that are geared to

reduction of future operational costs, that future value should be considered.

- If many of the requirements are technical, you may want to consider engaging outside help in reviewing the requirements with the Technical Team for necessity.
- As part of the final signoff process, make sure that The Business and Technical Leads/managers, understand their role in certifying business necessity of each requirement.

ADDRESSING THE QUESTION WITH THE PROJECT TEAM

Project Manager- Ask The Project Manager to describe the requirements validation process being followed. Ensure that this process includes not only a mechanism to determine if requirements are properly worded and documented, but also a way to determining whether each requirement is individually justified.

Business Team- Emphasize in discussions with The Business Lead and Executive Sponsor their role in controlling scope and ensuring business value at the requirement level. Make sure that whoever approves the requirements for The Business Team has taken the time to actually read the requirements in sufficient detail to validate that it is needed.

Technical Team- Make sure that the Technical Team understands that one of their roles is to help The Business Team understand how easy/hard requirements might be to implement. Also, the Technical Team needs to understand that they should ensure each of the technical requirements are individually justifiable.

Steering Committee- Make sure that the Steering Committee understands their role in challenging individual requirements for business value. This may be an unfamiliar role for some Business Leaders.

LESSONS LEARNED FROM PAST PROJECTS
- It is not enough that to approve The Project at the macro level, it is the details at the micro level that truly drive cost and duration.

Q13: Does <u>Each</u> Documented Requirement Have Real Business Value?

- It is often difficult for people to articulate what they need a system to accomplish and to write that in a clear and concise manner. You should use experienced Business Analysts trained in extracting good requirements from users to facilitate the process.

> You can't just ask customers what they want and then try to give it to them. By the time you get it built, they'll want something new. - Steve Job

- It takes more effort, but there is often value in developing cost estimates for each requirement or logical grouping of requirements versus one overall project estimate. This facilitates a review of cost vs value at the requirement level.
- Often Business and Technical Team members have little understanding of how much individual requirements on a project cost to develop. They are usually not privy to hourly rate/cost information or even software cost information. **Numerous times, I have been told by users that if they had known how much a particular feature would cost or how long it would take to implement, they would not have wanted it.**
- When looking for unnecessary requirements, pay particular attention to requirements that are short and vague. These requirements are often very high level and less thought out than the more completely documented requirements. An example of this might be "Must have flexible reporting capability". While undoubtedly useful if properly developed, if you don't define this more precisely, you could literally spend a year + and millions of dollars on these innocent 5 words.
- Many Technology Projects include approved requirements that when fully implemented are rarely if ever used. An example of this is shown

121

in a study by the Standish Group in 2004 showing how often features in XP2002 were being used. It determined that only 20% of the features were used often while 64%f the features were rarely if ever used. These are the type of requirements that you want to ferret out of The Project. Doing so can result in significant cost and time savings.

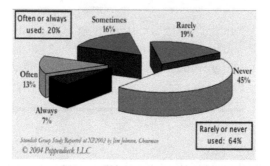

- There are a few "buzz words" that often only defined at the high level but which ultimately can increase cost dramatically as details are added. Examples of these include- simulation engines, automated workflow systems, data warehouses, mobile applications, decision dashboards, trend analysis, and proactive business alerts. These are all useful and powerful components that can add great value to systems. However, they are also usually very complex, expensive, and time consuming to build. Examine these types of requirements carefully to insure they are sufficiently detailed and have clear business justification.
- Unrelated requirements are just as likely to be slipped into already funded projects by Senior IT/Business Managers as they are to be added by users. I was on one military project where Technology Projects were only being funded as part of one major initiative if they were "field deployable to help the soldier in the field". To get funding under this program, the Senior Officers on The Project approved a plan to strap some servers, printers, terminal, generators, etc. to a pallet and push it on a helicopter to show that our central office based payroll system was in fact "field deployable".

122

Q13: Does <u>Each</u> Documented Requirement Have Real Business Value?

- Organizations that will negotiate hard to get a savings of ten cents per part will often approve a requirements document with little negotiation as to business benefits versus cost
- It is worth mentioning again. The person who signs their name as approving the detailed requirements document is going to commit the organization to significant cost and time expenditure, so they should actually take the time to read the document in enough detail to perform their business oversight function. Alternatively, they could have a trusted proxy review the requirements in detail prior to their being approved.
- It is important to create a culture where it is not only OK to challenge requirements, but where it there is an expectation that everyone will do so.
- Once requirements are fully documented, validated, and approved, carefully control the requirements baseline to ensure that items that could not get approval as part of the formal requirements process don't get added back into The Project covertly. This happens more often than you might think. All changes after requirements approval need to go through a formal Change Management process.

RELATED QUESTIONS

1. Are The Project objectives clear to all?

15. Is there a holistic view of required business and technical changes?

21. Who is really speaking for The Business on The Project?

23. Are project business requirements well documented?

14. IS THE COST OF UNWILLINGNESS TO MODIFY BUSINESS PROCESSES UNDERSTOOD?

"Resistance at all cost is the most senseless act there is. "- Friedrich Durrenmatt

WHY IS THIS QUESTION IMPORTANT?

One of the most expensive decisions a company can make on a large software package implementation project is whether to change the purchased software to align with current business processes or to change business processes to align with the best practices embodied in the software package. This decision will impact system usability, how long The Project will take to reach initial deployment, the cost of that initial deployment, and maintenance costs far into the future.

Significantly modifying purchased software often changes the fundamental way that the software works and changes how data is stored. It also often adversely affects system performance, and greatly increases project cost. Just as importantly, the changes must be carried forward as new versions of the purchased software become available requiring what is often significant on-going software maintenance effort just to keep the software working.

Often The Business Team is not made aware of the cost impact of making major changes to purchased software and so logically will want to retain

Q14: Is the Cost of Unwillingness to Modify Business Processes Understood?

familiar current business processes even if this involves making significant software changes.

While this may be the right thing to do in many cases, you should not decide to make major package software modifications lightly. It is prudent in these situations to examine your existing business processes to see if there are opportunities for improvement. This should include allocating time to examine The Business processes that are built into the software you have purchased.

These business processes are usually well thought out, comprehensive, and represent industry "best practices". **You should robustly challenge the team to explain why The Business processes built into the software will not work for your organization. An explanation of "that is not how we do it" is not sufficient to explain why the new processes will not work for your company.**

REAL WORLD EXAMPLE

A large manufacturing company was implementing a new financial system. This company had a long-standing way of doing month end processing with reports that were generated in a certain formats and routed to different departments for review and creation of closing entries. This existing process was cumbersome, time consuming and often put month end closing at risk. However, it was considered "how things **had** to be done". In planning implementation of the new system, The Business Team was adamant in insisting that the system be significantly modified to support the current closing process albeit with automation support to make it more efficient.

This would have nearly doubled the cost of the financial system part of The Project and would have perpetuated the inefficient manual process. Ultimately, company Executives decided to use the closing process/reports built into the software which were being used by many similar companies.

This resulted in significant savings in cost, time and future effort. Once all parts of The Business became accustomed to the new processes, monthly closing became much smoother requiring less time and effort than it had previously.

BEST PRACTICES

- Implement package software "out of the box" to the greatest extent possible. All major software packages require configuration such as adding chart of accounts, addresses, etc. as a normal part of the deployment. These changes are normal and make good business sense. What you want to avoid to the greatest extent possible is making code/database changes to the purchased application. These are expensive to implement initially and require continue effort to maintain of the life of the system.

Any requirements that result in a need to significantly customize the software package should be accompanied by a clear justification and be approved by senior project sponsors. Keep a log of all requirements that result in software customization including recording which sponsor approved the customization

ADDRESSING THE QUESTION WITH THE PROJECT TEAM

Project Manager- Ask The Project Manager to see the customization log periodically to ensure that it is being maintained and to keep a sense of how much customization is being done to the purchase software. Additionally, you should have The Project Manager include information about approved customization periodically in Steering Committee presentations.

Business Team- You should periodically remind The Business Team that software customization is expensive in terms of time and money. If there is an insistence on keeping current business processes, ask how that gives the company a competitive advantage and ask them to explain why the out of the box processes cannot work.

Technical Team- Early in The Project make sure that Technical Managers understand your organization's view on customization. It is not uncommon for the Technical Team to build significant customizations

126

without even telling The Business Team or Management the costs involved. Some see this not as a cost to the company but instead as being responsive to The Business. Developers like to develop software and often are reluctant to push back on The Business Team when it comes to business requirements due to cost and complexity. However, it is in the best interest of the organization as a whole to do so when justified.

In discussions with the Technical Team, you should ask how difficult it will be to maintain the customizations as new versions of the software are installed. They should be able to articulate their strategy and staffing needs to maintain customizations going forward. The answers to these questions should guide how much software customization you will approve.

Executive Team- It is critical that the Executive Sponsors/Steering Committee responsible for The Project are made to understand the cost and time impact of being inflexible on changes to business processes. This is the group that The Business Team will approach to argue for the necessity of keeping all existing business processes so they need to understand the impact.

LESSONS LEARNED FROM PAST PROJECTS

- It is not an exaggeration to state that extensive customization of packaged software can more than double the cost of the implementation over the life of the system and delay deployment significantly. This is difficult for an organization to justify when the only argument for extensive customization is "that is not how we do things" or "that will not work here" without solid reasoning as to why that is the case.
- Create a culture where it is not only acceptable for people to question customizations, but where it is expected that people will do so. In the end, it is the domain of The Business Team/Business Sponsors to decide what is required.
- A cost/time estimate should be made for each customization effort. This estimate should be

127

shared with The Business Team and sponsors for approval.

- Having an Executive Sponsor deliver a strong message on minimizing customization at the beginning of The Project to both The Business and Technical Teams is crucial to setting the tone for The Project.
- Package software customizations often are forced to use relatively inefficient ways of integrating into the core software and are historically prone to performance issues.
- A cost/time estimate should be made for each customization effort. This estimate should be shared with The Business Team and sponsors for approval.
- One good way of evaluating requests for customization is based on whether the area is a strategic differentiator for the company. If your

There's a way to do it better - find it. -
Thomas A. Edison

business is steel processing and you are customizing software to implement a proprietary manufacturing process that no other company has, that may be a good candidate for customization. However, in that same instance, significantly customizing the payroll process is probably less supportable since all companies have payroll that follow fundamentally the same rules.

- Make a conscious decision that the excuse "we have always done it that way" is not sufficient to justify the cost of customization and that additional justification is required.
- Any assumption from The Business Team that the objective of The Project is to "just automate what we do now" should be thoroughly challenged. Existing processes are often tied to existing software and forms. Take this as an opportunity to improve these processes and tailor them in such a way that the software will be support them.
- Make sure you ask the question "why can't it work out of the box" to The Business Team. Sometimes the answer given by business users is as unsupportable as "we don't like how the screens look".

128

Q14: Is the Cost of Unwillingness to Modify Business Processes Understood?

- Often The Business Team will not expend sufficient time trying to understand how the software is intended to work before they push for modifications. Do not approve any customization unless The Business Team can demonstrate to you that they understand how the system functions without customizations. If they cannot demonstrate how it works, they probably have not taken the time to fully understand what you have purchased.

- Although assurances from the software vendor should be carefully evaluated, they are a good source to help the team understand what is possible without customization. Usually such advice is provided at no cost as part of the "pre-sales" process up to the point you sign a purchase contract. After that point, expect to pay for assistance from the vendor and even then, it is usually money well spent.

- Ensure that one or more experienced resources with expertise in the software package being implemented are part of The Project Team. This will nearly always significantly reduce the amount of customization requested as they are able to explain to both The Business and Technical Teams how to configure the system to best meet The Business requirements. Although such expertise is usually not cheap, it nearly always saves money in the end and more importantly reduces the time it takes to deploy.

- In spite of everything above, sometimes customization is unavoidable. Don't entirely reject the idea of software customization. Instead limit customization to what is truly necessary. There should be a balance between the desire to continue following current processes and the costs of doing so. The goal is to make an informed decision based on the costs and benefits.

RELATED QUESTIONS

13. Does each documented requirement have real business value?

15. Is there a holistic view of required business and technical changes?

15. IS THERE A HOLISTIC VIEW OF REQUIRED BUSINESS AND TECHNICAL CHANGES?

"I cannot say whether things will get better if we change; what I can say is they must change if they are to get better."- Georg C. Lichtenberg

WHY IS THIS QUESTION IMPORTANT?

In today's highly integrated business environment, Business and Technical processes are tightly intertwined. It is increasingly difficult to make technical changes without needed to make corresponding business changes and vice versa. This is especially true if one of the goals of The Project is to make processes more efficient.

One of the challenges this presents is coordinating the changes between The Business and Technical Teams. This is especially true with respect to the timing of changes. If business processes are changing, the design of the new business process must be well underway when the Technical Team begins to build the system or it is likely that the new system will not fully support the revised business processes. Likewise it may not be possible to fully implement new business processes until the accompanying system changes are in place.

Q15: Is There a Holistic View of Required Business and Technical Changes?

Therefore, it is important that there be a single view of the timing of The Business and Technical changes so that the dependencies between the two can be managed.

REAL WORLD EXAMPLE

A company approved a major project to change from manual assembly of promotional coupon books to automated assembly and publishing of physical books. For the first time, the organization was also planning to electronically publish coupons to the web/mobile devices. Since The Business processes related to the new technology were still being determined, initial system requirements were created to merely automate the existing manual processes as they were. This included automation of workflow and processing steps that were no longer needed using the new system.

Fortunately, this process misalignment was discovered before significant amounts of time and money were spent on software development. The development effort was delayed slightly until the new business processes were agreed to and requirements could be changed to reflect the new procedures. If The Business and Technical Teams had not been working closely together on process change, this may not have been discovered until the testing process resulting in considerable time and cost waste.

BEST PRACTICES

- The Project Schedule should include the tasks/ milestones/ dependencies required to ensure Business and Technical changes are made as needed. This will help ensure that progress can be monitored throughout the duration of The Project.
- A simple one page pictorial timeline view of the inter-relationship between the timing of The Business and Technical changes helps all participants understand the overall timing.

ADDRESSING THE QUESTION WITH THE PROJECT TEAM

Project Manager- In discussions with The Project Manager, state your expectation that The Project Manager is responsible for ensuring that all required changes are managed, not just the technical changes. Ask to see the tasks in The Project Schedule that explicitly cover Change Management.

Business Team - The Business Team should be able to explain how they have determined which business process changes are necessary and how they intend to validate the overall system supports these new processes. Additionally, you should ask if the approved requirements for the new system reflect The Business processes that are intended to be in place at the point of deployment or the current business processes.

Technical Team - The Technical Team should be able to articulate the process changes that The Business intends to make and how the system will support these changes. If either group cannot readily discuss how change will be coordinated within The Project, you should insist upon a meeting between The Business and Technical Teams to discuss the process changes anticipated. This meeting should be facilitated by The Project Manager.

LESSONS LEARNED FROM PAST PROJECTS

- The Business Team often continues to refine the new business processes after system requirements are agreed upon. While this is inefficient in that it often necessitates re-work, it is probably inevitable. Any required changes discovered after requirements are approved should only be approved using formal Change Management processes including an estimate of the cost/time impact of the change.

- If major business process changes are anticipated, you should consider engaging a consultant specializing in Change Management to help shepherd the change process. Their expertise in getting consensus on change is well worth the cost and will result in an overall smoother development and deployment processes

- Making process changes especially in a larger organization is often very difficult and quickly becomes "political". Often people and organizations have a vested interested in continuing current processes and will try to thwart change either actively or passively. This is especially true when the resultant changes have the potential to impact jobs or reporting structures. Executive assistance is often required to keep the change process on track.

- You want to ensure changes are agreed upon (however reluctantly) all the way from the clerk level to the Executive level early in The Project. Keep in mind that anyone between these levels usually has the capacity to derail the implementation of change either covertly or overtly.

- Often the Technical Team wants to make business process decisions for The Business. Members of the Technical Team sometimes have also worked in The Business organization and/or have been working in a particular area so long they begin to believe that they know what is best for The Business. While their suggestions are both valuable and expected, all business changes must be fully embraced by The Business or there is a high likelihood of failure.

- Likewise, The Business Team is inclined to want to make technical change decisions on a project. Business Team member insight on technical changes is often very valuable, but ultimately, the Technical

Team will be responsible for creating and maintaining the solution and thus should have the final say in all technical decisions.

- Ensure that all new business processes are fully documented in enough detail that there is a clear understanding of what was agreed to. Lack of clarity in written requirements is a common cause of strife within The Project Team. It can also cause users to refuse to accept the new system, and is a significant caused of cost and time overruns.

RELATED QUESTIONS

1. Are The Project objectives clear to all?

19. Are all impacted Stakeholders actively involved in The Project?

22. Are customer and Supplier impacts of The Project understood?

23. Are project business requirements well documented?

16. IS THERE A STRATEGY FOR STATUTORY RECORD RETENTION?

"By some estimates, the data-storage curve is rocketing upward at the rate of 800 percent per year. Organizations are collecting so much data they're overwhelmed." Jeff Davidson

WHY IS THIS QUESTION IMPORTANT?

A sometimes neglected aspect managing electronic data is the need to ensure that your Project Team retains data necessary to satisfy legal and regulatory requirements. This can be more complex than either The Business or Technical Teams may understand. There are numerous factors that may influence how long you need to retain certain types of data such as the type of business you conduct, Federal and State Regulations, etc. Examples of this include Dodd-Frank Act for financial records, Sarbanes-Oxley for audit related papers and other information, HIPAA rules for health related data, etc.

The question of data retention becomes considerably more complex if the organization also conducts business or has operations outside of the United States. In that case, a clear understanding of sometimes conflicting rules must be understood especially if the data is generated in or related to operations in one country but stored in another country.

Your organization must also ensure that the data retention policies consider business needs in additional to the regulatory requirements. For each type of data in the system, there should be a formal decision as to how long this data should be retained taking into account all retention needs.

Section 2: Business Related Questions

Paradoxically, there is a competing emerging trend to set maximum retention periods for certain types of data in companies. This is especially true in the case of emails, text messages, etc. which are more informal in wording than official documents and sometimes contain personal viewpoints rather than corporate policy. In a number of very public instances, this type of electronic data has proven very embarrassing and expensive to organizations during litigation. There are many companies whose legal teams strongly advise that certain types of electronic data be retained only for the minimum required period and then be promptly deleted from all systems and backup tapes.

The best way to address the retention issue is to assemble a team of legal, business, and technology managers to establish specific minimum and if necessary maximum retention periods for all major categories of electronic information. These retention requirements should be clearly documented, agreed to by all parties, and incorporated into The Project activities. This is especially important if a selective data migration of data to a new format is being considered as part of The Project.

REAL WORLD EXAMPLE

A major steel processing company provides corrugated steel sheets in certain specification to a company that in turn uses the steel to manufacture culverts that go under roads. There are federal rules that these steel culverts must be traceable back to the original steel mill and batch of steel it originated from. This is required so if  structural problems are discovered in one culvert all similar products made from that batch of steel can be identified and inspected. Steel culverts under roads can potentially be in place for decades until they are replaced so this is a long term data requirement.

As a result of this, the steel processing company needed to retain data about the steel that they purchased from the steel mill and the customers that they sold the processed steel to for a number of decades so that traceability can be maintained. Similar data for non-transportation related customers may only be

136

needed for a few years, so the steel processor had to decide whether to do long term archiving of data for only a few customers or all customers.

REAL WORLD EXAMPLE TWO

A large global company wanted to consolidate data centers as a cost savings measure. One of the existing data centers was in Germany where it had been operational for a number of years. The desire was to move the servers and the data residing on them to the United States. It was discovered that German/European privacy rules would not allow any data that contained "personnel information" to be stored outside of the country of origin. The data that was being moved did not include traditional personnel data, but did contain names and email addresses of personnel that approved purchase orders, etc. It was determined that this personnel related data must be purged from the systems before the remaining data could be moved to the United States. The company would have been subject to significant fines if this had not been resolved prior to the data being migrated.

BEST PRACTICES

- Data retention can have significant legal and financial implications, so retention decisions should be made only with the participation of expert legal counsel.
- There should be a documented Data Retention Plan clearly defining how long each major type of data in the system should be maintained.
- The data retention policy should be reviewed with and approved by the Steering Committee and then implemented as part of The Project.
- The Data Retention Plan should be reviewed and updated periodically as business conditions and regulatory requirements change.

Section 2: Business Related Questions

- There should be one person on The Business Team designated as being responsible to managing and implementing the Data Retention Plan.

ADDRESSING THE QUESTION WITH THE PROJECT TEAM

Project Manager- If there are significant data retention implications of the current project you should ask The Project Manager to see a copy of the Data Retention Plan for review. You should also ask to see the tasks in The Project Schedule that have been added to implement and test the data retention processes.

Business Team- It is highly recommended that you appoint someone on The Business Team to be responsible for data retention coordination/oversight on The Project. You should discuss the Data Retention Plan with this person to validate that it has been adequately reviewed and agreed to by all affected parties.

Technical Team- You should ask the Technical Lead if they have seen the Data Retention Plan. You should also ask them how this strategy is being implemented in the system being implemented in The Project.

Legal Team- You should ask the lead counsel for the company if they have reviewed the Data Retention Plan in detail and whether they concur with the strategy.

Audit Team- You should ask the internal audit lead for the company if they have reviewed the Data Retention Plan and understand its impact on audit related data. You should also ask how the audit team will verify data is being retained in accordance with the strategy.

LESSONS LEARNED FROM PAST PROJECTS

- Data retention is a very serious matter but even large companies sometimes do not give it proper attention until they are involved in litigation, major warranty claims, or have a need to examine historical data.

Q16: Is There a Strategy for Statutory Record Retention?

- The regulatory environment related to data retention is fluid, confusing, and sometimes contradictory. A good example of this is the massive pendulum shift in views about what that can/should be collected following the 9/11 attacks in the United States versus current thoughts based on recent disclosures of what data is been collected.

- Data retention policy, by default, is often determined by mid-level business managers because "they know the data best". This is a mistake because retention is both a Business and Legal Issue.

- Experienced legal advice is required especially if the organization is multi-nation, works in the financial, manufacturing, health related or government domains. Do not hesitate to bring in outside assistance with expertise in data retention to help ensure legal requirements are understood.

- If the current project involves significant data migration that will result in less data being retained than was previously, consult with corporate legal counsel to ensure that any data needed to support active on-going litigation is retained. This is usually called a "records hold" and there can be significant consequences if you delete data pertaining to on-going litigation regardless of the reason.

- The data retention policy must be written, approved by all parties involved, built into systems operational practices, tested/audited periodically, and updated on a regular basis as business needs and regulatory environments change.

RELATED QUESTIONS

44. Is there a strategy for project data protection?

48. Is data migration planning adequate?

17. IS THE STRATEGIC IMPACT OF PROJECT TIMING BEING EFFECTIVELY MANAGED?

"Timing in life is everything." **Leonard Maltin**

WHY IS THIS QUESTION IMPORTANT?

It is important to understand the impact of project implementation on The Business. This is especially true if project implementation is tied to some business event. An example of this might be that The Project must be completed before a new product launch or The Project must be implemented prior to quarter-end financial reporting.

Experience shows that most projects can change their implementation data without major business impact. This is not to say it is acceptable to have project delivered late, since missing a deployment date usually implies increased cost and results in ill feelings over the failure to meet time commitments. What you want to do is identify when delays in timing will have major business impact and respond accordingly with increased project oversight and perhaps additional resources as necessary.

Carefully review key project dates in conjunction with the timing of other major business activities to ensure that there are no major conflicts. You don't want to be the company cited elsewhere in this book that implemented a major new inventory system just before one of its biggest sales seasons with disastrous results. I am talking here about Hershey not being able to ship candy to many customers in the lead-up to Halloween 1999 resulting in an 8% drop in share prices.

REAL WORLD EXAMPLE

The Sarbanes Oxley Act implemented in 2003 was aimed at improving the reliability and accuracy of corporate financial reporting. It holds corporate Management personally responsible for certifying accuracy of financial statements. One major impacts of this complex set of laws on Technology Projects is that most companies impose what they call a Sarbanes "quiet period" from October – December of each year. During the period, most systems changes impacting corporate financial reporting (inventory, purchasing, finance, etc.) are prohibited.

This allows a period of system stability before end of year processing. I have been involved with projects at a couple of companies where major system changes were scheduled in late September so that they would be implemented just prior to the Sarbanes freeze on October 1st.

In cases where deployments were delayed even a week or two, the impact was significant. The usual outcome of even minor delays was to change the implementation date until early February so that the deployment would come after completion of both the Sarbanes Quiet period and year-end financial closing. This turns a one or two week delay in deployment in to a 4 month delay significantly increasing cost and delaying business benefits.

BEST PRACTICES

- Early in each project, there should be an analysis of the strategic impact of project timing. The Steering Committee and Project Team should clearly understand these impacts.

Section 2: Business Related Questions

- If project deployment is extremely time critical from a strategic perspective, then the level of project monitoring and oversight needs to be increased accordingly.
- In general you want to schedule a major technical deployment with at last a month's buffer between any critical business events. In this way, you have some time cushion if delays occur.

ADDRESSING THE QUESTION WITH THE PROJECT TEAM

Project Manager - The Project Manager should be able to explain what "slack time" is in the schedule. Slack time serves as a contingency if tasks get delayed. If there is no slack time in the schedule, then a delay in any critical part of The Project is likely to impact the deployment date.

There should also be a discussion over the level of confidence the team has in the time estimates. A big red flag would be if the timing is especially critical and the team has low confidence in the date estimates. You should also discuss with The Project Manager how increased oversight will be put in place to manage risk and status to ensure the critical dates are achieved.

Business Team- The beginning point of discussions with The Business Team should revolve around the impact to the organization if they project is deployed late. You should also explore how confident The Business Team is in the work estimates and ability of the team as a whole to deliver The Project on time.

Technical Team- Just as there are business critical timing impacts, there can be similar critical technical timing. For example, you may be in a situation where a project must be completed by a certain date or it will result in need to renew expensive hardware/software licensing. Another example is if The Project must be implemented by a certain data to meet new encryption standards. The Technical Lead should be able to articulate the timing of any critical technology dependencies so that they can be considered.

Steering Committee- Ultimately, the decision on when to deploy based on business and technical time dependencies should be in the hands of the

Q17: Is the Strategic Impact of Project Timing Being Effectively Managed?

Steering Committee. You should ensure that all necessary information is presented clearly to the Steering Committee so that an informed decision can be made. This decision should be well documented and communicated to all project Stakeholders.

LESSONS LEARNED FROM PAST PROJECTS

- There are three common project practices that are significant red flags if The Project is especially time critical. If these occur on your project, then the schedule estimates are suspect and should be closely reviewed.
  - o The Project Team is given the deployment date before estimates are complete and told to make The Project fit in that time period.
  - o The Project Team has provided estimates based on the work to be done and are then directed to cut X number of months/weeks from the schedule to deploy on a certain date.
  - o The Project Team has been directed to remove all slack time and contingency from the schedule/budget
- Often the first time/cost estimate produced by The Project Team turn out to be the most accurate. **If your organization has a culture of pressuring Project Teams to shorten all time and cost estimates as a matter of common practice, then you are unlikely to get estimates that you can rely on.** Make sure you understand the schedule estimates before prior to pushing to significantly shortening them.

If you must compress the schedule to achieve a particular date, it should

Fast is Fine, But Accuracy is Everything-

Wyatt Earp

be because you have truly removed some of the work originally anticipated and/or you have increased resources to support getting the work done faster.

Section 2: Business Related Questions

- On time critical projects, ensure that you have established an atmosphere that supports honest status reporting so that you always know the real status of The Project.
- Some organizations create an atmosphere where "bad news gets you killed" and then wonder why people misrepresent project status until just before deployment.
- For the most time sensitive projects, ensure that you have very experienced senior level Project Managers, Business Leads, and Technical Leads. This not only helps speed The Project along, but also helps ensure personnel experienced in identifying and managing risks/issues are part of the team.

RELATED QUESTIONS

3. What Is the impact if The Project fails?

22. Are customer and Supplier impacts of The Project understood?

18. IS THE TACTICAL DEPLOYMENT PLAN ACCEPTABLE TO THE BUSINESS?

"Expect the best, plan for the worst, and prepare to be surprised." Denis Waitley

WHY IS THIS QUESTION IMPORTANT?

Beyond the strategic timing issues discussed in the prior chapter, there is a need to understand the tactical plan for the deployment. Regardless of when a Technology Project is deployed, there is almost inevitably some disruption in business operations- perhaps over a weekend or holiday period, sometimes longer. These business disruptions need to be well planned and communicated so that overall impact is minimized.

One key area for consideration for on-line systems to understand the timing of when access to the current system be disabled to start deployment activities and when the new system will become available after deployment is complete. It is not uncommon that during this period of system unavailability, some business operations must be suspended or be accomplished "on paper". In these cases, the manually recorded transactions are input into the system manually when the system again becomes available. The Business Team will have to be strongly involved in this discussion to identify what can be done when the system is not available and how The Business will "catch up" later.

Additionally, for larger projects, there are often issues of whether you deploy the complete solution at one time or perhaps deploy incrementally over a period of time. Sometimes, it makes sense to implement The Project one Division of the Organization at a time or one geographical region/plant at a time.

These decisions can have a significant impact on business operations and are clearly not decisions to be made by the Technical Team alone. There needs to be a clear shared view of the tactical aspects of the deployment documented in a Deployment Strategy. The Deployment Strategy needs to be formally approved by The Business and Technical Teams, and reviewed by the Steering Committee. Once approved, it must be, fully comprehended in The Project Schedule, and communicated as early as possible to all potentially impacted parties.

REAL WORLD EXAMPLE

A large manufacturing company was doing a major system consolidation involving movement to a new data center. Once the systems were disabled to start the cutover migration, shipping labels could not be printed, online loan applications could not be created, products could not leave plants, etc. In total, The Business projected millions of dollars of impact an hour and that was if everything went correctly.

Once the period of downtime was identified, The Business Team worked closely with the Technical Team to identify actions that could be taken to lessen the impact on business operations such as printing orders early, pre-printing labels, re-scheduling logistics providers, etc. While the impact was still significant, by planning for the inevitable outage well ahead of time, disruption was minimized and well understood by all involved both inside and outside of the company.

BEST PRACTICES

- The Deployment Strategy must be written and include both strategic timing and tactical considerations.

146

Q18: Is the Tactical Deployment Plan Acceptable to The Business?

- After approval, the Deployment Strategy should be shared with the Steering Committee. Since some of the Steering Committee members likely represent some of the affected business areas, endorsement of the concept by the Steering Committee is critical.
- There should be a frank discussion of what could go wrong with the deployment and what The Business impacts of these issues might be.
- There should be a written back-out strategy that would be executed in case of a deployment failure. This back-out strategy would return systems and data back to the point immediately before deployment began and should be tested prior to the deployment cutover period.

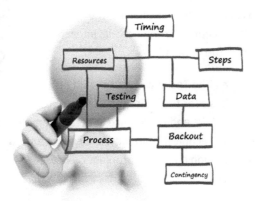

ADDRESSING THE QUESTION WITH THE PROJECT TEAM

Project Manager- Ask to see the Deployment Strategy. If one has not yet been created, ask The Project Manager when it will be created. Ensure that there have been discussions between The Business and Technical Teams about deployment.

In particular, you should ask to see the details in The Project Schedule surrounding the deployment period including seeing how/when the deployment concept will be tested prior to go live. If there is little detail in the schedule other than a milestone showing the deployment date, this is a significant red flag about the level of deployment planning.

Section 2: Business Related Questions

Business Team- Discuss with The Business Lead how the production cutover will occur and what impact this will have on business operations including what steps will be taken to minimize impact. Try to gauge whether sufficient thought has been given to the deployment impacts. Additionally, to stimulate discussion, try to understand from The Business Team the impact if the deployment takes longer than planned.

For example, if deployment is scheduled to be completed by 5:00PM on Sunday, ask what the impact will be if problems are encountered and the system does not become available until say noon on Tuesday. It is critical that The Business Team understands the deployment concept and the potential impacts of deviating from the timeline.

Technical Team - The Technical Lead should be able to explain the basis for the estimates of how long deployment will take and confidence in these estimates. You should also explore with the Technical Team how they will return the system to its original configuration if a major problem is encountered and the deployment has to be aborted.

Steering Committee- It is not uncommon for the Steering Committee on major Technology Projects to be ill informed about the impacts and risks of deployment until something goes wrong. Oversight of business impacts is a key Steering Committee role, so the Steering Committee must be made to understand The Business impacts of the Deployment Strategy including not only the impact if everything goes well, but also the impact if the deployment does not go well. The Steering Committee should be provided access to the Deployment Strategy and encouraged to fully understand the impacts.

LESSONS LEARNED FROM PAST PROJECTS

- Usually early in a project, the extent of deployment planning is somewhat vague such as "deployment must be complete by the end of March". This is probably adequate until requirements have been fully documented and a system design has been agreed upon. After that, there should be significant discussion on how The Project will be deployed.

- The Deployment Strategy needs to be in writing and include details on business impacts along with the technical activities.
- The Deployment Strategy should be placed under Change Management after it is formally approved and changed thereafter only through a formal Change Request agreed to by all Stakeholders. This Change Request should include and analysis of the impact of the change to The Business.
- There should be one person designated as the Deployment Lead for The Project. In a smaller project this could be The Project Manager or a Business Manager. In larger projects this is often a full time job or even a multi-person job if there are phased deployments.
- The Deployment Strategy is often decided upon at the Central Office level of an organization. If you have remote locations, ensure that you solicit and consider input their input before finalizing the Deployment Strategy. In my experience, failing to get plant/remote office input to the deployment strategy is easily avoided by including personnel from those areas on The Project Team on a part-time basis. This will likely also pay off in additional areas such as requirements, testing, data conversion, etc.

> I've learned over decades of building that a deadline is a potent tool for problem-solving.
>
> Adam Savage (Mythbusters)

- Often the majority of effort in deployment planning revolves around what happens if things go well. Significant consideration also needs to be given to what will happen if things do not go well. In particular, the

> Deployment Plan should include some detail on how the system will be "rolled back" to the original software/data if there is a deployment failure.

- It is not always possible to fully test deployment activities to ensure they are viable and determine how long they will take. However there is no excuse for not performing deployment testing. The Business needs to understand how long deployment/data conversion will take and the only real way of determining this is to do a mock run.
- In some extreme cases it is not possible to stop deployment after it begins or to roll back to the old environment if the deployment fails. In these rare cases, the organization needs to have a very experienced Deployment Lead in place and strong oversight of testing and deployment planning.
- Ensure that the Deployment Strategy including any approved changes is clearly communicated to all impacted organization units and external affected suppliers/customers.

RELATED QUESTIONS

17. Is the strategic impact of project timing being effectively managed?

21. Who is really speaking for The Business on The Project?

22. Are customer and Supplier impacts of The Project understood?

19. ARE ALL IMPACTED STAKEHOLDERS ACTIVELY INVOLVED IN THE PROJECT?

"Effectively, change is almost impossible without collaboration, cooperation and consensus."- Simon Mainwaring

WHY IS THIS QUESTION IMPORTANT?

This issue may seem so intuitively obvious that you wonder why it is included in the book. However, more often than not, actively impacted parts of the organization are not included in Technology Projects until late in the process or even after deployment. This is especially true if the organization is large and geographically diversified.

Some of this stems from how projects are approved and funded. Often a single Business Unit or office determines a project is needed and gets funding approval. This originating Business Unit expects to make the key project decisions because they are paying for it. While on the surface it is hard to argue with this logic, it is rather short-sighted because the needs/inputs of the organization as a whole should be considered not just the needs of one individual Business Unit. This approach provides the greatest possible value to the organization as a whole.

Let's take an example of a financial institution implementing a new mortgage system enhancement to better track mortgage applicants. The mortgage group provides the funding and logically takes the lead in crafting the solution.

However, they fail to consider that there could be legal implications of collecting this data so Legal should be involved, the data collected could be of great value to groups marketing financial products to customers, the banking group might find value in this data to try and get the customer to open a bank account, etc.

By not soliciting the input of all potentially impacted parts of the organization, value to the company as a whole from the investment in the upgrade may not achieve its potential. Merely involving all areas of The Business would have increased value to the organization as a whole

To address this issue, there needs to be a concerted and objective effort at the beginning of each project to identify all potentially impacted parts of the organization including both technical and business segments. Then once the affected organizational units are engaged, efforts should be expended to keep the engagement throughout the various projects phases.

REAL WORLD EXAMPLE

An unfortunate example of this comes from a large military systems project. This was a multi-year project involving many different parts of the organization. Stakeholder mistakes were made in two different areas. One of the goals of this project was to consolidate important but unclassified data from a number of sources into a single "one stop shop" where authorized users could go to view the data. Since none of the data was especially sensitive, no thought was given to involving the Data Security Organization in The Project.

Just prior to deployment however, it was determined that while the individual data elements were not classified, when you consolidated the data in one place and provided linkages to provide context to the data, it became classified data. If the security organization had been engaged in The Project from the beginning, this would have been discovered well before testing began. This

Q19: Are All Impacted Stakeholders Actively Involved in The Project?

led to a significant delay in deployment and considerable cost overrun.

On the same project, there was a logistics group that was to provide a small amount of valuable data to the new system. This data was part of the overall cost justification of The Project and although small in quantity was of great interest to the end users.

The organization that maintained this data was engaged at the beginning of The Project and a detailed data exchange agreement was developed and formally signed. Since their data was not needed for nearly a year and a half after project startup, they did not actively participate in Project Meetings and apparently did not ready any of The Project status reports or other materials provided weekly.

When it came time for testing, the organization was re-engaged and it was only then that it was discovered that organization Management had changed. The new management had shifted priorities and resources to other projects and no work had been done on the interface in over a year. This delayed full deployment of the new system for a considerable period of time while resources were re-engaged and development completed.

The solution to these issues is simple. Identify all parts of the organization early on that could be impacted by The Project. Once it is determined who should be involved, ensure the groups remain engaged for the duration of The Project.

BEST PRACTICES
- Early in the concept phase of The Project there should be a Steering Committee discussion to determine which parts of the organization should be involved in The Project.
- In addition to the Stakeholders identified as having direct technical and business involvement in The Project, at least consider involving the following organizations in all Technology Projects- Legal, Finance, Purchasing, Marketing, Help Desk, Infrastructure, Systems Architecture, Audit, Security, Testing, Quality Assurance, and Training. It may ultimately

be determined that some of these groups do not need to be involved, but they should at least be considered on all Technology Projects.

- If The Project involves both central office and remote office/plant/store changes, make sure that you include representatives of the non-headquarters units. They are often the intended user and can bring helpful insight to The Project.

- Once you have decided which organizations are to be involved in The Project, you should identify organizational representatives by name. These representatives should be empowered to either make decisions or get decisions made for their part of the organization. They should attend Project Meetings and review project communications.

- Ensure that all communications for The Project are distributed to each of the identified representatives.

- Monitor participation in reporting status, attendance at meetings, participation in Steering Committee sessions, etc. to ensure each organization continues to participate in The Project. If they are not, take steps to ensure participation. If a representative is unable or unwilling to participate, get the organization to identify an alternative representative.

ADDRESSING THE QUESTION WITH THE PROJECT TEAM

Project Manager- Explore with The Project Manager how The Business and technical Stakeholders will be identified. There should be a document (usually called The Project Charter or something of a similar nature) that defines the scope of The Project and all involved parties. Prior to approving The Project Charter, carefully review the list of which parts of the organization will be involved in The Project..

Business Team - The Business Team should be encouraged to think outside of the box when considering other parts of the organization that might have an interest in The Project. If some types of data currently being gathered will change during The Project, they should consider what other parts of the organization might be impacted by this change. If The Project significantly changes a capability (interfaces, reports, access) that has been stable in the past encourage the team to determine what other parts of The Business may be relying on these capabilities and need to be involved in the change.

Technical Team- In discussions with the Technical Lead, make sure that they have considered all technical areas that might be impacted by The Project. A particular area of interest might be to explore whether any parts of IT are considering standards or infrastructure changes that might impact The Project. It is very discouraging to a Project Team after spending time and energy in defining a solution for a project to discover that there is a new corporate standard that dictates a different technical approach.

LESSONS LEARNED FROM PAST PROJECTS

- Inter-organization turf wars, organizational politics, personal ambitions, and ill feelings often combine to keep organizations from working together on projects of joint interest. You need to ensure that parts of the organizations are not excluded for these type reasons.
- It is an organizational decision whether all participants in The Project have to participate in the funding of The Project or not. However, who pays for what should be clearly established and formally agreed to early in The Project to prevent confusion as The Project progresses.
- For longer projects it is important to ensure that all organizational units that are participating in the funding of The Project follow through and get The Project included in their approved funding requests. It is very disruptive to have to stop a project because one of the funding organizations did not get approval for the required funds.

- It is natural for parts of the organization that contribute the most funding to The Project believe they should have the greatest say in its direction. However, you should always keep the best interests of the organization as a whole in mind in making decisions.

- Work hard to keep all affected parts of the organization involved throughout the life of The Project. Tailor meetings and status reporting to be absolutely as minimalistic and efficient as possible to minimize the amount of time it takes to participate in The Project. When you are completely replacing existing systems with new systems, you should pay particular care to identifying organizational units that rely on the existing system. You may find that over time the system usage has evolved far beyond its original intent. A good example of this is an inventory system that allows data to be downloaded into Excel.

  I have seen numerous situations where data like this is then electronically uploaded into another system to support business critical functions creating an ad hoc system interface that IT may not even be aware of. If you change the data available or change how it has to be accessed, you likely will "break" these informal but critical "shadow IT" systems.

  I call them shadow IT since they are as important to The Business as a whole as the more formal systems developed and deployed by IT, but which are created and operated without IT support deep in the shadows of the organization.

- The later you discover that you have failed to actively include some impacted part of the organization in The Project, the more likely it is to impact cost and the deployment date. Examine the portfolio of current and future projects that are planned to see if any of these are likely to impact this project.

  One area of particular concern should be to see if there are any Regional/Local/Plant/Store level projects underway that might impact Central Office/Global projects. It is both embarrassing and inefficient to find that you are spending organizational resources on multiple projects with conflicting goals/processes in the same business problem area.

> *The* difference *between involvement and commitment is like ham and eggs. The chicken is involved; the pig is committed*
>
> *Martina Navratilova*

- Help all parts of the organization that are affected understand the WIFM (what's in it for me) so that they can justify to their management why time and resources should be expended supporting The Project.
- The joke among Project Teams when evaluating who is impacted by a systems change is **"just turn it off and see who screams"**. This is a very poor (but unfortunately not uncommon) way of identifying impacted parts of the organization. This approach is definitely not recommended, but ultimately will occur at deployment as groups you failed to identify as being impacted notice the changes. Be prepared to quickly deal with unintended impacts when The Project is deployed.

RELATED QUESTIONS

8. Who would like this project to fail?

20. Does The Business really support this project?

21. Who is really speaking for The Business on The Project?

20. DOES THE BUSINESS REALLY SUPPORT THIS PROJECT?

The keystone of successful business is cooperation. Friction retards progress.- James Cash Penney (Founder of JC Penney)

WHY IS THIS QUESTION IMPORTANT?

Each Technology Project should in support a Business objective. This is true even in the case of such traditional Technology Projects as PC upgrades, server replacements, etc. These types of projects extend the life of the infrastructure needed to support The Business, possibly reduce maintenance costs, and/or increase system performance. Each of these projects are beneficial to The Business. It is important to identify The Business value of each project. If there is no business benefit to a project then you should not authorize it.

It is important that The Business understands and supports each Technology Project. Even on the most technical of projects, there is often need for business participation in testing and perhaps even training and rollout. Even if no business resources are needed to directly support The Project, there is still an overall impact since IT resources working on this project are not available to work on other projects The Business perhaps thinks have more value.

In some cases you find projects are forced upon a particular business group such as when a central office system is mandated for use at remote locations. This also happens when the edict for major changes comes from Upper Management or outside consultants rather than from The Business themselves. In these cases, it is important that The Business be allowed to provide input into The Project and are given a chance to understand the purpose and benefits.

It is not uncommon for Upper Management to bring in a team of consultants to suggest organizational, process, and systems changes. The resulting recommendations then are mandated for implementation regardless of whether the managers/ workers that are "in the trenches" so to speak support the changes or not.

While it is best to convince Business Units of the value of the changes being considered, sometimes that is just not possible and a forced implementation is required. Even in these cases, you should strive to make The Business Units understand why the change is being made even if they do not agree with the changes. Sometimes the best that can be hoped for is that key people do not actively work to derail The Project. It is the job of Business Management to raise reasonable objections to ideas that they don't agree with. However, once a decision has been made, they need to support The Project actively.

It is important to understand to what extent The Business supports changes being made. This must be understood all of the way from the Executive level to the clerk level of the organization. By understanding the level of commitment of each part of the organization to the changes being considered, you can determine actions that might be required to have a *successful* project.

It is one of the unfortunate realities especially in large organizations that often people put the self-interest of themselves and their immediate work group ahead of the interests of the organization as a whole. This is understandable to some extent as we hold profit centers responsible for achieving cost/revenue targets and other business results. Sometimes it is deemed necessary to spend time and resources on a Technology Project that a particular Business Unit believes may not provide direct tangible benefit to them or in the worst case even degrade business efficiency. There is often an understandable and noticeable lack of enthusiasm for these types of projects.

If you anticipate active or passive resistance to the change, taking the time to explain the justifications for the change could be useful. It may also be necessary to have a frank and direct discussion about the value of The Project to the organization as a whole and your expectation of project support. In these cases, additional oversight may be required to keep individuals from derailing The Project.

REAL WORLD EXAMPLE

A large global manufacturing company that had grown through acquisitions

> Self-interest makes some people blind, and
> others sharp-sighted
>
> Francois de La Rochefoucauld

and joint ventures found itself with multiple parts management systems each of which was separately developed and maintained and which collected data in different manners. Going to a single global parts system would dramatically decrease costs of software development and maintenance, would standardize how data is stored, would ultimately decrease cost by consolidating buying power, and would ease reporting.

However, some regions/countries/plants already had local systems with capabilities that the new system would not have for a number of years at minimum. Additionally, implementing the standardized global system would require significant amount of local resources for data conversion and would require that local processes be modified to the corporate standard.

There was understandably considerable pushback in some areas against implementing the system since it was considered expensive to implement and a step backward in capability for some locations. Once the resistance was identified and understood, it was addressed with a top down push from Upper Management indicating that deployment was mandatory and emphasizing the significant benefits to the company as a whole. Additionally deployment teams were formed at the central office level to travel to each location (sometimes for months) to assist with data conversion and process change. By understanding the reasons for The Business pushback and designing both a "carrot and stick" approach to pushing the deployments, the system was implemented successfully in location after location.

BEST PRACTICES

- Effort should be taken to ensure that all Business Stakeholders understand the value of each project to the company, even for those projects that are considered purely Technical Projects.

- Passive resistance to a project is perhaps even more impactful than active resistance since the active resistance can at least be discussed and dealt with. Actively monitor progress on The Project to ensure that project opponents are not using delaying tactics such as diverting resources to other projects or failing to meet deadlines.

- Take the time to try and understand why The Business areas are resistant to The Project and see how these concerns can be addressed. Projects are often a negotiation process where groups compromise in order to craft a solution acceptable to all.

- If a project is critical to the organization and there is business apathy or even resistance, direct senior Executive intervention may be required.

- One highly effective technique I have seen Project Executive Sponsors use on a project is to get all involved parties in a room, discuss The Project concerns, and then poll all of The Business and technical areas one by one as to whether they will support The Project. This puts each area "on record" with their support of The Project.

ADDRESSING THE QUESTION WITH THE PROJECT TEAM

Project Manager- Discuss communication plans with The Project Manager to make sure that all affected business areas are being actively included in The

161

Project. Also discuss with The Project Manager whether issues are arising where Business Units are not providing committed resources and/or information. Any such resistance should be escalated to the Steering Committee if it cannot be resolved by The Project Manager.

Another key area to cover with The Project Manager is ensuring that issues raised by anyone on The Business Team are faithfully recorded in The Project Log and tracked until resolved. This ensures that everyone has a voice on The Project even if the issue is not resolved to their liking. When a decision is made on the issue, the resolution should be recorded in the log.

Business Team- Discuss concerns with each Business Unit and take steps to ensure that any concerns they have about The Project are being actively considered by The Project Team. Encourage The Business Team to formally raise issues by including them in The Project Log/issues management process, rather than just raising them in hallway conversations where they are quickly forgotten.

Steering Committee - The Steering Committee is key to resolving the worst cases of lack of project support. The Steering Committee should review and discuss any legitimate objections to projects. Then if the decision is made to pursue The Project, it is their role to ensure that the areas they represent provide needed support to The Project Team and not work behind the scenes to make The Project fail.

LESSONS LEARNED FROM PAST PROJECTS

- Often resistance to projects is a simple as groups feeling that their input is not being heard on a project so why should they support it. Formally recording and addressing their input is an effective way to ensure their input is considered.
- Even if a project is mandated from the top, you need to find ways to make people feel that it is not being "jammed down their throats". One way of doing this is to ensure that each area understands the importance of The Project and its overall value to the organization.

- One of my favorite sayings is that "the world only has the appearance of being a democracy". Everyone should have their say in major project decisions, but once a decision has been made, all areas should support the decision even if they do not agree with it. It often takes Senior Executive involvement to make this happen in the worst cases.
- One surprisingly effective way of overcoming resistance to projects is to find the people who object to aspects of The Projects the most and make them an active part of The Project Team. What usually occurs thereafter is that they see their concerns are being at least discussed. They often come to understand why things are being done a certain way and find ways they

> My father taught me many things here — he taught me in this room. He taught me — keep your friends close but your enemies closer."
>
> Michael Corleone The Godfather Part II

can support The Project. Also, The Project Team usually finds at least some merit in the concerns of the detractor as they work to resolve them.
- If there is significant passionate disagreement about a project that cannot be resolved through negotiation or Executive fiat, then you should consider not doing The Projects. If there is not at least grudging support for The Project from the major involved areas, it is unlikely to be successful.

RELATED QUESTIONS

5. Is there sufficient Executive oversight?

8. Who would like this project to fail?

19. Are all impacted Stakeholders actively involved in The Project?

21. WHO REALLY SPEAKS FOR THE BUSINESS ON THE PROJECT?

"You have to listen to the people who have a negative opinion as well as those who have positive opinion. Just to make sure that you are blending all these opinions in your mind before a decision is made" - Carlos Ghosn

WHY IS THIS QUESTION IMPORTANT?

This is an area that will surprise most senior Executives. Most people assume that projects decisions are made and directions are set by senior Business Executives who have broad knowledge on how The Business currently operates, the challenges The Business is facing, and the future direction. While it is true that this level of the organization usually signs off on things like scope and requirements, the details which really shape how the system functions nearly always come from the rank and file of the organization which I call the Yeoman level.

Yeoman is not meant to be a derogatory term by any means. The dictionary defines Yeoman as someone who has—"performed or rendered in a loyal, valiant, useful, or workmanlike manner, especially in situations that involve a great deal of effort or labor". It is an umbrella that includes payroll personnel, purchasing agents, accountants, assembly line leads, stock traders, registered nurses, etc. These are the people that the organization relies upon to keep things running day in and day out.

Q21: Who Really Speaks for The Business on The Project?

The Yeomen rightly feel that they best understand what it takes to keep The Business running and changes that need to be made. There is usually so much trust in the judgment of the Yeoman that their managers often sign off on their work with only cursory oversight.

There are several potential issues in having the Yeoman speak for The Business that you want to consider.

- Yeomen usually understand all aspects of their current role in great detail but may have little knowledge of how changes in their area might impact other areas.
- Yeomen sometimes are not privy to the future strategy of their department much less the Organization as a whole. As a result there may be lack of alignment with these strategies.
- Often you see Yeomen so entrenched in the status quo that they are unable and/or unwilling to objectively consider doing things any other way.
- While they understand what they would like to see, Yeomen are often not involved in the organizational budget process and may not be the best stewards for deciding what is worth funding and what is not.

For these and other similar reasons, although Yeoman participation in The Project is essential, there also must be active participation and detailed review of their work by The Business management team which perhaps has a different perspective on strategy and priorities. You want to ensure that Business Managers in the affected organizational units get a clear message that they personally are responsible for speaking for The Business and they are expect to ensure alignment of scope, requirements, etc. on The Project.

REAL WORLD EXAMPLE

I was once asked to review a financial systems project. This project was the result of significant strategic discussion among top Executives about the need to change fundamental practices and move in directions as radical as identifying and driving away customers that were unprofitable to the organization. Although there had been several meetings where the Executives explained the new strategy, not everyone fully understood and/or support this concept. As systems changes began to be made to support these policy

> As a decision maker, you rely on information being passed to you by the people who report to you. As the CEO, however, you cannot rely solely on this information. You also need to 'dip' down into your organization and learn directly from employees at all levels and virtually all skill sets.
>
> Scott Weiss

changes they sometimes did not support this new corporate direction.

In digging into the details, I found that Segment Leads in the marketing group were financially compensated for achieving year over year of customer growth and had not embraced the idea of shedding unprofitable customers. As a result the formal system requirements (which were documented in considerable detail) were designed to deliver a system that continued down the existing path of encouraging growth. There was only the most cursory attempt at implementing the new direction.

When I interviewed several managers of the marketing group, they admitted that they had signed off on the several hundred page requirements document without even reading them. They did this because they trusted the judgment of the Segment Leads. One manager went so far as to say that these were the people who did the work every day and who best understood what the company needed.

For this project, it was not the Senior Executives or the Marketing Managers that spoke for The Business, but rather team leads with a personal financial stake in the status quo that de facto decided business direction. The result of this was considerable delay in implementing the system because of significant and costly design changes that were required to implement the corporate strategy. I would like to say that this was an isolated case, but it is not. In my experience, it usually the mid-level Yeomen of the company that really dictate business direction.

BEST PRACTICES

- Documents that describe The Project (especially things like the scope and requirements documents) are in reality the voice of The Business on a Technology Project and must be reviewed carefully and completely to ensure that they align with overall strategy.
- While it is appropriate and desirable for The Business Yeoman to actively participate in The Project, managers in the affected Business Units must understand that they personally are responsible to all decisions made
- There should be one Manager, Director or Executive identified who will be the voice of The Business on The Project and who should be both responsible and accountable for project decisions from a business perspective

ADDRESSING THE QUESTION WITH THE PROJECT TEAM

Project Manager- Discuss with The Project Manager how involved The Business Executives and Managers are in The Project. Find out who is really providing The Business requirements. Get an opinion on whether Business Management is sufficiently involved in the details of The Project to make the necessary decisions they will be called upon to make. Ask The Project Manager to report to you any instances where they believe that management is not sufficient engaged and where key decisions are being pushed to lower levels in The Business structure.

Business Team- Ask The Business Managers how much time they are spending on The Project and how involved they are. Inquire about the depth of their understanding of the scope and requirements details. It is also a good idea to re-iterate key strategic directions and remind The

167

Business Managers that they are both responsible and accountable for implementing this direction.

Steering Committee- Ensure that the Steering Committee understands the importance of the details in the scope and requirements documents in defining what the resulting system will be capable. Emphasize the role of the Steering Committee in ensuring the agreed upon strategy is embodied in these document.

LESSONS LEARNED FROM PAST PROJECTS

- It is not uncommon for people writing requirements to never openly challenge the strategic direction of a project but to instead create detailed requirements in conflict with that direction because they did not agree with it.
- Often the first time a manager/Executive sees a scope/requirements document is the day that they are asked to sign it. Over and over I have witnessed the conversation where the manager asks the Yeoman if they agree with the requirements and then sign it without reading based on the answer.
- Managers should review requirements and scope drafts periodically as they are being developed so that they will understand the content when called upon to approve it.
- The real voice of The Business is not the PowerPoint strategy slides or the motivation speeches on strategic direction. It is the details in the documentation The Business produces. Whoever writes that documentation is the one that really speaks for The Business.

RELATED QUESTIONS

7. What are key roles for project success?

9. Am I sufficiently engaged in The Project?

20. Does The Business really support this project?

22. ARE THE CUSTOMER AND SUPPLIER IMPACTS OF THE PROJECT UNDERSTOOD?

 *"There is only one boss. The customer. And he can fire everybody in the company from the chairman on down, simply by spending his money somewhere else". - Sam Walton*

WHY IS THIS QUESTION IMPORTANT?

Project Teams often focus so much on making technology changes that they fail to properly consider the customer and supplier impacts until often very late in The Project timeline. Suppliers and suppliers can be affected by Technology Projects in several different ways, each of which require careful coordination. The Project may require changes to the data that they provide to your company. Or it may require business process or technical changes. It often even may involve periods of system downtime during deployment.

The Project Team needs to anticipate these impacts early in the process and ensure that they are incorporated into communications planning, testing, training, deployment, etc. Keep in mind that The Project may be more important to you than it is to the impacted suppliers/suppliers. This is especially true if your organization will reap the financial benefits but not have to incur supply and customer implementation costs. As a result, tact is required in approaching those impacted to convince them to make the changes required.

REAL WORLD EXAMPLE

A major manufacturing company was consolidating servers in a new data center. This was originally believed to be a simple change with suppliers only having to change the internet IP address (this is like the telephone number used to connect devices over the internet). As The Project progressed, it was discovered that the manufacturing company did not have technical contacts in a number of their customer's companies. Additionally, in some cases the customer did not have technology people available to make the change.

Testing of changes needed to be done very carefully so as not mingle production and test data which was confusing to some suppliers. This was especially burdensome on the suppliers since The Project Team wanted to do that testing at night and on weekends when the smaller suppliers did not have staff available to support testing.

Communications about the required changes were drafted by the Technical Team and were very technical in nature confusing many of the smaller companies. Testing with all suppliers was not completed prior to deployment and as a result the first few weeks after deployment were disruptive  to The Business and some suppliers. Despite heroic effort on the part of The Project Team, there were persistent issues for several months on at least an occasional basis for some suppliers. The net result was significant supplier impact at the end of a fiscal quarter and angry internal and external Executives.

Most of the issues encountered could have been predicted if the issue of customer impact had been discussed more thoroughly between all parties early in The Project.

BEST PRACTICES
- The Business owns the customer and supplier relationship and should be the focal point of all external communication.

Section 2: Business Related Questions

- A Manager/Executive on The Business Team should be accountable and responsible for ensuring external impacts are identified and addressed within The Project.
- Specific tasks should be added to The Project Schedule outlining timing of customer communications, testing, training, deployment, etc.

ADDRESSING THE QUESTION WITH THE PROJECT TEAM

Project Manager- You should ask The Project Manager to see the tasks in The Project Schedule related to customer and supplier impact and as The Project progresses, ensure that status against those tasks is being reported.

Business Team- A manager from The Business Team should be designated as accountable and responsible for ensuring customer impacts are assessed and dealt with. A good practice would be to discuss the impacts with the designated manager to ensure that the impacts have been considered and how these impacts will be communicated to your suppliers.

Technical Team- If The Project will require any technical changes by suppliers, explore with the technology team how complex these changes will be and how the Technical Team will be prepared to extend technical assistance to suppliers that might require it.

LESSONS LEARNED FROM PAST PROJECTS

- If your company has a significant number of suppliers/suppliers and/or churn in your customer base, it is likely that you will have some difficulty constructing a list of technical contacts for your current active suppliers. Make sure the effort to create the contact list begins early in The Project.

Q22: Are The Customer and Supplier Impacts Of The Project Understood?

- Keep in mind that "suppliers" can also include internal departments, subsidiaries of your company, joint ventures, etc. Do not forget them in your communication planning.

- Especially in large companies and/or geographically dispersed companies, the impact on internal suppliers can be as significant as the impact on external suppliers. Make sure that the impact on internal suppliers is also taken into consideration.

- Many smaller suppliers/suppliers do not have dedicated IT departments or even significant IT expertise. Often, these companies may not have a detailed understanding of how their internal systems are configured. You should be prepared to offer technical assistance to help external companies understand and in extreme cases even make the required changes.

- Your company expects a return on investment for completing The Project and as such understands why it is important. The Project may have little or even no value to your suppliers/suppliers so they may be reluctant to dedicate financial and/or personnel resources to technical, business process, or data changes. Be prepared to answer the question "what is in it for me" from the suppliers.

- Sometime suppliers will request reimbursement for the cost of making changes mandated by The Project. If they have to bring in IT help to make changes, pay overtime for testing outside of normal business hours, encounter significant business impacts during deployment downtime, etc. asking for reimbursement is not entirely unreasonable if there are no concrete benefits for the customer.

- Sometimes it is not practical or cost effective to test some changes with each customer. In that case, a good practice is to focus on the small number of suppliers/suppliers that have the greatest impact on your sales and profits.

- Occasionally, testing with external suppliers/suppliers results in "data leakage" where test data intended for the soon to be

173

deployed system instead ends up in the current production system. On one project that I worked on, we tested the purchasing interface by "buying" the largest American flag the supplier had to sell from its catalog.

Due to confusion over network addressing, the data went out as live and a week later a thirty by fifty foot flag costing several thousand dollars showed up in The Project Office. Considerable care must be taken by all parties involved when testing external connections to ensure that test data does not inadvertently get processed in production systems.

- If the impact on suppliers/suppliers is potentially great, it makes good business sense to have direct Executive Level conversations with the most important suppliers/suppliers describing The Project and how they will be supported through testing and deployment.
- To the extent possible, take key customer and supplier business cycle constraints into account when scheduling testing and deployment. A classic example of poor timing of a deployment is the implementation of a new Supply Chain System by Hershey's just before Halloween in 1999 which resulted in failure to deliver $100 million worth of candy for Halloween that year causing the stock to temporarily dip 8 percent.

While this deployment disaster would have been very impactful at any time of the year, it was exacerbated by the ill-advised timing of deployment during one of the busiest seasons for the company and its suppliers.

RELATED QUESTIONS

1. Are The Project objectives clear to all?

17. Is the strategic impact of project timing being effectively managed?

18. Is the tactical deployment plan acceptable to The Business?

Q22: Are The Customer and Supplier Impacts Of The Project Understood?

23. Are project business requirements well documented?

24. Are external access requirements understood?

41. Have system interfaces been adequately planned?

23. ARE BUSINESS REQUIREMENTS WELL DOCUMENTED?

Good Requirements

"The most difficult part of requirements gathering is not the act of recording what the user wants, it is the exploratory development activity of helping users figure out what they want. – Steve McConnel"

WHY IS THIS QUESTION IMPORTANT?

It is not uncommon for The Business Team to be disappointed during testing at the end of a project as they discover that the system that was built or enhanced was not what they had in mind. In the best of cases, the issues are small and easily resolved. However in some cases, the requirements disconnect can have significant cost and schedule impact. The problem is often related to incomplete and/or insufficiently detailed requirements.

Donald Firesmith of the Software Engineering Institute did a study that found that "requirements errors cost US businesses more than $30 billion per year and often result in failed or abandoned projects and damaged careers".

There is a general rule of thumb for software development that if a requirement problem costs $1 to fix during requirements gathering, it will cost about $10 to fix during the coding process, it will cost $15 to fix if not found

176

until testing has begun, and will ultimately cost $80 to fix if not discovered until deployment.

VACATION EXAMPLE

Let's look at a non-IT example. At Christmas a family of four sits down in a family meeting and agrees to go on a vacation to "somewhere fun during the summer". All four people are glad the vacation issue is settled and leave the meeting with a sense of accomplishment.

The father is excited that the family will spend the 4th of July weekend going camping at the lake. The mother is excited that they will take a trip in late August to see all the museums in Washington DC. The son is excited that they will leave for vacation right after school is out in late May and go scuba diving in the Caribbean and last but not least, the younger daughter is eager to finally go to Disney World in Orlando and spend an entire 3 months riding It's a Small World.

In May when it is time to begin packing, the difference in perception of what was agreed to becomes apparent and everyone is disappointed.

While humorous, this example is not all that different from how the process of writing business requirements sometimes turns out unless care is taken. The difference in perception is not intentional, but has more to do with how people view conversations from their own unique perspective.

Assumptions are made based on these perspectives- ie to the young daughter obviously fun means Disney World. People are so entrenched in their perspectives that they do not even see the need to document the details. However, documenting requirements in clear, unequivocal wording is a key part of project success.

WHAT MAKES A GOOD REQUIREMENT

There are 8 characteristics of a good requirement. The requirement should be:

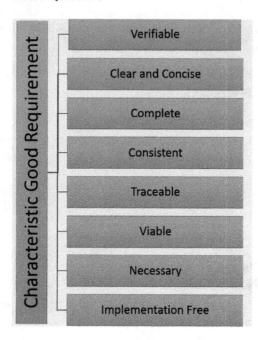

1. **Verifiable** - There must be a way of testing that this requirement has been met by the development team.
2. **Clear and concise**- The requirement should be short and clearly written. There should not be any subjectivity, or open ended statements.
3. **Complete** – The requirement statement must contain everything needed to understand what is being asked. It should be as exact such as saying the screen should return data in 5 seconds not the screen should return data quickly.
4. **Consistent** - There needs to be no conflict or confusion when you look across requirements. For example, you don't want to have one requirement say the system run on Internet Explore and another one say it much work with any browser. Likewise you need to use standardized consistent terminology so that you don't call something a shovel in some places, a spade in others, and a trowel in even others.
5. **Traceable** - Each requirement should be given a reference number so that the

Team can show the relationship between the various requirements. This will also allow the eventual tracking of how that requirement was implemented in the design and where it was testing. This traceability is key to being able to validate that all the approved requirements have been implemented in the system.

6. **Viable** - Requirements also need to within the realm of possibility. You should not have a requirement that the system "can never be down" since some downtime is unavoidable. Nor should you have a requirement that the system must respond to complex simulations within 2 seconds. Addressing unrealistic requirements as they are being discussed is much better than ignoring them until the systems is being tested.

7. **Necessary**- Each requirement should relate back to the objectives of The Project. This will help ensure that each feature is truly needed to support The Project.

8. **Implementation Free**- The requirement should tell the developer **what** needs to be done, but avoid telling them **how** it should be done. While The Business Team owns the "what of The Project" (requirements), the Technical Team owns the "how of The Project" (design). You want to leave the Technical Team enough latitude to design and build the best system possible.

REAL WORLD EXAMPLE

A company approved a project to replace a very old/mature legacy mainframe based inventory system. The legacy system allowed a user to move around the screen and between the screens using function keys and experienced users had developed techniques of multiple quick keystrokes to quickly move between screens, Each of these screens processed information very quickly since they performed little data validation or formatting. This system could only be used within the walls of the company on terminals/PCs connected directly to the mainframe since it had no real security.

The replacement system was to be browser based so that it could be used both within the company and externally by a user with proper security credentials. The proposed system was very mouse/graphically based and performed

179

significant data validation/formatting to correct data issues at the time data was entered. Overall, the new system was much more powerful, resulted in better data, and allowed vendors to remotely review and manage their inventory at the plants they were contracted to service.

Overall, the new system was a great success with most users. However, a small but vocal group of very experienced users at the central office were very unhappy with the new system. The function key based navigation was not included in the new system and speed with which the screens processed data was considered too slow for  experienced users that did not often make data errors (at least in their minds).

It turns out these very experienced users never wanted the new system in the first place and felt threatened by it since it decentralized part of their work to the plants. Therefore, they did not actively participate in the requirements process and in fact never reviewed the drafts of the requirements for completeness and accuracy. They did however repeatedly say in and out of meetings that the new system needed to "do everything the old system did".

As a result of this lack of involvement in the requirements process, the function key capability that they felt was critical to their job was not included and the performance requirements which were documented and which the system performed to were not to their liking. They however, argued that since these capabilities existed in the old systems, they should have been included in the new system.

The situation was ultimately solved through a combination of some small but costly system changes, changes in organization/processes of the central inventory office, and in some cases personnel changes.

The clear message is that people who have a significant stake in the outcome of a new system or system upgrade need to be involved in the requirements process either personally or through a trusted representative. This will help ensure that if the system is built as it has been described in the requirements; it will be acceptable to the users.

BEST PRACTICES

- There are a variety of formats that can be used to document business requirements. You should worry more about the content than on using a particular format. The key is that requirements must be in writing and must meet the requirements criteria described above.

- Sometimes organizations ask business users to "write down what you want the system to do" and call that requirements. Requirements gathering and documentation is very much a learned skill. It is well worth the investment to have trained Business Analysts (BAs) be responsible for collecting and documenting requirements or at least provide requirements gathering training to those who need it.

- The organization needs to ensure that sometimes lengthy requirements documents are actually read and verified for accuracy and completeness prior to approval. This needs to happen at both the user and manager level.

- After requirements are formally approved, they become the basis for estimating cost and schedule, determine system design. The Requirements Document is a contract of sorts between The Business and Technical Teams defining what the systems must be able to do. After approval, requirement changes regardless of how minor must go through a formal Change Management process so that the impact of the change can be evaluated and the timing of when implementation timing can be determined.

- If the organization has a Quality Assurance or Testing Group, they should be involved in the requirements process from a quality perspective. They should evaluate requirements from the perspective of whether the requirements are clearly written and whether they can be objectively tested.

- Creation of requirements is primarily a business function, but there should be some participation from the Technical Team to ensure that the requirements are sufficiently detailed to support system design and development.

181

- Requirements issues discovered early in the process can be remedied quickly and cheaply. The same error not discovered until testing is likely to be much more expensive and often result in implementation delays.

ADDRESSING THE QUESTION WITH THE PROJECT TEAM

Project Manager- Make sure that The Project Manager is actively involved in the requirements process. The Project Manager role is to ensure that all involved parties are actively engaged, that the requirements meetngs are an efficient use of time, and that there is a good process in place to document/ validate/ approve requirements as they are being developed.

Business Team- In discussions with The Business Team, strongly emphasize the expectation that The Business is prepared to dedicate sufficient resources to support the requirements process. Ensure they understand how important it is to have good requirements and that you are going to hold them accountable for requirements accuracy.

Technical Team- Ensure that the Technical Team is at least somewhat involved in the requirements process. A key role of the Technical Team is to ensure the requirements are adequate to drive the design and development processes and that the requirements are practically implementable.

The Technical Team needs to be proactive in identifying any user requested requirements that are expensive, take too long, or are not technical feasible within the existing project concept. Identifying these problematic requirements does not mean that they must be eliminated from The Project. Instead the objective is to ensure that The Business Team understands the impact of complex requirements on time and money. This will allow The Project to balance The Business benefit of the requirement against its time and cost impact.

182

LESSONS LEARNED FROM PAST PROJECTS

- When you are replacing an existing system, one common (and reasonable) user assumption is that all functions the old system can perform will automatically be included in the new system Often there is little or no documentation of current system functionality, so It is not enough to write a general requirement saying the new system must do everything the old one could do.

- Drill into the Technical and Business Teams and the Sponsors the mantra that if the requirement is not in the final approved requirements document, it will not get built. During the give and take of requirements gathering, requirements are sometimes mentioned verbally in early meetings, but do not get documented in the written requirements. Additionally some requirements included in early drafts are rejected or modified in later meetings.

  It is impractical to assume that all project participants will be able to attend all requirements meetings. It is easy to understand people's assumption that if a requirement was verbally discussed at a requirements meeting or included in an early draft it is going to end up in the system. However, this is not the case. All involved parties need to carefully review the final requirements draft because if a requirement is not in the final approved draft it is likely not to be built into the system regardless of how many times the requirement was mentioned verbally in a meeting.

- It is not uncommon that parts of the organization will chose to not participate in the requirements process because they do not agree with the overall project objectives/goals. Or perhaps they do not agree with the strategy Management has selected. A major group not supporting the requirements process is is very likely to result in incomplete requirements and a system that will either fail at deployment or require costly enhancements to be usable. Be vigilant in ensuring that all affected groups are actively participating in the requirements process.

183

Section 2: Business Related Questions

- One technique that has been found to be very successful in ensuring that all affected parties have reviewed the requirements prior to their being approved is to bring the leads of all The Business functions together in a meeting and have a senior Executive poll them individually as to whether they approve the requirements. If the team understands that this will happen, they are much more likely to take requirements approval seriously.

RELATED QUESTIONS

1. Are The Project objectives clear to all?

13. Does each documented requirement have real business value?

14. Is the cost of unwillingness to change business processes understood?

19. Are all impacted Stakeholders actively involved in The Project?

21. Who is really speaking for The Business on The Project?

24. Are external access requirements understood?

24. ARE EXTERNAL ACCESS REQUIREMENTS UNDERSTOOD?

"Protecting yourself is very challenging in the hostile environment of the Internet. Imagine a global environment where an unscrupulous person from the other side of the planet can probe your computer for weaknesses and exploit them to gain access to your most sensitive secrets". - Kevin Mitnick

WHY IS THIS QUESTION IMPORTANT?

A significant trend over the last few years has been to increasingly allow customers, suppliers, and other outside entities to directly access organizational data and systems. For example, many manufacturing companies now allow their supplier access to on-line inventory information so that the supplier can monitor inventory levels of the products they sell the company and automatically ship additional product when on hand quantities get low. This process called Vendor Managed Inventory increases efficiency at both the plant and at the supplier.

Also, there is a strong expectation on the part of customers that you have an eCommerce capability or a website that allows consumers to order products. To facilitate this, you will need a robust and secure capability to allow external access to your data. As the need to give customers and suppliers deeper and deeper access into organizational data continues, so does the need to ensure you have adequately planned for current and future access requirements?

Section 2: Business Related Questions

When your organization embarks on a major Technology Project, you should carefully consider both current and future plans that might include external access to your organization's data. There are at least five major aspects of external access that you will want to make sure The Project Team has considered as discussed below.-

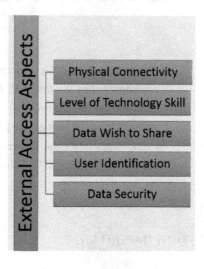

1. Physical Connectivity to systems should be carefully planned by an expert in computer security. This is an area where I think companies go too far in opening up systems to external access.

An appropriate mental model of this issue is the old castles of the Middle Ages in Europe. They had big imposing walls with just a very few methods of ingress/egress surrounded by a moat. The way to access the castle is through the big public access point across the drawbridge and through the massive front door that is highly defended. This is the public view that most see of your systems and perhaps how you have been led to believe represents your system. You log onto your website and are met with this significant layer of security.

However, if you harken back to the medieval castle movie metaphor a little deeper, you remember that the enemy often finds out about the hidden tunnel you had dug under the castle, the hidden sewer, the small door on the back wall, or used grappling hooks with ropes thrown over the castle wall, etc. Unfortunately, IT often turns your massive well protected castle into Swiss cheese by opening holes into it for special access. These holes through the corporate firewall are often needed and usually well intentioned, but can represent significant security vulnerability.

Over time, organizations tend to forget what holes have been opened and/or why they are there and who is authorized to use them. You as an Executive providing oversight to a project cannot be expected to understand all of these physical access issues, but the best advice is to make sure that the person your organization has put in charge of computer security for your organization is very up to date on security and that you have followed their advice. This is not an area to try and save time and money.

2. Level of Technology Skill of External Entities needs to be considered if you are considering extending sophisticated external connectivity to Suppliers and Vendors. Most consumers will access your information through web browsers over the Internet. This is common well understood technology thanks to ESPN, Amazon, and eBay. It is reasonable to expect that external users will understand how to connect to your web site without significant technical support.

However, if you are considering sophisticated direct data interchange with external organizations such as electronic submission of shipping data, allowing direct access to your corporate systems, transfer of files, etc., it requires more technical sophistication on the part of your suppliers and perhaps customers to accomplish this safely.

Do not assume that the organizations that you do business with have full time IT staff or access to technical expertise to help make changes to their systems as that is often not the case. Many smaller companies know little about the technology that they use than how to make it work every day. If changes are required, they will often need technical support that your Project Team may need to provide. Otherwise the vendor/customer may have to engage outside help to complete technology changes, raising issues of who will pay to make the necessary changes.

3. Deciding What Data to Share also needs to be carefully considered. Many legacy corporate systems were designed with rather simplistic security. In older systems, often if you are a trusted member of the organization you can see and perhaps update everything. If you are not an authorized user you can see nothing. When you start allowing external access, this security model will probably prove to simplistic.

For example if you have a paint supplier that you wish to give access to inventory data, you probably don't want them to access electrical parts data. You may want to go farther even and only let them see data about the type of paint they supply to you. An even more granular view may be that several supplies provide that paint and you only what them to have access to the shipments that come from their company.

The Project Team may have to temper what they would like to make available based on the access control capabilities of your systems. Complex access schemes may be beyond the capability of older systems without significant enhancements. There should be considerable dialog between The Business and Technical Teams to ensure that the system is capable of supporting the external access vision.

4. User Identification is a critical component of granting access to systems remotely. There is a now standard expectation that consumers accessing you website will be able to create users IDs/passwords, manage log passwords, etc. in an automated way. You want to make sure that your development team is using the most current login protocols and security mechanisms to protect this form of access including mandating hard to guess passwords.

The more challenging aspect of user identification relates to supplier/vendor access. This kind of back door access where you give suppliers access directly to your corporate systems is usually much more powerful in terms of accessing bulk data, but paradoxically is sometimes much less secure.

Sometime it is as easy as someone getting your helpdesk phone number, calling up and saying that they are from ABC Paint Company and need their password reset, and seconds later you have access. Or they call and say they need to see the paint data from all plants instead of only the one you are currently providing paint and are granted access to the additional data.

You want to ensure that company to company access goes through at least as much scrutiny as does the consumer access and that there written authorization to change access rights of Suppliers and Vendors.

5. Data Security is a catchall for most of what you read about in the news. This is where Target incurred significant costs, loss of sales, and loss of reputation due to stolen data. This is also where employees lose USB data drives with personnel data resulting in significant fines.
The ways in which unauthorized users attempt to access your data are many and constantly evolving. The range from brute force (i.e. the battering ram that eventually makes it through the castle gate even as you are pouring boiling oil on the invaders) to the elegant.

If you are storing customer financial data, personnel data, company proprietary secrets, government information, etc. on servers even remotely connected to external users, **no amount of paranoia is excessive**. This is any area where you need extremely competent personnel in your organization and you need to strongly champion the time, effort, and money it take to provide the security needed to keep you off of the front page of the newspaper.

REAL WORLD EXAMPLE

A large manufacturing company wanted to improve handling of indirect and direct material purchasing by automating the purchasing, shipment, and invoicing process through the implementation of standard Electronic Data Interchange (EDI) processes. This has been common practice among larger companies for decades and is a proven technology. However, some of the materials vendors the company dealt with were small local companies. The first indication of a problem came when it was discovered that the company did not have phone numbers or email addresses for supplier technical contacts at a number of suppliers. It was eventually discovered that this was because there were no technical personnel at the companies.

The Project Team discussed just eliminating these small vendors and moving to larger suppliers. However, due to the community oriented nature of the organization, the desire to locally source materials where possible, and long-standing good relations with small suppliers, that was rejected.

Because of this, the scope of The Project had to be expanded to include buying and configuring PCs with software to generate EDI transactions already installed and providing them to a number of the smallest suppliers. Without this assistance, the goal of automation of the new corporate-wide purchasing process could not have moved forward.

BEST PRACTICES

- If you are allowing any external access to organizational data, make sure you have someone on staff that truly understands information security and keeps abreast of trends in that area. If you do not have an absolute expert, then go hire one and/or bring in an expert for the duration of The Project.
- External access to organization data is implemented by The Project, but the need to support it extends for the life of the system. Best practice is to have one person identified within your organization who owns coordination of all external access.
- There is usually both a business and a technical aspect of coordinating external customer access to data/systems. This can be confusing to outside organizations if they receive communications and questions from multiple groups in your company. Consider pairing one person in your organization with each of your involved suppliers and customers to coordinate the changes so that there is a consistent message.
- Ensure that the requirements for external access are well documented and included in the overall project requirements document.

ADDRESSING THE QUESTION WITH THE PROJECT TEAM

Project Manager- Ask to see the tasks in The Project Schedule related to implementing external access including timing of testing with suppliers and customers. Additionally ask to see where in The Project Communications Plan communications with outside organizations is covered.

Business Team- In general, The Business Team should take the lead in interacting with the affected suppliers and customers. Make sure that they have planned how to accomplish this. Also challenge The Business Team to look at best practices in other parts of your industry and look at industry trends to identify innovative ways you may want to allow data access in the future. These should be included in the requirements documentation.

Information Technology Team - Challenge the Technical Team to explain the mechanics of external access to you in layman's terms. This should also include the technical changes that suppliers and customers will likely have to make. If you cannot understand the issue, then your outside suppliers and customers probably won't understand it either. Make sure you review communications to your outside suppliers and customers to ensure it is understandable.

A sensitive but critical topic that you need to broach with the Technical Lead is the level of expertise of the IT security personnel you have within your company. If you don't want to face the potential of having your company on the front page of the paper with a data security issue, you need to ensure that your organization has top notch highly trained IT security personnel that keep current on industry trends. Have an honest discussion to ensure you have that expertise in the organization. If you are not comfortable that you have the right level of expertise in the organization insist that outside help be engaged as you work to increase the skill level of existing personnel.

191

LESSONS LEARNED FROM PAST PROJECTS

- Changes to outside connections should be tested prior to deployment. Make sure that you have considered this in The Project Schedule and coordinated it with your outside suppliers and customers. While Project Teams often like to test connectivity over the weekends or late at night to not disrupt normal production operations, you may find suppliers and customers reluctant and/or unable to support testing outside normal business hours.

- For larger organizations, there are sometimes difficulties in determining which suppliers and customers currently have external access and which will need it in the future. Additionally, while individuals in your organizations probably have a good personal relationship with individuals at the suppliers and customers, you may find that there are no accurate electronic lists of contacts with email addresses that you can use to distribute information about The Project in bulk. Ensure you have sufficient time and personnel allocated in The Project Schedule to refine supplier/customer contact information.

- The desire to implement sophisticated data exchange with external suppliers, vendors, customers, etc. may be of higher priority to your organization than it is to the external organizations. Do not assume that these outside organizations will enthusiastically embrace the change. This is especially true if it requires major changes to their technology.

- If the new external access mechanism requires technology changes on the part of the external organizations, be prepared for a discussion on who pays for the change. The costs may include purchase of hardware/software, monthly telecommunications fees, need to hire outside experts to implement the change, etc.

Often the position of large organizations is that outside organizations must pay for changes required on their end of the connection. Common sense should prevail however. If you are spending large sums of money each week on a project that could be delayed over external access issues, dedicating one of your technology team members to help with configuring/ troubleshooting vendor issues or

192

spending a small sum of money to provide software licenses to a few vendors may be a good investment.

- Special attention should be paid to the timing of external access changes. Make sure that you are not making the changes at times that are bad for the suppliers and customers. For example, a prime time to implement large corporate systems in the  US is the week of Thanksgiving since you have as much as a 4 day window to implement changes. However, if you have retail customers that need continuous access to your systems, you probably don't want to implement on "Black Friday") which is one of the busiest shopping days of the year.

- The IT staff best understands the technology involved in setting up external access, but often are not the best at communicating what is required to non-technical outside users. Make sure that all communications to your outside suppliers and customers are well reviewed and appropriate for the audience that it intended for. The first three emails sent to suppliers explaining the change on one project I was involved with were extremely technically accurate, but made little sense to The Business contacts at the suppliers that received the email. As a result, many of The Business contacts just deleted the emails. Make sure that the communications you send are understandable to the audience.

- If the external access changes involve international suppliers and customers, complexity and time/cost often increases very dramatically. Depending on where you need to establish connectivity, there are hurdles of language, versions of communications software, connections speed/quality issues, and never ending delays/regulatory challenges. Make sure you dedicate sufficient time and experienced resources to resolve international connectivity issues.

Some of my most frustrating weeks have been spent trying to resolve issues where connectivity works in one plant but won't work in another plant just across a national border.

RELATED QUESTIONS

15. Is there a holistic view of required business and technical changes?
24. Are external access requirements understood?

SECTION 3: WHAT PROJECT MANAGEMENT QUESTIONS SHOULD YOU ASK?

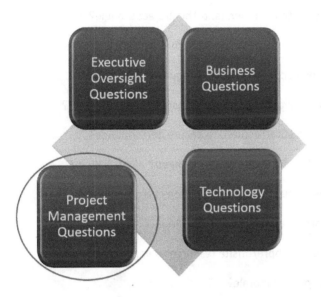

The Project Manager is responsible for organizing and leading The Project Team in pursuit of The Business objectives. They must be sufficiently connected to The Business and technical areas that they can understand and guide The Project. However, they should not become so deeply involved in the details that they lose the big picture view of The Project. This big picture view is needed to maintain the objective perspective needed to make good decisions and provide honest assessments of status. The Project Manager also needs to interact closely with the Steering Committee.

Section3: Project Management Questions

This section focuses on various areas that Executives should explore with their Project Manager in order for the Executive to understand how The Project is being managed.

25. How well are project costs being tracked?

26. Are The Project risks understood?

27. How were project estimates determined?

28. Does your team understand The Project triangle?

29. Are intellectual property rights contractually protected?

30. Are project contracts being adequately managed?

31. How is quality being assessed/assured on The Project?

32. Are contracts structured to ensure performance?

33. How is Project Scope being managed?

34. How will you know when The Project is complete?

35. Are part time resources on The Project really available?

36. How are offshore/offsite resources being managed?

37. How is project morale?

38. Do we have the right Project Team composition?

39. Are project issues being adequately managed?

25. HOW WELL ARE PROJECT COSTS BEING TRACKED?

"A budget tells us what we can't afford, but it doesn't keep us from buying it."- William Feather

WHY IS THIS QUESTION IMPORTANT?

Understanding how much a project costs and managing these costs as The Project unfolds is one of the keys to getting good value for your project investment. A process should be established to ensure that all project costs are included in project financial reporting.

Unfortunately, it is not unusual for project costs to be substantially under-reported. This is not to say that the costs are not reported somewhere within the company.

However, costs are often not accumulated in such a way as to make it easy to understand the true costs associated with The Project. Here are a few areas where project costs are prone to be under-reported.

Internal Business Labor - Very few of the large projects I have been involved with have accurately captured the true cost of business personnel assigned to The Project. Business personnel are often involved in gathering requirements, design review, status meetings, testing, training creation and delivery and a variety of other tasks.

Over time, these efforts can total thousands of hours on a large project. They are hours that The Business personnel are not able to devote to their normal job. In some cases the company may have to back-fill for these workers with new hires or temporary workers. Failure to allocate these costs to The Project, understates the cost of The Project.

Sometimes, groups justify this as not being an incremental cost to the company as a whole. However, if you are backfilling positions or using temporary workers to cover for time spent on The Project, this is absolutely not the case. Even if there are no direct incremental costs to the company, it is important to understand the true cost of projects so that management can make an informed decision as to whether The Project is justified or not.

If you are capitalizing significant portions of The Project costs, identifying all costs becomes even more important so that the company can accurate determine the amount to be capitalized.

Internal IT Labor - It is also not uncommon for time spent by internal IT personnel to not be reported as part of The Project cost. Full-time IT resources on a project are generally reported against The Project. However, you should ensure that part-time hours spent on The Project IT personnel are also included in The Project costs. This category of support which includes database administrators, system administrators, network support, system architects, etc. can be substantial and should be captured as part of the overall project cost.

Facilities Costs- If The Project incurs significant incremental facilities costs, you should ensure that these are also associated with The Project instead of being buried somewhere in the IT Department or even Corporate budget. These costs can include office rental/utilities, desks and cubicles, computers and printers,  wiring and cabling, moving expenses, etc. These can add up to a significant amount and should be budgeted for and tracked as part of The Project costs.

Accrued vs Paid Expenses- This is often one of the biggest surprises on large projects especially if you have significant external consulting expenses. It is not uncommon for there to be a 3-4 month delay between when work is performed and payment goes to the vendor due to billing cycles, invoice questions, expense audit, 30/60 day payment terms etc.

While your corporate accounting department certainly understands this and takes it into account in terms of corporate reporting, many Project Managers only report paid expenses. As a result when they issue a report of expenses to date, it may not include several months of often expensive consultant billing. When this occurs, it can significantly understating project costs at a given point in time. Several times, I have seen projects reported as being on budget until the end when several million dollars in bills are paid after deployment.

It should go without saying that you cannot financially manage a project unless you know exactly how much you are spending on The Project as it is being spent. However, I would go so far as to say most mid to large sized Technology Projects do not have a complete picture of project finances on a regular basis.

REAL WORLD EXAMPLE

I was once reviewed a financial services project that was steadily slipping behind schedule. The Executive in charge was concerned that project delays were delaying achievement of planned benefits. However, he was comforted by the belief that costs were still in line with the approved budget.

It didn't take too long to discover that the company was spending far more on The Project than was being reported. Only costs paid to external technology product and service providers that had been actually paid were included in the cost reports he was reviewing.

The cost of internal personnel (both IT and business) working on The Project were not included, even when temporary personnel were brought in from a staffing firm to backfill the work of these employees.

Additionally, the cost of renting office space for The Project Team was buried in the overall IT department costs as were PC/Networking costs incurred in the new workspace. Most importantly, The Project was only reporting costs as bills were paid with several million dollars of expenses for consulting services and computer hardware having been incurred but included on the cost reports since invoices had not yet been paid.

The bottom line for this company was that costs were being substantially under-reported to the Management Team. Combining this with the schedule slippages (which were also substantially worse than reported) projected a total cost at completion of nearly double what was originally approved. Due to the importance of The Project, the company decided to go forward, albeit with a new Program Manager, enhanced financial controls, and better Executive oversight.

BEST PRACTICES

- Finance personnel should be engaged in accumulating and reporting on the financial condition of The Project not The Project Manager if at all possible. This is increasingly important as project size and complexity grows.
- For larger projects, establish a family of charge numbers to which all project expenses are associated. This makes it easier to budget, accumulate and report project costs.
- Financial reporting should include both accrued and paid expenses or should contain prominent explanations of what is not included.
- To the extent possible internal labor costs should be included both in The Project budget and in reported costs.

ADDRESSING THE QUESTION WITH THE PROJECT TEAM

Project Manager- Work with The Project Manager to ensure that all types of costs are included in The Project budget and that these costs are captured and included in project financial reporting. Set the expectation with The Project Manager that they are responsible for working with Finance to ensure costs are being accumulated and reported correctly.

Business Team - Set the expectation with The Business Team that they will be expected to keep track of the time they spend on The Project and report that time as directed.

Information Technology Team- As with The Business Team, you should set the expectation that all time spent on The Project will be charged to that project.

Finance - Coordinate with the Finance Department to have someone assigned to The Project to ensure costs are being adequately captured, categorized, and reported.   All financial reporting should originate with the Finance Team.

LESSONS LEARNED FROM PAST PROJECTS

- Business personnel often do not record their time against individual projects like IT personnel routinely are asked to do. Therefore, capturing their project time will require some mechanism for capturing actual time or at least estimating the time each resource spends on The Project.

- For internal personnel with differing salary/benefits packages, collecting accurate actual costs for a number of people can be difficult and time consuming. I have worked with a number of organizations that instead defined an average fully loaded labor rate that was then used for all internal effort.

  This average internal labor rate which includes benefits is usually in the $80 -$120 per hour range and while not 100% accurate for any given person, is surprisingly accurate when spread across a number of internal personnel assigned to The Project.

- A key number that both you and The Project Manager needs to know at all times in the "burn rate"

Q25: How Well Are Project Costs Being Tracked?

for The Projects. This is the current actual project cost per day/week/month. I was on one large project with a burn rate of about $1M per month which works out to $250K per week or around $50k per day. Knowing this, if we had a decision/issue/problem that delayed us 2 days, I would challenge the team to justify that this was a $100K problem. As a result, we often got quick escalation and attention to problem areas.

RELATED QUESTIONS

5. Is there sufficient Executive oversight?

27. How were project estimates determined?

26. ARE THE PROJECT RISKS UNDERSTOOD?

"The biggest risk is not taking any risk... In a world that changing really quickly, the only strategy that is guaranteed to fail is not taking risks." - Mark Zuckerberg

Why is this question important?

While you hope that everything goes well on a project, you should always be vigilant in identifying things that might go wrong. By identifying and tracking potential risks, you are much more likely to be able to either avoid them or reduce their impact. Here are some key areas to consider in understanding project risks:

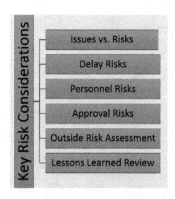

Issue vs. Risk - Risks are potential concerns that may or may not materialize. Issues are events that are currently impacting The Project. It is important to understand which category each item falls into. Issues need immediate attention and focus from The Project Team and Stakeholders as appropriate. Risks on the other hand should be carefully guarded against and discussed. It may be appropriate to take actions to prevent risks, but they lack the immediacy of issues.

To understand the difference think of a waterfall. If your canoe is a mile or so upstream of the waterfall and you think you are beginning to feel the tug of current, that is a risk. You can easily mitigate the risk by paddling to the side of the river.

If on the other hand, you ignore the tug of current until you are about 10 feet from the waterfall; that is an issue. These is no way to avoid what if going to happen. All you can do is try and figure out how to survive the next few minutes.

Delay Related Risks - When examining risk, consider the impact of delays in achieving key milestones/events. While any task being late potentially has an impact on The Project, some tasks are both more likely to cause overall delays and are more impaction to The Project such as delays in signing contracts, delays in getting site changes completed, late hardware delivery, etc. It is harder to predict the timing of these type things making them candidates to consider when identifying risks that should be managed.

Personnel Related Risks- Two of the most significant risks on many projects are the risk of personnel not being available to commit time to The Project as promised and the loss of key project personnel. You should consider what risk you have in these areas and take appropriate action to keep the risk from materializing.

Approval Related Risks- Also, consider the impact of delays in getting financial approvals or approval of less funding than

205

requested. If you do not get funding approval in a timely manner, it nearly lways has an impact on your resource plan and Project Schedule.

Outside Risk Assessment- If you believe that The Project is especially risky and/or large in size, it may make sense to bring in outside resources to conduct a formal risk assessment. This has the advantage of the assessment being conducted by someone who is skilled in identifying risks. Additionally, an outside risk assessment does not have a vested interest in the outcome and can be more open and honest in their approach than is possible within some organizations. Outside risk assessors can ask the "impolite" questions about The Project that people within the organization may not be comfortable asking.

Lessons Learned Review- Another good method of identifying risks on a project is to review the lessons learned from other similar projects. If you organization conducts Lessons Learned Reviews as project conclude, review the lessons from other similar projects to determine if they provide insight that you might take advantage of.

REAL WORLD EXAMPLE

A company had a project to replace a legacy information processing system with a commercial off the shelf software package from a small vendor. The vendor had been selected through a comparison of competing products based on a number of innovative features. As soon as the product was selected The Project Team eagerly began to configure the software using a trial copy provided by the vendor.

As this was occurring, the Purchasing Department diligently worked to negotiate an acceptable purchasing contract. It was obvious from early in the contract negotiation

process that this would be a difficult negotiation due to the small size of the vendor and their reluctance to agree to high dollar product liability indemnification levels required by the Company. Some on The Project Team questioned allowing the development team to begin to work with the product prior to finalization of the purchase agreement, but were basically told to keep working.

There was no risk identification/management process on this project so the risk was not documented nor shared with the Steering Committee or Executive Stakeholders. After nearly 4 months of negotiation, it was determined that an agreement was not possible and Purchasing began to negotiate with the second choice vendor. That negotiation was concluded quickly as the second choice vendor had a prior relationship with the Company and was familiar with the mandatory contract terms and conditions.

Unfortunately, The Project Team had to go back to the Steering Committee for additional funding since they had spent over $1M of The Project budget over the 4 months they worked with the original product. The Steering Committee was understandably upset that significant funds had been spent without notify them as to the risk being taken to move The Project forward prior to conclusion of the purchase negotiations. It should be noted that even if the Steering Committee had been notified, they may well have approved moving forward, but would be doing so with cognizance of the risks involved.

BEST PRACTICES

- The Project Manager should maintain a Risk Log documenting all project risks and the steps to be taken to deal with the risk.
- Key project risks should be listed on all status reports and Executive presentations so that they can be discussed and reviewed.

- Periodically throughout The Project, The Project Manager should set aside time to openly discuss potential risks.
- You want to ensure that there is a culture where risks can be openly discussed. People that raise risks are usually not trying to derail The Project or to paint it in a bad light. If you create a culture where "bad news gets you killed", The Project Team will be very reluctant to raise and attempt to deal with risks until they have materialized.
- If your project has major risks, these should be closely and continuously monitored and proactive action taken to prevent their materialization.
- As soon as a risk begins to manifest itself, it becomes an issue that needs to be dealt with immediately. Make sure that your risk list does not contain items that are really Issues.

ADDRESSING THE QUESTION WITH THE PROJECT TEAM

Project Manager- On a periodic basis, ask The Project Manager to review the Risk Log with you. This will help set the expectation that Risk Management is important and risk are to be identified and actively managed across the duration of The Project. The Project Manager should take the lead in risk identification and management and should set an example by raising risks and discussing them both at Project Meetings and Steering Committee meetings.

Business Team- As you are discussing The Project with The Business Team, ask them what risks they see and what aspects of The Project worry them. Then ask if these areas of concern have been passed to The Project Manager for inclusion in The Project Log. Ensure that The Business Team understands the importance of formally raising risks and ensuring they are included in the Risk Log.

Information Technology Team- In a similar way as with The Business Team, discuss risks and concerns with the Technical Team and ensure they are included in The Project Log.

Steering Committee- You should ensure that the Steering Committee is informed of major risks as they arise and periodically thereafter. If risks turn into issues, then the Steering Committee should provide assistance as appropriate in resolving. While you don't want to paint too grim a picture of project risks, you should ensure that there is a candid discussion on risks and the worse-case scenario impacts if they materialize. I have often heard Steering Committee Members lament that there were are that something was a risk, but never were made to understand the impact if the risk occurred.

LESSONS LEARNED FROM PAST PROJECTS

- Some standard risks apply to all projects. These include tasks may take longer than estimated, additional requirements may be discovered as work progresses, data quality may be worse than expected, etc. While you should document these risks, do not spend too much time or effort on type of risk that are inherent in any

Technology Project. Instead, focus on factor that are unique to your project.

- Risk identification is like brainstorming in that it is best done without too much filtering by Management. If someone raises a risk item, resist quickly dismissing it, but rather record the item and spend some time trying to understand why it is perceived as a risk.
- People and organizational units tend to get defensive when you suggest items they are responsible for are a risk to The Project. Set the appropriate tone that risk identification is aimed at bringing attention to possibilities versus identifying current deficiencies.
- Once a risk has been identified, it should be tracked and reported on until there is no long a chance that it will impact The Project.

RELATED QUESTIONS

9. Am I sufficiently engaged in The Project?

33. How is Project Scope being managed?

39. Are project issues being adequately managed?

27. HOW WERE PROJECT ESTIMATES DETERMINED?

"Facts are stubborn, but statistics are more pliable"- Mark Twain

WHY IS THIS QUESTION IMPORTANT?

When a project is proposed, one of the first questions usually asked is often how much will it cost and how long will it take. The answers to these questions quite often are the primary determining factor as to whether The Project is approved or not. However, if you cannot rely on the accuracy of the estimates, you could be making a poor decision. Therefore, it is important to understand how the estimates were determined.

Estimates are one of the primary yardsticks against which we measure project success. However, the harsh truth is that estimates have no real impact on how much The Project will really cost or how long it will take. Good project management and financial management practices will ultimate determine how long The Project will take and how much it will cost.

An example that I like to use when I teach classes in estimating involves two Project Managers on virtually identical projects for two companies. Project Manager A estimated The Project would take 10 months and cost $150K. Project Manager B estimated The Project would take 14 months and costs $300K. In both cases, The Project actually took 12 months and cost $200K which is what is was always going to cost regardless of the estimate.

However, Project Manager A will be seen as a poor Project Manager since they were significantly off in the estimate.  Conversely, Project Manager B will likely be considered a good Project Manager because they will be seen as being able to bring in The Project faster and cheaper. Keep in mind though that they were equally skilled in Project Management since they both got the same work done for the same cost and time commitment. Hitting estimates speaks much more to your skill as an estimator than it does to your skills as a Project Manager or your ability to manage project budgets.

At best, estimates are an informed guesses. Estimation is a combination of skill and art. There is a mechanical part of estimation where you identify the work components, estimate each of them, assess dependencies to determine timelines, etc. However, in my experience, this mechanical rigor alone is not enough.

The art of estimation comes into play when the estimator adjusts these numbers based on their experience on other projects, evaluation of personnel capabilities, assessment of risk potential, etc. Having an estimator that is experienced in estimating projects of a similar size and complexity is critical to developing a credible set of estimates.

I have a reputation for creating good credible estimates for large Technology Projects. This comes from many years of experience in

212

creating and reviewing estimates and managing large Technical Projects. I could even do a pretty good job estimating how long it would take and how much it would cost to build a dog house with a fence around it in our back yard.

However, if asked to provide estimates for scaling this up to building a zoo to house thousands of animals, I would probably not be a good choice nor create a very good estimate. So when you are evaluating the estimate, look at the skill and experience of the person creating the estimate. Pay particular attention to experience on projects of similar size and complexity.

There are several components of any estimate that you should be aware of when asked to review/approve the estimate. Here are a few.

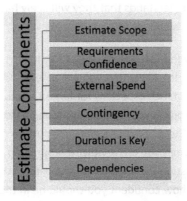

Scope of the Estimate- Examine what is included in the estimate scope closely. Even if the estimator does a good job in creating estimates for the items they included in the scope, if they leave out items such as data conversion, testing, hardware, etc., the estimate is likely to be inaccurate.

Throughout this book, I identify items that should be included in most Technology Project estimates. The related questions at the end of this chapter also identifies items that you should consider when creating estimates.

Requirements Confidence- If you have not determined exactly what you want to do, it is hard to estimate how long it will take to do it. If your requirements are very high level such as I want to implement a new sales force automation product, you should consider any estimate created to be correspondingly rough.

On the other hand, if your team has laid out the 32 key functions the new sales force system must perform, you should expect the estimates to be much better. Sometimes to keep The Project moving along, you have to produce estimates when all you have is high level requirements. If that is the case, produce the best estimates possible, but ensure that everyone who reviews the estimates understands that they will likely have to be revised as more detail is added.

External Spend Estimates- Unless you have a large IT staff sitting around idle, it is likely that you will at least consider bringing in in outside assistance especially for large Technology Project. Also, on many projects you will be purchasing hardware and/or software. These can be a significant portion of the overall project costs. So when you are reviewing/approving estimates, you should question the source of these external spend estimates to determine how confident you should be in them. Obviously the best situation is when estimates are based on firm proposals or negotiated pricing. The estimates with least confidence are those your team makes when they have yet to select vendors.

Another aspect of this to consider is the mix between internal and external personnel. There is usually a substantial difference in costs between internal and external resources As part of the estimate you will need to decide which tasks will be accomplished by internal resources and which by external resources. If the mix of personnel is significantly incorrect, you will likely have a budget that is not very realistic.

Contingency- Regardless of how thorough your planning is and the skill of your estimation team, unexpected events arise on Technology Projects especially as size and complexity increases. To account for this uncertainty, it is common to add a contingency factor to all estimates. The percentage of contingency should be related to the uncertainty of requirements, lack of finalized contracts, etc.

There are two types of estimating contingencies that you might want to consider adding. The first is contingency in the event a decision is made to increase scope such as adding additional functionality or additional deployment locations, etc. The second type of contingency is to account for changes in pricing/duration of items already in the budget such as travel costs being greater than originally anticipated. You should consider including both in your budget.

Duration is the key- In my experience, the key to good estimation is to estimate the duration of the effort correctly. If a project is significantly over budget, than it is most likely also past its scheduled deployment date. There is no great mystery to this. . The single greatest variable cost on the Technology Projects is nearly always labor cost. You assemble a team of people to work on a project, and while you may add and release people from The Project as it progresses, there should be a core team that remains from the beginning of a project until the end. If the end moves out, then you nearly always incur additional internal and external labor costs.

To understand how significant the impact of this is on your particular project, you should calculate your "burn rate" as part of the estimation process. The burn rate is the total labor dollars you spend on your project each week. For example, if you have a 20 person Project Team with an average fully loaded labor cost of

$100 per hour, then your burn rate is $80K per week. So if your project is two months late, you are likely to be about $640K over budget. Knowing your projected burn rate will help you understand the importance of The Project time estimates and upon project launch will reinforce how important it is to hit all of the key project dates.

Understand the Dependencies- If you are building a new plant and the foundation takes 2 months, framing takes 2 months, mechanical systems take 2 months, and finishing takes 2 months, then you can build the plant in 2 months right? Obviously that is not the case since there is a natural progression of these activities that keeps you from starting framing until the foundation is complete.

Most IT estimating techniques rely on estimating individual parts of The Project such as a screen takes 1 month, a report takes 2 weeks, configuring a new server takes 3 weeks, etc. However, to string these individual items into a real estimate, you need to understand the dependencies between them so that you can estimate total project duration. Ensure that you Project Schedule takes into account these dependencies so that it the resultant timeline will be reliable.

REAL WORLD EXAMPLE

I was the Program Director of a large Enterprise Resource Planning (ERP) Project. Phase 1 of the program including implementation of Financials, Indirect and Direct Purchasing, Human Resources, and Payroll. Overall, this was about a $30M project for this Company. At the end of the phase, we were approximately $60K under budget for this year-long effort that at its peak had over 100 internal and external resources working on it. The company was happy because they assumed that being this close to the estimate meant that everything had gone exactly as planned on The Project, but that was not the case.

216

Q27: How Were Project Estimates Determined?

We were successfully in estimating because we had locked down areas of major cost during the estimating process including software licensing, hosting expenses, and external labor rates. These allowed me to estimate costs pretty accurately based on the burn rate for The Project Team with a modest amount of contingency built in.

As The Project unfolded, we had issues with data quality/conversion, connectivity with external companies we exchange data with, and changes in scope. By working hard to meet the 4 major deployment dates, I was able to control labor expenses and bring The Project in slightly under budget.

BEST PRACTICES

- Ensure that your estimating team is experienced in estimating projects of a size and complexity similar to your project. Estimating large multi-phase, multi-year Technology Projects is a learned skill. If you do not have sufficient internal expertise to create such an estimate, seek out external assistance with the estimation process.
- A project cost estimate is useless without a high level Project Schedule. The schedule will help you understand how long each major activity is expected to take and the dependencies between the activities. If your team is not ready to produce at least a high level project timeline, they are not able to give you a credible cost estimate.
- There are a variety of software tools available to help with project estimates based on estimating system features (sometimes called function points). These tools can be helpful, but take experience to properly use and to evaluate the results. I would not recommend that the first time you use one of these estimating tools be in estimating an important large project.
- All estimates should go through a peer review process where you bring in members of The Project Team and even others in

the company that may have experience doing estimates. This peer review process often discovers cost/time components the estimating team may have overlook and helps get buy-in from The Project Team.

- The estimate should be divided into cost areas and not just be one aggregate number. For example, you should not give a Project Team $1M for a project. You should give them $150K for software, $250K for hardware and $500K for labor. Then you should track actual costs against each of the cost components so that you will understand actual expenses by each of these areas. Just because the team spends less than anticipated for hardware should not automatically mean they get to spend that money on something else.

ADDRESSING THE QUESTION WITH THE PROJECT TEAM

Project Manager - The Project Manager usually takes the lead in creating The Project cost and time estimates. You want to have frequent discussions with them as the estimate is being created so that you will understand in some detail the things that are included and those not included in the estimate. This will also help you understand which areas of the estimate are firm and which areas are softer due to uncertainties.

Business Team- The Business Team should provide input to the estimation process relating to the level of business resources that are necessary to support the major project tasks. Prior to approving the estimates, you want to have a frank conversation with The Business Lead as to their agreement with the cost and time estimates. Set the expectation with The Business Lead that they need to fully understand and support the estimates.

Information Technology Team- The discussion with the Technical Team is very similar to The Business Team. You want to set the expectation that the Technical Lead will review and understand the cost and time estimates and support them.

Steering Committee - The Steering Committee ultimately should be the group that approves the estimates allowing The Project to move forward. You will want to ensure that the Steering Committee members understand their role in this process. Also you need to help the Steering Committee understand the role of contingency in costs/time estimates and the importance of this in having a credible estimate.

LESSONS LEARNED FROM PAST PROJECTS

- The first tendency of most Steering Committees is to strip out project contingency. This is a mistake. I absolutely support putting special rules around the use of contingency funds to make it difficult to access them. This keeps control of the funds in the hands of the Steering Committee while still keeping them as part of the official project budget. However, if you eliminate contingency you put the entire project at risk.
- A good rule of thumb is to allow 5% contingency for small well defined projects. Increase contingency to 10% if The Project is large or more complex. Finally, increase the contingency to 20%+ if duration is over 2 years, if it is large package software implementation, or it The Project involves significant business process change.
- Estimates should be developed from the bottom up rather than the top down. If the sponsors already have a definite cost and duration target for The Project and intend to badger The Project Team until they get an estimate that supports this, you are likely to end up over budget, create a poor quality product and miss delivery dates.

219

- In those cases where you must reduce cost/duration, you should do so by removing scope from The Project rather than just beating on the estimates until they get to the numbers you like. Reducing scope is a legitimate way to reducing cost.
- Be careful in letting your hardware/ software vendors provide overall project time and cost estimates. While they can certainly provide estimates for the activities they are involved in, they are likely to not include good estimates for activities that they are not involved in like data conversion and training. Also, experience shows that vendors tend to want to low-ball estimates to get The Project approved and moving.
- It is worth stating again that a project cost estimate without a supporting high level Project Schedule is unacceptable.
- Labor burn rate is always a significant component of overall cost and if you do not understand how long you will need to keep The Project Team engaged and their costs, you will not have a good cost estimate.

RELATED QUESTIONS

1. Are The Project objectives clear to all?

15. Is there a holistic view of required business and technical changes?

23. Are project business requirements well documented?

25. How well are project costs being tracked?

28. DOES YOUR TEAM UNDERSTAND THE PROJECT TRIANGLE?

"Pure mathematics is, in its way, the poetry of logical ideas."- Albert Einstein

WHY IS THIS QUESTION IMPORTANT?

There comes a time in many projects where someone suggests the need for a fundamental change in The Project. This could be to decrease cost, speed up The Project, or change scope. Many things can trigger such a discussion such as budget constraints, change in Management, etc.. If your project reaches such a point, it is important to understand the inter-relationship between cost, time, quality and scope. It is nearly impossible to change one of these factors without changing at least one of the other. There are numerous names for this relationship. Here we will call it The Project Triangle.

PROJECT TRIANGLE

If you remember high school geometry, you may remember that you cannot change one of the legs of a triangle without changing the length of at least one of the other legs if you want to keep the area of the triangle constant. In our Project Triangle example, you cannot decrease cost without changing scope/quality or time.

Understanding the relationship between these factors, is critical to avoiding what I call the perception of the "free change". This is where someone (usually Senior Management) wants to make a change without it affecting anything else. If you allowed The Project Team to build a modest amount of contingency into The Project estimates, you can absorb some change without affecting the other factors. That is why you want to allow contingency in the estimates.

However, if there is no contingency in the budget, changes in one area such as late deliverables which extends the overall delivery date, will increase cost and/or require a scope or quality decrease.

FAST GOOD CHEAP

Sometimes it takes a while for people to wrap their head around the idea of The Project Triangle and understand how important it is in understanding why it is difficult to change project dimensions. A less elegant but easier to understand way of describing the same concept is the idea of "fast, good, cheap- pick any two".

In this case, fast represents The Project Schedule, cheap The Project budget, and good the scope of The Project. If you want it faster and cheaper, then it will not be as good (the scope will have to be decreased). If you want to make it better (increase the scope) you are going to have to increase either cost or time or both. This is the same conceptually as The Project Triangle, but easier for many to understand.

Whichever version resonates best in your organization, you want to ensure that everyone on your Project Team from the team members to The Project Manager to the Steering Committee understands the concept as it relates to the impact of changes to The Project. All but the smallest changes are going to have an impact on project delivery.

One other aspects of project change that sometimes surprises Executives is how sluggish a project can be to react to these types of changes. If  you want to increase speed by adding budget, it will take some time to bring new people on The Project and acclimate them to the environment.

If you want to decrease cost by reducing scope, you may find that there are contractual issues with external Vendors that impact your ability to quickly remove resources from a project. This sluggishness to react to change is important especially if you are in the later stages of a project. You may find that it will take so long to implement the changes, it will not have the intended effect in the time left before deployment.

REAL WORLD EXAMPLE

In one of my earliest consulting engagements, a mid-sized regional wire manufacturing company wanted to migrate from what was fundamentally an index card in a file box method of

managing inventory (they had relatively
few distinct products but large quantities
of each) to an automated inventory
system tied directly to their accounting
system. The initial estimates required
much longer to implement and would
cost much more than the company was

willing to commit. There were a few rounds of Executives pushing
to reduce the estimates that did not change the answer
significantly.

Then I drew The Project Triangle on a whiteboard for them and
explained the inter-relationship between cost, schedule, and
scope. They immediately began to understand the issue and
requested I come back with a proposal they could afford by
reducing the scope of the initial project.

Their intention was to hold off on funding other parts of the
system until the initial project proved successful. We were able to
divide scope into multiple projects. The first phase has very
successful leading to eventual funding of each additional phase at
the appropriate time.

BEST PRACTICES

- Whenever there is an event on a project that changes cost,
  schedule, or scope, a formal analysis of the impact of that
  change on the other factors should be completed. This
  applies whether it is a deliberate change such as adding new
  functionality or a consequence of something happening on
  The Project such as late deliverables. It is important to
  understand the impact of each change on the other project
  factors.
- Major project changes should be presented to the Steering
  Committee with an understanding of the impact of the
  change on The Project including- time, cost, and scope.

ADDRESSING THE QUESTION WITH THE PROJECT TEAM

Project Manager - The Project Manager should take the lead in identifying events that change one or more of The Project dimensions. You and The Project Manager should regularly discuss how The Project is progressing in terms of these three dimensions so that you can understand the impact of changes.

Business Team- Ensure that The Business Team understands the concept of The Project Triangle. This is especially relevant when The Business wants to add new functionality to The Project Scope or is unable to provide the level of personnel support originally anticipated. This will help The Business Team understand the impact of these on other aspects of The Project.

Information Technology Team- The Technical Team also needs to understand the concept of The Project Triangle. This will help the Technical Team understand the important of controlling the scope of what is included in the system and the importance of meeting the key project deliverable dates.

Steering Committee- Perhaps even more important than having The Project Team understand The Project Triangle, the Steering Committee needs to understand it and how it affects project Change Requests.. This will help them understand the impact of requested changes or help in understanding the importance of project issues like late milestones. It is difficult for the Steering Committee to perform its oversight function without understanding the relationship between these project dimensions.

LESSONS LEARNED FROM PAST PROJECTS

- It is not uncommon for Business Team members to work directly with the Technical Team behind to scene to covertly add functionality beyond the approved scope. Technical Teams in their desire to keep The Business satisfied will often accept this scope creep. In doing so, they put the schedule and cost of The Project at risk. Understanding The Project Triangle can help contain (but probably not prevent) scope creep.

- The cultural of some organizations is that Executives are expected to significantly drive down the cost estimate for all projects. Because of this, they will push the team until the team produces a lower estimate as requested. Frankly, these Executives deserve what they get as a result.

Either The Project Team will begin to intentionally inflate all original estimates so that they can "reduce it" to what it always should have been, or the team comes in with an honest estimate and then is forced to cut it to a level that either guts quality or results in costs/time over-runs.

This is not to say that estimates should not be questioned and closely examined by the Executive Team. That is their oversight function. However, arbitrary demands to slash the budget without changing scope or schedule are unlikely to turn out well.

- The best way to reduce project costs/schedule is to reduce scope. If your organization is unwilling to invest the amount of money it would require to do the full project, consider doing a much less expensive Proof of Concept or divide The Project into distinct phases that can be individually implemented and which can begin to show business value. These types of approaches will limit the initial investment while still producing a quality system albeit at a lesser scope.
- If you reduce The Project time/cost estimate by dividing scope into multiple individual projects/releases, keep in

226

Q28: Does Your Team Understand The Project Triangle?

mind that each project has some overhead and the total of the parts will likely be more than the cost of having a single project.

- If you take a project estimated at $1M and one year and divide it into two parts, do not be surprised if you get two projects at 7-8 months each requiring $600K - $700K each because of the impact of project overhead such as project startup/shutdown time. Splitting project into multiple parts nearly always increases the total cost/time, but can greatly reduce risk and get at least some functionality to The Business earlier.

RELATED QUESTIONS

31. How is quality being assessed/assured on The Project?
33. How is Project Scope being managed?

29. ARE INTELLECTUAL PROPERTY RIGHTS CONTRACTUALLY PROTECTED?

"I am always up to steal secrets from smart people."- Jim Rash

WHY IS THIS QUESTION IMPORTANT?

Imagine your surprise at the end of a long and expensive software development project to find that the software development company you paid so much money is selling software very similar to what they built for you to other customers. Imagine surprise turning into anger when your corporate lawyers tell you that there is nothing you can do to stop this because of the contract that you signed with the developers. This is not a far-fetched scenario by any means.

The standard contract wording from most software developers (large and small) often talks about joint ownership of the software code or shared intellectual property rights. I even saw verbiage once that gave the developer complete ownership of the code and gave the company that paid for the software development only the right to use the system. This prevented the company from even enhancing the software they had paid for.

It is important that you protect your intellectual property rights in the contracts that you sign with your software and consulting service providers. Intellectual property rights preservation is a specialized area of expertise.

You should ensure that your legal team either has specific experience in this area or engage outside assistance to review technology contracts. There are four areas in particular that you want to ensure are taken into account when protecting your intellectual property rights.

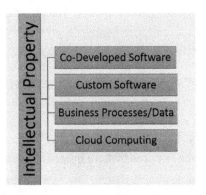

Co-Developed Software- If a software vendor believes that some of the customizations or configurations you want to make to their product may be of commercial value, the may offer to co-develop the software changes with you.

This is usually accompanied with a vague offer that they will lower their fee in return for the right to use/resell the software that comes out of the "collaborative" development process. This is an intuitively attractive offer with you believing that you will get what is perhaps their more experienced developers plus a reduced price.

However, you should be cautious about such an arrangement. I have looked at a few instances where this type of partnership was used. Call me cynical, but I could never get the vendor or the company  commissioning the software to be able to document exactly how much money the deal saved.

One of the reasons for the lack of quantifiable savings is agreeing to co-develop software changes the nature of the software being built. It changes the software from a custom fit to the exact needs of your organization into a generic product that could be applicable to multiple companies. The effort to create a generally implementable software package is greater than the effort required to develop one meant only to support your company.

Additionally, when you agree to co-develop software, you at least partially give up your control over functionality and look and feel. The vendor will push for features that they feel will have wide applicability across their customer base and may balk at implementing features that are only of interest to your company.

If you decide to enter into a co-development agreement, be sure that the contract clearly states the extent to which you will be able to control the intellectual content of the system and how development costs will be shared.

Custom Developed Software - Even in those cases where you are paying all of the development costs of a system, some software development vendors may attempt to put wording in the contract that gives them the right to use the software developed for other purposes.

Ensure that the contract language clearly states that none of the code developed for The Project can be used by the vendor for any purpose after

230

conclusion of The Project. Additional ensure that you own all rights to both the source code for the software and the software itself.

There should be penalties that extend beyond the end of the contract that apply if it is discovered that the vendor is using the software they developed for you in demonstrations, inclusion in their product line, as a jump start for development work for similar clients, etc. These are very common practices even among reputable software companies.

Business Processes/Data- During the course of a project, the external development team will be exposed to information about how you do business. These internal business processes may well represent part of your competitive advantage so you want to take safeguards against a vendor disclosing these business processes to other customers.

It is not uncommon for a company to provide data to the vendor as part of the development and testing process. This data could well be of use to your competitors. In any case, you want to ensure that you are contractually protected against the vendor disclosing your business process and/or data to other customers.

Cloud Computing- The big trend recently has been to move to "Cloud Computing". Cloud computing is where vendors deliver computing power as a service rather than as a product.

Cloud computing attempts to minimize cost by sharing resources across locations and clients creating a scenario where you are not supposed to care or even know where your data is located. Depending on the type and sensitivity of your data, some day you may care very much where your data is stored. The reality is that there is no "cloud". Eventually, you programs and data are placed on a physical server located in a data center somewhere. Where this is could make all the difference.

Keep in mind that there are different data privacy laws in the European Union than in the United States and even different rules on how US intelligence agencies can snoop on data not in the United States. If you were to find that your data was on servers in countries with civil unrest such as Egypt and the Ukraine, you may have additional concerns about data privacy and accessibility. In both of these counties, servers and data storage devices were looted from companies during the unrest never to be seen again. If your data happened to be on one of these, you would have a significant problem

The bottom line is that if you are considering moving sensitive data to a cloud computing provider, do some homework about where the data will really be stored and make sure that you are comfortable with the physical and legal protections offered your intellectual property in that location.

REAL WORLD EXAMPLE

A small "boutique" software development firm specialized in developing add-ons to a major Enterprise Resource Planning (ERP) System and had developed a reputation for delivering high quality customizations at a reasonable price. A major manufacturing company engaged them to create a significant enhancement to the product. This enhancement was significantly bigger than most of the work the company had previously been involved with, but an agreement was reached and work began. Over a year into the two year effort, the vendor announced that they had been acquired by the ERP vendor and were ceasing work on our project.

This left the company with half-finished software that was of no value and which could not be implemented. Due to a poorly worded (from the company's perspective) contract, there was no recourse available to remedy the situation and the company wrote off The Project costs.

However, this was not the end of the issue by any means. About a year later the ERP vendor officially launched a new module based on the code written for The Project and attempted to sell it to the company who had originally funded the work.

Again, the poorly written contract did not protect either the software written or even the detailed business processes that were incorporated into the new module. Make sure that any contract you sign protects the valuable intellectual property rights of your company.

BEST PRACTICES

- You should never grant others rights to your company's intellectual property with getting something equally valuable in return.
- If there is not a section in the software or development services contract related to intellectual property rights, create one. If there is a section on intellectual property, review it carefully to ensure that it completely protects you property rights with sufficient penalties that survive the end of the contract.
- If the vendor is suggesting some type of partnering/co-development or joint ownership arrangement, ensure that you get competent legal counsel skilled in those types of agreements to draft/review the language.
- It is good practice to have vendors certify in writing at the end of The Project that they have physically removed all of your data from all vendor systems.

ADDRESSING THE QUESTION WITH THE PROJECT TEAM

Project Manager- Ensure that your Project Manager is fully aware of intellectual property issues and is vigilant in monitoring The Project Team for compliance. If you have entered into some type of co-development agreement, set the expectation with The Project Manager that they are responsible for monitoring that agreement and ensuring that your requirements are not usurped by the desires of the vendor to create a generic system.

Business Team- Discuss with The Business Team any limits you might find appropriate in what they can and cannot share with the external vendors. This includes both data and business processes. You should consider making The Business Lead the focal point for all data requests and emphasize that if there is any question about data sensitivity, The Business Lead should escalate the request.

Information Technology Team- Ensure that the Technical Team understands that they cannot release any data to the vendor without direct approval of The Business Lead.

LESSONS LEARNED FROM PAST PROJECTS

- If a vendor shows you a demonstration that includes data from another company, then you should assume that they are going to show your data to other clients. If this bothers you, then you need to ensure that your intellectual property rights are adequately protected.
- A good rule of thumb is that if would not freely share business process details or certain types of data with all internal employees, you should be cautious about sharing it with outside vendors.

RELATED QUESTIONS

30. Are project contracts being adequately managed?

44. Is there a strategy for project data protection?

30. ARE CONTRACTS STRUCTURED TO ENSURE PERFORMANCE?

"The best move you can make in negotiation is to think of an incentive the other person hasn't even thought of - and then meet it".- Eli Broad

WHY IS THIS QUESTION IMPORTANT?

Determining whether a vendor has satisfactorily performed their contractual obligated duties for a Technology Project is sometimes not nearly as clear cut as you would wish it would be. This is especially true of contracts that involve contracting for services such as developers, testers, etc.

There are often legitimate disagreements between companies and vendors over whether The Project requirements have been met or not. It is not uncommon for the vendor to continually scale back their Project Team towards the end of a contract to the point that work just stalls soon after the initial deployment due to lack of people to work on it. '

The best way to address vendor performance is with a well thought out contract. Below are six contractual considerations that want to consider in drafting your technology contracts.

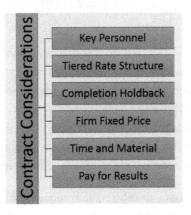

Key Personnel Clauses - There is a pretty standard rotation of expertise in most vendor engagements. During the sales cycle, the vendor tends to bring in their superstars. They are smart, experienced, personable and very adept at understanding your concerns and explaining how they could be addressed. These are the consultants that you know can make your project successful. Sometimes you agree to a contract just because of these superstars.

However, often you will rarely see them again after you sign the contract as they will be off marketing to other clients. Instead, the vendor will provide stand-ins that are "just as good". These are likely to have some experience, but are obviously not the superstars who sold you on the vendor.

Vendors will also provide a number of inexperienced consultants for whom this is their first or second project. These resources are here to get on the job training while helping with your project. Then about two thirds of the way through The Project, they will all begin to disappear slowly being replaced by a new group of inexperienced consultants brought on The Project to get their initial training. While there is admittedly a good bit of cynicism in

237

this timeline, it is actually a good representation of what to expect when you engage a large consulting organization to work on a long duration project.

One way to break this pattern is with a key personnel clause. I recommend that if there are individuals on the sales team or proposed delivery team that you feel understand what you are trying to do and have the necessary skills, add a clause in the contract that lists these key personnel by name as people that cannot be taken off of The Project without your express permission and approval of the proposed replacement.

Also, I suggest that you contractually require that you have the option to review the resume and/or interview all consultants billed under your contract. This will help insure that you are getting the level of consulting assistance that you are paying for.

Tiered Rate Structure- Often large consulting companies propose a single tier rate structure for personnel they provide. I.e., a database administrator (DBAs) might be $150 per hour. However, there are very experienced DBAs and much less experienced. If you are paying the same amount for both junior and senior DBAs there is little incentive for the vendor to provide their top talent.

I would recommend trying to negotiate a tiered scale where junior DBAs are perhaps $110 per hour and senior DBAs are the $150 per hour. This removes the financial incentive to provide less skilled personnel since they will be paid less per hour for them. Part of this negotiation would necessarily be a definition of what level of experience each tier of consultant will meet. Vendors usually don't like this type of arrangement, but it does help ensure you are getting what you paid for.

Completion Holdback- One technique that I recommend for all custom developed software contracts is a completion holdback. This is where you retain say 10% - 20% of all billed fees until the end of The Project to be paid when the software is accepted by the company. This leaves  enough money on the table that most vendors will ensure that work continues until you are satisfied with the result. Obviously these type holdbacks are not popular with vendors.

Firm Fixed Price Contract- This type of contract is are where you are paying a set fee for the performance of a defined set of deliverables. Many companies prefer this type of contract believing that it will give them predictable costs. However, this is usually not the case because of lack of detailed requirements and the power of the change order.

Usually contracts are signed early in The Project when details about functionality are still being worked out. Therefore, any description of the work to be proposed is of necessity high level. An experienced vendor Program Manager will leverage that lack of detail into a series of Change Requests that will drive up the cost of the contract, usually significantly beyond the originally agreed upon amount.

If you do insist upon a firm fixed price contract, ensure that there is sufficient detail in the contract to describe the work to be performed. Also you will want to engage an experienced Project Manager to negotiate change orders with the vendor to keep the price increases under control.

Most importantly however, you want to pre-negotiate the labor rates to be used for all change orders. Vendors sometimes will use higher labor rates on change orders than they would for regular project work. You should not sign the master contract until you have negotiated the best possible labor rates for work under change orders.

Time and Material Contract- These are contracts where you are paying the vendor for all of the authorized hours they expend on a project. This is my preferred vehicle for software development contracts because it eliminates all of the time and effort arguing about what is in or out of scope and the negotiation of change orders.

You can instead spend your time much more productively working on The Project and making sure you get good value out of the consultants working on it. Also, since you are usually buying a large number of consulting hours at one time you can generally negotiate better hourly rates for various types of consultants than you can with fixed price contract change orders.

Pay Based on Results Not Passage of Time- Next to completion holdback, I believe that this is one of the most powerful performance incentives you can put in a consulting contract. Whether you are paying on a fixed price or time and material basis, the vendor will be working on a set of deliverables. I highly recommend that you set up the contract to release periodic contract payments based on completion of agreed upon deliverables.

This gives the vendor great incentive to complete all of the milestones on The Project timeline on time and is a great tool to keep The Project on track. Sending the vendor a check just because another month has gone by does not send nearly as powerful a message as not sending the check until the design document is approved. This also brings visibility into delays in completing deliverable that can help you as an Executive provide project oversight.

REAL WORLD EXAMPLE

A manufacturing company was negotiating a large labor consulting contract with a vendor. Prior to the beginning of negotiations, the CIO did research of the rates this vendor charged its best customers and on how other companies structured their consulting contracts. Even though it was a time and material contract, a not to exceed amount was negotiated for major deliverables with payment tied to completion of the deliverables with a modest holdback. Billable hours were capped per week to keep down overtime billing and very favorable rates that were inclusive of travel expenses were negotiated to keep down effort needed to process expense reports.

Even though The Project was expected to last about 2 years, labor rates for approximately 5 years were negotiated as part of the initial package ensuring favorable labor rates for any desired follow-on work. Also key personnel were named in the contract and stayed engaged for the duration of The Project. This was all possible because of three key factors 1) a highly skilled negotiator 2) repeated indication that the company would move to the next vendor on the list if an agreement could not be reached 3) bundling a large amount of services over a long period of time into a single contract.

BEST PRACTICES

- Vendors will not be enthusiastic about any of these techniques to motivate performance as they will disrupt their booking of revenue, affect sales quotas, etc. However, they will keep the vendor more focused on your project and the successful and timely completion of deliverables.
- When negotiating with vendors make sure you send your best negotiator. This may not be your Project Manager or Business Lead. The vendor will send

their best so should you. One of the keys in any negotiation is to always indicate your willingness to walk away from the table and engage another vendor to do the work. If the vendor believes you have no options but the work with them, you have already lost the negotiation.

ADDRESSING THE QUESTION WITH THE PROJECT TEAM

Project Manager- Unless they are very experienced in contracts and negotiation, The Project Manager is generally not directly involved in vendor negotiation. However, they should be consulted about items such as deliverables, payment schedules, and key personnel. Also, The Project Manager should review the full contract prior to final agreement and be allowed to provide comments.

Business Team - The Business Team is generally not involved in the contractual process, but should be made aware of the incentives as the contract is finalized.

Information Technology Team - The Technical Team is generally not involved in the process, but should be made aware of the incentives as the contract is finalized.

Legal Department- You should have detailed conversations with the Legal Team on the incentives that you want included in the contract so that they can craft appropriate wording and negotiate the incentives with the vendor.

Steering Committee- Of course the Steering Committee needs to understand the contract in general, but in particular the performance incentives you are including.

LESSONS LEARNED FROM PAST PROJECTS

- Just putting incentives on a piece of paper and signing it is not enough. Refer to the chapter on contract

242

management for ideas on how the make sure that you get what you have negotiated for.

- Experience shows that if you insist a vendor agree to a fixed price software development contract, most vendors will add 20% or more to the price over what their bid on a time and materials contract would have been. This is to account for the risk they are assuming in provide the services for a set fee.

- Anything that you want the vendor to do should be negotiated and included in the contract. After the contract is signed, any changes are likely to be expensive.

- If you do chose firm fixed price as the type of contract vehicle, you should add at least 10% - 20% of the contract value into the budget to pay for the inevitable Change Requests.

- Be cautious about allowing the vendor to start work prior to agreeing on a contract. It is not uncommon for both your team and the vendor to want to begin work immediately in order to jump start The Project.

  While there is value to this from a project perspective, it can adversely impact contract negotiation in that it begins weaken your chances of walking away from the vendor during negotiations and begins to set a standard for rates, expenses, etc. If you do choose to allow the vendor to begin work prior to contract agreement, it should be for a fixed duration with no option to be extended. This puts pressure on both sides to conclude negotiations.

- If your Legal Team does not have expertise in Technology Contract, they should engage outside counsel to help with drafting/reviewing contracts.

RELATED QUESTIONS

5. Is there sufficient Executive oversight?

9. Am I sufficiently engaged in The Project?

32. Are contracts being adequately managed?

31. HOW IS QUALITY BEING ASSESSED/ASSURED ON THE PROJECT?

"Be a yardstick of quality. Some people aren't used to an environment where excellence is expected."- Steve Jobs

WHY IS THIS QUESTION IMPORTANT?

Hunter S. Thompson is quoted as saying the "Anything worth doing is worth doing right". I am not sure he particularly had Technology Projects in mind when he said this, but the sentiment certainly applies. If you system does not function properly when deployed, it may keep you from achieving The Projected business benefits. Additionally if quality is poor, you will likely have to invest additional time and money to resolve future issues.

The National Institute of Standards and Technology estimated in a 2002 study that in the United States alone, software bugs cost $59.5B annually. Obviously projects do not set out to have defects, so it is useful to examine where these defects creep into a project. Regardless of the type of Technology Project, there are 5 areas in particular that deserve special attention as related to ensuring quality.

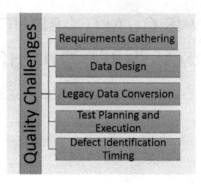

Requirements Gathering- Clear, well documented implementable requirements are the foundation upon which The Project rests. If you are missing requirements, have incorrectly documented requirements, etc. that error is likely to carry through until the end of The Project. Requirements are elicited at the beginning of most projects when the team is just forming and people are not as focused on the problem as they will be as The Project progresses.

Requirements are often documented by business personnel that while very knowledgeable in business operations, often do not have experience in concisely documenting requirements. Special care should be taken to ensure the quality of the requirements. There are a few key ways to ensure quality of requirements documents.

One of the most important keys is to ensure that there is at least one person on the requirements gathering team that has experience in documenting requirements. This includes understanding what level of detail is required, how to structure good requirement statements, etc. This will help ensure that the requirements that are captured will support the needs of The Project.

Additionally, ensure that there is at least one member of the Technical Team takes part in the requirements gathering sessions. This will help ensure that the requirements are captured at the appropriate level of detail to support the development effort. The final and hardest part of helping ensure requirements quality is the final requirements review.

You need to slow The Project down for a bit and ensure key business personnel take the time to actually read the requirements to ensure their accuracy and completeness.

Data Design - The Technical Team builds a system design based on the requirements and intended system configuration. This includes not only a design of how the system will be divided into components, but will also include a design of how data will be handled in the system.

Understanding what data is needed to implement project requirements and how this data is organized is another critical foundational element of a system. Poor data design can lead to inadequate system performance, difficulty in building reports, issues exchanging data with other internal and external systems, etc.

Usually The Business Team sees database design as one of those mysterious things which unfolds behind the curtain and which should not be questioned. This is often a mistake. Database diagrams seem complex and hard to understand on the surface. However, with a little help, anyone can understand how to read the design documents. If you take the time to review the data design with key Business Team members It will improve overall system quality. These are the people who can help identify data that may be missing from the design and/or data that is perhaps associated together incorrectly. This is a valuable quality check that can head off problems as The Project progresses and is well worth the investment of time and effort.

Legacy Data Conversion - Approaches to legacy data conversion are discussed elsewhere in this book. However, it is worth mentioning here in the discussion on quality that you need to create and  execute a strategy to deal with legacy data quality very early in The Project to ensure that you have sufficient time to cleanse data as necessary. Poor data quality can keep you from achieving business benefits and in my experience is one of the top things that keep systems from deploying on time.

Test Planning and Execution - It is an unfortunate reality that development often takes longer than anticipated resulting in chaos in the testing schedule. This often has the ripple effect of impacting the quality and thoroughness of testing. One way to mitigate this is to ensure that a detailed test plan has been developed so that testing is ready to begin as soon as system components are complete.

Key to this is to ensure you have testing environments and test data ready to go as soon as testing can begin. This is an area where attention to the quality of the planning can pay off by limiting testing delays.

Defect Identification Timing- One last thing to keep in mind when it comes to quality is the need to find defects as early as possible. There have been several studies on the cost of finding defects early in a project versus discovering them at deployment. While there are some differences of opinion on exactly how expensive errors found late are, the consensus is that it is very important to find and resolve errors early. A popular graphic documenting this was created by Steve McConnel in his 2004 book Code Complete.

Cost to fix a defect		Time detected				
		Requirements	Architecture	Construction	System test	Post-release
Time introduced	Requirements	1×	3×	5–10×	10×	10–100×
	Architecture	–	1×	10×	15×	25–100×
	Construction	–	–	1×	10×	10–25×

A key message from this study is that if you have a requirements problem that is not discovered until after deployment, it will costs 10 to 100 times what it would have cost if discovered during the requirements process.

REAL WORLD EXAMPLE

To save time on a mid-size inventory system, The Project Team decided to document the requirements concurrently with designing the database. The requirements gathering sessions were deemed business activities and there was little technical participation and the database design sessions were deemed technical sessions with little business participation.

Late in the requirements process, it was determined that there were too many parts in the inventory to effectively manage at the part level so they created the concept of a part grouping which associated related parts into groups which would be the primary way parts were ordered and managed. Management reports, dashboards, etc. would use part grouping to reduce the number of areas to watch to a much more manageable level.

Unfortunately, the database design team was not part of the discussion about part grouping and subsequently did not build the capability for that type of relationship into the database. In the end, the
Technical Team approved the requirements and The Business Team approved the design.

However, their reviews were very perfunctory and shallow and the issue was not discovered until late in the testing process. This quality issue resulted in a database re-design and an overall 3 month delay in implementing The Project which costs the company about $600K. If quality procedures had been in place and caught the issue as it occurred, the cost of fixing it would have been negligible.

BEST PRACTICES

- If the IT organization and/or Business has a Quality Assurance group, they should be engaged in The Project as early as possible to help ensure deliverables quality. If there is not a formal Quality Assurance group in your company, appoint someone on The Project Team to be responsible for monitoring and managing project quality issues. On smaller projects, this is often The Project Manager
- Ensure that there is a trained Business Analyst and/or other personnel trained in requirements documentation in charge of the requirements process. Poor quality requirement statements affects development, design, test, and even training.
- Take the time to train The Business personnel that are working on requirements in at least the basic of good requirements documentation.
- Make sure that time for Quality Assurance is built into The Project Schedule. All major deliverables should have tasks in The Project Schedules for reviews, revisions, and approvals.
- When quality issues are discovered, take the time to resolve them as they are found. Fixing them later will take much longer and cost much more.
- If you are using external resources on The Project, ensure that quality standards are built into the contract so that you do not have to pay for sub-standard work. Too often contracts concentrate on timing of deliverables without having a way to ensure the quality of those deliverables.

ADDRESSING THE QUESTION WITH THE PROJECT TEAM

Project Manager- Ask to see the tasks in The Project Schedule related to Quality Assurance. These should include document reviews, peer reviews, formal signoff of key deliverables etc. If these have not been included, insist that they are explicitly built into the schedule so that sufficient time will be available to produce quality products.

Business Team - Stress with The Business Team the importance of having well documented requirements and the cost of having poor requirements. Set the expectation that The Business and Technical Teams will both actively participate in the requirements process and review the results in detail prior to giving requirements approval.

Information Technology Team- Emphasize the need for quality standards throughout The Project and the role of the Technical Team in maintaining quality. This includes active participation in quality reviews and making time to review deliverables prior to approving them.

LESSONS LEARNED FROM PAST PROJECTS

- The more people that you have as official reviewers of a document, the less likely it is that anyone of them will actually read the document. Most will assume that other people have read it and will just sign off on it. It is much better to have a very small number of approvers that actually review and comment on the document.
- One of the most commonly type of missed requirements are what I call the "everyone knows that" requirements. This is where The Business Team fails to document business requirements because they assume everyone understands something. For example, they may fail to include a

251

requirement to make sure that a customer has paid for past orders before accepting new orders because everyone know you look at that. However, the development team that does not have the same level of business knowledge is unlikely to build that capability into the system without a written requirement.

- As The Project progresses and The Project Schedule begins to become more compressed, getting people to focus on quality becomes increasingly difficult. You need someone responsible for the quality function that has the personality and power to force the team to slow down at key points and focus on Quality Assurance tasks.

- After spending so much time talking about the importance of quality, it bears mention that quality is not an absolute, it is relative. I managed a development effort for software used on US Navy Trident Submarines where a system failure could result in the destruction of a $1B boat and the death of several hundred crew not to mention loss of a quite a number of very powerful nuclear missiles. In this environment, no amount of quality control or testing was deemed excessive due to the consequences of failure.

However, on another project I managed, we created a reporting package for an inventory systems that had to be implemented at the beginning of a month. This system had passed all of the mainstream testing, but had not yet completed all of the exception testing. The worse consequence of a failure here was that we would possibly order slightly too much inventory until the problem was fixed. Since the burn rate to sustain The Project Team was close to $75K per week, management made a decision that it was not worth $300K to delay the deployment another month and we deployed the system and quickly fixed the few problems that were encountered.

Q31: How Is Quality Being Assessed/Assured On The Project?

- For deliverables that are the responsibility of outside vendors, make sure you understand contract provisions related to quality and approvals. Many contracts will have wording indicating that if you do not provide feedback on the deliverable within say 5 days, it is considered accepted.

  When agreeing to contracts, ensure that they include sufficient time for deliverable review. Also, you should have a "warranty" period after deployment where any defects identified will be fixed at no additional cost.

RELATED QUESTIONS

5. Is there sufficient Executive oversight?

19. Are all impacted Stakeholders actively involved in The Project?

21. Who is really speaking for The Business on The Project?

32. ARE PROJECT CONTRACTS BEING ADEQUATELY MANAGED?

"Thoroughly read all your contracts. I really mean thoroughly."- Bret Michaels (Rock Star)

WHY IS THIS QUESTION IMPORTANT?

In several areas of this book, we have discussed areas that should be carefully addressed prior to signing technology contracts. However, contractual concerns do not end once the contract is signed and the vendor begins to perform the work or deliver the hardware/ software.

Once The Project begins, it is not uncommon for both you and vendor to stop thinking about the contract and focus on The Project. In fact, since contracts are often considered Executive and Legal Department concerns, key project personnel on both sides may not even seen the final version of the contract.

It is important that your Project Manager, Business Lead, and Technical Lead all have an understanding of the contract provisions and that they are provided with a copy of the contract itself for reference. It is understandable that you might be reluctant to share some information like costs and rates with the team, but that information can be easily redacted from the document prior to sharing it with them if you desire. It is important that team leaders understand the deliverables, terms and condition, intellectual property protections, etc. for them to effectively monitor contract execution.

While some Executive or Purchasing Manager may "approve" contractual payments on a project, they usually only do so after Project Leaders indicate the work has been performed. If these Leaders do not have access to the contractual document, they may provide invoice approval recommendations that do not align with the contractual agreements.

REAL WORLD EXAMPLE

A financial services company embarked on a significant effort to develop a new customer service application. Because of the aggressive timeline, they engaged a large software development company with significant expertise and experience in the type of system being built. The company lawyers were very experienced and understanding the aggressive deadlines inserted a system of financial incentives and penalties into the contract to help motivate the vendor to deliver key components in a timely manner.

The Project proceeded on track for a period of time, but about two thirds of the way through The Project, the vendor pulled some of their most experienced people off of the job to staff a new contract with another company. The replacement personnel while not totally unskilled had a significant learning curve to become productive due to the need to understand the requirements and work that had been done to date. Within a month, The Project was in real trouble from a deliverable date perspective and ultimately was deployed about 3 months late.

Remembering the penalty clauses in the contract, the company attempted to recoup some of the loss by invoking the penalties. However the contract had a defined process for resolution of poor performance involving notifying the vendor of the deficiency, meeting with management to attempt to resolve issues, approving deliverables in a timely manner, etc. that had not been followed. As a result, not only was the company not successful in invoking penalties, but actually had to pay some of the timeliness incentives due to failure to follow the contractual provisions. In a lessons learned session at the end of The Project, it was noted that no one on The Project Team had even read the contract much less had a copy to refer to and thus had no way of knowing the procedures to be followed.

BEST PRACTICES

- One active project participant should be tasked with understanding the contractual provisions for each vendor and in ensuring that both parties remain contractually compliant.
- All key Project Leaders on both the company and vendor side should have a copy of the contract with any sensitive information removed.
- There should be a meeting between Vendor and Company Leadership on a periodic basis to review contractual compliance and address any issues
- As The Project moves forward, sometimes situations changes such as scope or timing changes. If this occurs on your project, make any necessary contractual changes in a formal manner. Agreeing to contract deviations with "just a handshake" is ill advised unless your Legal Department approves.

ADDRESSING THE QUESTION WITH THE PROJECT TEAM

Project Manager- Discuss with The Project Manager the key components of each of your vendor contracts and ensure that they have a copy of the contract to refer to. Set the expectations that they are to monitor the activities of both the company and the vendor to ensure both are complying with the contract provisions.

Business Team- Ensure that The Business Lead also has a copy of each of the major vendor contracts relating to delivery of services to The Project. Set the expectation that The Business Team must follow the contract provisions and escalate any situation where the contract is not being followed and/or the contract requires amendment.

Information Technology Team - The Technical Lead should have a copy of all major hardware/software contracts and all services contracts for The Project and should be responsible for ensuring both the company and the vendor adhere to the provisions.

Steering Committee - Executives on the Steering Committee need to be aware of the general structure and scope of each of the major vendor contracts. They should also have available to them copies of the actual contracts to refer to as needed.

LESSONS LEARNED FROM PAST PROJECTS

- If The Project reaches the point where lawyers for the company and vendor are arguing about contract compliance, it is unlikely that you are going to get anything of value implemented anywhere close to your planned deployment date. You want The Project Leads to manage/monitor contract compliance so that issues can be resolved well before the lawyers get involved.

- If the relationship between the company and vendor begins to get strained, it is preferable to attempt to solve it with high level Executive meetings between leaders of the two organizations rather than getting the legal team involved. Having said that, it the issues cannot be resolved between the Executives of the respective organizations, don't hesitate to involve Legal to enforce the contract and protect your investment.

- Vendor and company teams on projects work very closely together often in a high stress fast moving environment. It is natural in such an environment for the formal barriers between vendor and company to go away to be replaced by an atmosphere of working together to get the job done.

I believe that when you reach such a stage, work gets done much faster producing a better result. However, it is easy to fall into the trap during the heat of a project to begin to "horse trade". For example the contract calls for the vendor to build two interfaces, but the Technical Lead proposes that the company build those interfaces instead and the vendor in return will write 3 new reports.

In my mind, this is a great way for the vendor and company to work together, but it can become a contractual nightmare if problems are encountered and/or the relationship sours. Then, the lawyers get involved and everything grinds to a halt. I encourage horse trading on a contract, but there needs to be at least minimal formal documentation of the change in the contract. I call these zero cost change orders. They document what was agreed to, but do not affect timing or amount of payment.

258

RELATED QUESTIONS

5. Is there sufficient Executive oversight?

7. What are key roles for project success?

9. Am I sufficiently engaged in The Project?

30. Are Contracts Structured To Ensure Performance?

36. How are offshore/offsite resources being managed?

33. HOW IS PROJECT SCOPE BEING MANAGED?

"By increasing the size of the keyhole, today's playwrights are in danger of doing away with the door."- Peter Ustinov

WHY IS THIS QUESTION IMPORTANT?

Your teenager comes to you asking for $10 to buy a used guitar at a pawn shop which seems very reasonable to you so you agree. Roll the calendar forward a year and the used guitar has become an expensive new electrical guitar with amplifiers, you have spent a fortune on guitar lessons, you have to park in the street because you teen now has a garage band that practices at your place, and they all want tattoos so they can have street credibility.

You sit and wonder how something as simple as a used guitar became a new reality that you would have never agreed to if you know where it was really headed. This is what a failure to manage

Project Scope feels like and you why you want to avoid it on your Technology Project.

When you approve a project to proceed, you are approving a defined set of activities, costs, benefits, goals, involved parties, etc. that in total can be called The Project Scope. If any of these areas change significantly, then it is likely to affect cost and/or schedule (See the chapter on The Project Triangle). Very significant changes may well make you question the value of The Project as a whole.

There are three aspects of scope management that you want to understand and manage.

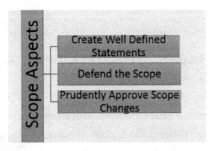

Create a Well Defined Scope Statement- Prior to approving a project, The Project Team should define The Project Scope. This should include not only what is "in the scope" of The Project, but also what is "out of scope".

The in-scope definition should cover things like functionality, data, training, involved Business Units, etc. You should also outline The Business benefits and costs so that the Steering Committee understands how much they are expected to invest in The Project and what benefits the company will receive from having made this investment.

Just as important as defining what is in-scope, the Scope Statement should define what is out of scope. This should include any feature that people might logically assume or hope is part of The Project. Examples of out of scope items might be- server replacement is not in-scope, creation of a data warehouse is not in-scope, end user training is not in-scope. Listing the out of scope items removes confusion over whether the items are included or not.

The Scope Statement should be concise, but sufficiently detailed to clearly define the boundaries of The Project. Once approved by The Project Leads and the Steering Committee, the Scope Statement will become the basis for The Project Schedule, budget, staffing, etc., so it needs to clearly define The Project.

Defend The Scope- In my Project Management Class, I have a slide showing an ancient castle surrounded by a moat being attacked by invaders from the next kingdom. The label on this slide is "Defend the Scope". I think that this is a very fitting metaphor for how you should treat the scope of your project.

Hopefully, you will have developed a well-written Scope Statement that has Project Team and Sponsor approval. What you will find is that almost immediately people will begin to chip away at that scope often behind the scenes.

They may argue with the Technical Team that since the scope included writing a few reports, it obviously included building a data warehouse, buying sophisticated and expensive end-user reporting tools, and training hundreds of people in how to use the tools. Another common approach is for one of The Business Managers to approach the team and request that their pet idea be added to The Project even though it was purposely not included in the approved scope.

However, you not only need to guard against scope additions, you should be careful to guard against unapproved scope subtractions. Reducing the scope of systems sometimes limits their usefulness. Once the scope has been approved, it should be defended against any change without a formally approved Change Request.

Prudently Approve Change Requests - Sometimes change is unavoidable. Nothing in the discussion above should be interpreted a message to never change Project Scope. The message is to only change it in an informed manner with an understanding of the impacts to time, cost, and personnel resources.

If there is a compelling reason to change the scope, then analyze the impact on The Project, adjust the budget/schedule as needed and approve the Change Request. This should be done as sparingly as possible since any significant Change Request interrupts the flow of The Project.

REAL WORLD EXAMPLE

On an inventory system project I reviewed, The Project was running over budget, so The Project Team unilaterally decided to remove all of the warehouse location tracking features from the system to reduce cost and get The Project back on track. They did not inform the Steering Committee or the Warehouse Manager of this decision and The Project moved steadily towards deployment over the next 8 months. During the final User Acceptance Testing, the warehouse tester discovered that you could not track inventory to its storage location bringing progress to a screeching halt.

Since this was one of their top reasons for supporting The Project, the warehouse team was understandably upset that this key feature would not be available. Ultimately, they refused to certify the test and refused to install the new software until the feature was added. This resulted in a delay of several months and a significant additional investment of resources on the part of the company.

BEST PRACTICES

- Change Requests should be in writing and should include estimates of the impact on schedule, budget and staffing. They should be approved by the same Stakeholders on the Steering Committee that originally approved the scope.
- Once a Change Request is approved, it should be communicated to all involved in The Project
- All project participants should be educated in the process to request changes and the need to only implement changes that are formally approved.

ADDRESSING THE QUESTION WITH THE PROJECT TEAM

Project Manager- In general, The Project Manager should take the lead in establishing and defending the scope of The Project. Set the expectation that you will look to them to identify and deal with attempts to introduce out of scope items into The Project.

Business Team- Ensure that The Business Team understands that the only way to add/change/delete system functionality is through the Change Request Process. Set the expectation with The Business Lead that they are be on watch for attempts to change Project Scope.

Information Technology Team- As with The Business Team, you should discuss the process for changing Project Scope set the expectation that the developers are not to work on items that are not in the approved scope regardless of who asks them to do so.

LESSONS LEARNED FROM PAST PROJECTS

- When a Senior Business Manager comes up to a junior developer and asks them to add something to the system, it is difficult to turn them down. To combat this, both the developers and The Business Managers need to understand that this is inappropriate and will not be tolerated. Additionally, you want to create an atmosphere where developers are comfortable with escalating issues such as this to their Project Leaders.
- Projects sometimes die the "death of a thousand cuts". This is where no single unauthorized change is terribly impactful, but the sum of hundreds of these changes dramatically increases project cost and delays deployment.

If something is suffering the death of a thousand cuts, lots of small bad things are happening, none of which are fatal in themselves, but which add up to a slow and painful demise.-

Old English Idiom

- It is not just The Business Team that will try to increase scope. The Technical Team sometimes has their own ideas of what the system should do that they will try and impose on The Project. You should also be vigilant to these changes.
- One of the best ways to defend your scope is to create the concept of the mythical release 2. Release 2 is the next set of work on the system that may begin soon after deployment of the initial release. This release is not currently funded or scheduled perhaps, but does represent a place where scope that cannot be fit into the initial release can be documented.

It is much easier to mark a change as "deferred to release 2" than it is to mark it as "denied". Whether Release 2 is ever actually built and implemented depends on The Business value of the items contained in it and their benefit to the company. Regardless of this, having a Release 2 gives users at least the hope that their pet item may eventually be added and is not just being forgotten.

RELATED QUESTIONS

1. Are The Project objectives clear to all?

13. Does each documented requirement have real business value?

21. Who is really speaking for The Business on The Project?

23. Are project business requirements well documented?

28. Does your Project Team Understand The Project Triangle?

34. HOW WILL YOU KNOW WHEN THE PROJECT IS COMPLETE?

"Disneyland will never be completed. It will continue to grow as long as there is imagination left in the world."- Walt Disney

WHY IS THIS QUESTION IMPORTANT?

This is another of those questions that you might think is very simple, but turns out not to be. Small projects are relatively simple to shut down. There is usually a single deployment, followed by a short amount of cleanup and then close The Projects.

The larger and more complex a Technology Project becomes, the harder it is to bring to a close. Somewhat paradoxically, the more successful a large Project Team is, the hard it is to disband it. Often, there is an Executive that wants to keep a successful team together to continue working on some new problem.

However, keep in mind prior discussion about labor burn rates and their effect on the total project budget. One of the most controllable costs on a project is the labor cost. Even a small Project Team of say 12 people will usually cost about $50K per week. If you keep them on The Project for an extra month you will incur $200K for costs that probably were not in the original budget. One of the keys to managing costs on a project is to create a firm definition of project completion in the Scope Statement at the beginning of a project. Then close The Project as soon as that is achieved. It is helpful to examine some of the dynamics that make a project difficult to shut down.

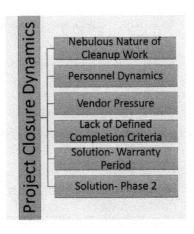

The Nebulous Nature of Cleanup Work- The end of a project can resemble an untidy house after a frat party. Clear heads looking at the situation can easily create a list of perhaps dozens of individual things that "need" to be done to put the house in order.

Certainly, the broken windows need to be fixed and the trash collected and taken out. However, as you look at the list, you begin to find things that have little or nothing to do with the party like the need to repaint the basement which has needed painting for years. And you find items like buying a ladder then using it to get the Frisbee out of the tree which while related to the party will take so much time and money that it is just not worth doing.

The list of "cleanup" items at the end of a large project can have much in common with this. It is inevitable that smart Executives will want to try to get The Project Team to take care of some long-standing items that do not have sufficient priority or business value to warrant being funded on their own  merits. There also may be a number of things which fall in the category of "nice to do" or even "important to do" items. These items have importance in some people's minds, but may not have sufficient business value to justify their costs.

You should ensure that the cleanup list at the end of The Project is carefully scrutinized to ensure that items on it are part of the original scope of The Project and that they provide business value greater than the costs to keep The Project Team moving forward. Applying a practicality filter to the cleanup list usually slashes many items of little value to the company as a whole.

Personnel Dynamics - At the end of a long high pressure project, there are many people that are more than ready to return to their regular job in the organization. However, there are usually a number of people, often in project leadership positions, that would prefer The Project continues. The reasons for this can range from honest desire to not stop until "everything is done" to loss of status in the real world compared to their perceived status on The Project Team. Someone who is a Business Lead on a project that everyone respects and depends upon, may be hesitant to returning to their old Business Unit to process purchase orders. Based on these motivations, innovative people can find many reasons/ways to keep The Project in place.

Vendor Pressure- Vendor Client Managers are compensated on their success in selling additional work to clients. They would not be doing their job if they did not push an agenda designed to extend the length of The Project. These are sometimes difficult to combat since the proposal is likely to be well structured and will usually contain defined business benefit. Additionally, the Client Manager will certainly use their contacts among the Executives to socialize the need for additional work. Even if the additional work is deemed beneficial, it should only be added to The Project through formal change order or better yet a new project.

Lack of Defined Completion Criteria- Scope Statements created at the beginning of a project should always include completion criteria. I like to include a statement to the effect that- "This project will be considered complete when A, B, and C have been completed".

Then, periodically through The Project, I remind The Project Team and Steering Committee of this definition of project completion. As The Project begins to reach its scheduled end date, start releasing un-needed personnel from The Project Team and when the completion criteria are met you stop The Project.

One Solution is a Warranty Period - While you want to control the amount of cleanup work at the end of a project, some amount of it is inevitable. One solution is to build a set amount of time into The Project budget/schedule that I call the warranty period.

This is a set period of time (perhaps a month depending on the length of The Project) where you will keep at least part of The Project Team intact to deal with any defects found in the system and to take care of key residual cleanup items. It is not a bad practice to let The Project Team work on just about anything that

271

they or The Business wants them to work on as long as it can be accomplished in this set period of time. At the end of the warranty period the rest of The Project Team is disbanded.

It is also important to include a warranty period in vendor contracts during with they will resolve emerging issues usually at reduced or no charge.

Another Solution is Phase 2- One technique that I describe elsewhere in this book to control scope, contain excessive cleanup efforts, and divert vendor proposals is what I call Phase 2 of The Project. I usually introduce about half way through The Project.

Phase 2 is an artificial construct used to accumulate items that people would like The Project/Project Team to work on before the end of The Project that are not in scope and/or have undefined business value.

As The Project draws closer to the end, I bundle up the Phase 2 items along with a cost estimate and present it to the Steering Committee as a new project. If the work stands on its merits and the Steering Committee gives formal approval, then we launch it as a new project. If not, the work remains unfunded. In any case, we close the original project as soon as the approved completion criteria have been met.

REAL WORLD EXAMPLE

I was asked to look at a State Government Project that successfully deployed the anticipated system but which still had a huge backlog of "required work" and was projected to go very significantly over budget. It didn't take too long to understand the problem, which was no one wanted The Project to end for varying reasons.

Q34: How Will You Know When The Project Is Complete?

The vendor had an extremely skilled Client Manager that know how to keep The Project alive and funded. In my opinion, there was nothing illegal or even unethical about the situation; the vendor just made it seem like the most natural thing in the world was to keep the team together working on problems.

The Vendor "seduction" started early in The Project when the vendor offered to host the development work at their facility versus working at the Government location for a very modest facilities fee. This took the Government Project Manager and several other agency personnel out of their small dark cubicles into much nicer office space.

The Project Manager literally went from an 8 foot square cube in the basement of a State Building to a corner office overlooking the river. The government team quickly became so enmeshed in the vendor culture that had lost the ability to objectively manage the vendor. All key project decisions including what was in or out of scope had been abdicated to the vendor.

The vendor Client Manager spent significant time in the offices of the Agency Managers and Executives. They came to understand the Agency's business and their problems and quickly began to provide free advice which eventually turned into change orders to add totally un-related work to their contract on The Project.

The successful deployment only made this worse as now the vendor had a cadre of experienced consultants that had great understanding of the Agency ready to work on new tasks. The scope of work that I discovered The Project Team was working on had very little to do with the original scope approved by the State Technology Council and funded the by the Legislature.

During my discussions with the Agency, I was asked several times why people were concerned about this since all of the work the

Vendor delivered was high quality and on-time and all of it had been approved by various Agency Executives.

The answer was very simple. Inside their world, they had what they considered a well-oiled machine that was stamping out system improvements that had been requested for many years. In the real world, The Project was very significantly over budget and considered a big problem because it was still going far after the expected completion date. While the current work being complete had been long requested, it had been denied funding multiple times as too expensive and as having little value to the State and the taxpayers.

The recommended solution was simple; stop all project work immediately and bundle all desired additional work into a new project which would have to go through the standard project approval process. This was implemented by the Agency and not surprisingly the work that was deemed critical enough to extend a very expensive vendor contract several times was never submitted for funding because sufficient justification could not be created to justify it.

BEST PRACTICES

- In the Scope Statement at the beginning of The Project agree on a firm set of completion criteria and as soon as these are met close The Project.
- Make sure that all the internal personnel working on The Project will have meaningful jobs to return to at the end of The Project. This will make people much more comfortable about closing down The Project.
- As the Executive Sponsor, caution Vendor Client Managers that any proposals for follow-on work are to be discussed directly with you prior to discussion with business and/or technical Managers.

Q34: How Will You Know When The Project Is Complete?

- Create a formal list available for all to see of out of scope items and/or items with undefined business value that are deferred to future releases. I call this the Phase 2 list.

ADDRESSING THE QUESTION WITH THE PROJECT TEAM

Project Manager- The Project Manager should take the lead in monitoring progress towards project completion. They should be able to show you verbiage in the Scope Statement documenting the completion criteria and tasks in The Project Schedule working towards project shutdown.

Business Team- In your discussions with The Business Team re-enforce the agreed upon completion criteria for The Project while encouraging the team to document any new ideas beyond the scope of The Project in the Phase 2 list which is to be reviewed for inclusion in a potential new follow-on project at the appropriate time.

Information Technology Team- When deadlines loom, it is not uncommon for the Technical Team to agree among themselves to defer things like documentation, tuning, reporting, error handling, etc. until after deployment. You should ensure that the Technical Team understands that after deployment, The Project will end so all key tasks need to be accomplished either prior to deployment or prior to the end of the warranty period.

LESSONS LEARNED FROM PAST PROJECTS

- Especially on long projects, make sure that your internal personnel have a job to return to. I have seen plant personnel sent to corporate offices to work on a project for a year then finding their job at the plant had been backfilled. Therefore, there was no need or place for them to return to when The Project ended.

275

Worrying about post-project positions can begin to consume significant time and attention on Project Teams toward the end of a project. Ensuring everyone has a job to return to is the least that Senior Executives can do for

employees that have worked long hours on a project. It is not much of a reward to a person that helps build a great system in an impossible timeframe to find that they no longer have a meaningful role in the organization at the end of a project.

- Each person on The Project should have a projected end date on The Project showing when they are expected to leave The Project. A spreadsheet or other document should be created about two thirds of the way through The Project showing the roll-off date for each project participant.

  This will allow both the individuals and their managers to work out a transition plan for moving them off The Project. This is also a powerful tool for managing consultant costs. Each consultant should have a set exit date based on their work assigned so that you do not pay for them longer than necessary.

- Ending a project takes leadership because the natural inertia once a well-functioning project machine has been created is to keep it working.

RELATED QUESTIONS

1. Are The Project objectives clear to all?

Q34: How Will You Know When The Project Is Complete?

15. Is there a holistic view of required business and technical changes?

23. Are project business requirements well documented?

33. How is Project Scope being managed?

35. ARE PART TIME RESOURCES ON THE PROJECT REALLY AVAILABLE?

"Baseball is ninety percent mental and the other half is physical."- Yogi Berra

WHY IS THIS QUESTION IMPORTANT?

Most companies do not have sufficient excess staffing to assign numerous people to be on a Technology Project on full time basis. Additionally, the nature of some project tasks is such that there is not sufficient work to consistently keep a person busy on a full time basis.

As a result, a significant portion of the staffing of many Technology Projects is made up of part-time resources. This is especially common with business experts and niche technical experts like database administrators and architects. Use of part-time labor is a very cost-effective way of completing project work and is considered a best practice.

However, too often, the part-time resources may not be available when they are needed the most, disrupting the flow of The Project and potentially and extending the schedule. If your Project Team is considering use of part-time resources (which again most projects do), there are a couple of factors to consider.

Timing of Resources Needs- It would be great if you could predict exactly when you need each resource months in advance, but that is not always possible. Due to the ebb and flow or Project Schedules, it is often not possible to predict exactly when you will need certain part-time resources until a week or two before they are needed. This requires a good bit of patience and flexibility from the part-time resource and their Manager. The commitment should be to provide as much notice as possible, keeping in mind the realities of projects.

Another issue that often arises with resource availability is what I think of as "blackout" periods. These are times when people will not be available regardless of needs of The Project due to competing needs. On one financial reporting project for a mid-sized company with a very modest sized accounting department, we needed part-time resources periodically for requirements definition, prototype review, testing, training, etc.

The Accounting Manager was very supportive of The Project, but told us up front that their personnel were not available the first and last weeks of each month because of month end closing, they would not be available every Friday because of Accounts Payable runs, and would not be available every other week on Wednesday and Thursday because of payroll processing. Even though we were promised resources at the 50% level, there were not enough non-blackout days in a month to get much more than 10% - 15% of people's time.

Named Resources- One key way of helping ensure you have sufficient part-time resources when needed is to have them designated by name. It is helpful for a Manager to agree that you can have 2 people from their 100 person organization for a few days. It is much better however, when you get them to commit that you can have Bill and Suzy each Tuesday and Friday for the next 6 months. For any resources needed in the next 3-4 months, you should insist on having managers commit resources by name to The Project in writing, copying the involved employees on the commitment.

Approval Resources- The most important yet hardest to get part-time resources on Technology Projects tend to be people empowered to formally approve deliverables. Generally, these are Managers and Executives who have many other responsibilities in the company.

This causes two problems that are equally impactful on The Project. They often let the deliverable languish in their email inbox for a period of time until The Project Manager comes around and shames them into reading it, thus delaying The Project. Alternatively, the approver is so busy that they just sign the document without reading it which can lead to future problems if it is inaccurate or contains items the approver does not support. In any case, you need a strategy to ensure that people designated as approvers actually have time available to perform this critical function.

Q35: Are Part Time Resources On The Project Really Available?

Over Committed Part- Time Resources- Time over-commitment often affects technical personnel on your project. This tends to be especially true for those resources with more specialized technical skills like Database Administrators.

I have run into multiple cases where a Database Administrator was assigned say 25% of the time to 5 or 6 projects. This is considered pretty standard practice since not all projects need time from the Database Administrator every day. But on those times when all project need assistance at the same time it become a significant problem.

People With 1 ½ or 2 Jobs- Often part-time people that already have a full-time job are assigned to support a project. If you only need the resource a few hours a week, this may be a workable solution.

However if you need a resource say 50% of the time on The Project, it is unrealistic to expect them to do their regular job and The Project work for any significant period of time.

One or the other job will suffer and the resource is likely to be unhappy about the quality of work they are able to provide for both jobs. You want to ensure that there is a plan to transfer workload so that personnel are able to handle all of the work assigned to them. It is not realistic to expect people to just work harder for months on end to perform two jobs at the same time.

REAL WORLD EXAMPLE

A large manufacturing company wanted to document requirements for a new Capacity Management System. The need for personnel to represent various parts of the company was identified early in The Project consisting nearly entirely of part-time resources.

281

Section3: Project Management Questions

The Project budget and timeline was approved based on commitments from the various areas that the resources would be available as needed. As The Project was beginning to gain traction, it became obvious that many of The Business people involved did have the time to properly focus on The Project which included detailed discussions, documentation of requirements, and requirements review.

An attempt was made to bring in outside resources to fill the gap, but they did not have The Business knowledge to significantly move The Project along since they had to talk to the same business people to obtain the needed business information. The Project lagged significantly ending up taking nearly double the original 6 month estimate and costing well over twice as much due to the influx of expensive consulting resources.

BEST PRACTICES

- Keep a spreadsheet of all of the part-time resources, their time commitment to The Project, what they are working on, and when they will be needed next and when they will no longer be needed on The Project. This should be updated regularly and circulated among resource managers periodically to remind everyone of the time commitment for the part time participants.
- For any resource over 25% committed to The Project, there should be a plan for how their existing workload will be sufficiently decreased to allow them to participate in The Project.
- Each involved Executive should be aware of the part-time time resource commitments made by Managers in their areas and support those commitments.

ADDRESSING THE QUESTION WITH THE PROJECT TEAM

Project Manager - The Project Manager should take the lead in working with The Project Team to identify needed full and part-time resources. The need for these resources should be documented in The Project Schedule. Review the required resources with The Project Manager at the beginning of The Project and them periodically throughout The Project to ensure that resources are available as needed.

This helps ensure that part-time resources are actually providing the time committed to by their management. The Project Manager should be the first to identify resources problems and you should set the expectation that they are to quickly escalate any problems with part-time resources to you to help resolve.

Business Team- Ensure that The Business Lead understands the part-time resource commitment that The Business is making to The Project. They should understand when those resources will be needed and what they are expected to be working on.

The Business Lead should work with Resource Managers to ensure resources are available when needed. Set the expectation with The Business Lead that they are to be proactive in ensuring that committed resources are available as needed and escalate any resources issues that arise.

Information Technology Team- This is very similar to the discussion with The Business Lead. The Technical Lead should proactively work to ensure resources commitments are honored and to escalate issues as they arise.

LESSONS LEARNED FROM PAST PROJECTS

- Overtime (either paid or un-paid) is an acceptable and even time-honored way of keeping projects on schedule for short periods of time. However, extensive use of overtime over a long period of time eventually becomes counterproductive and destroys morale on a project.
- Part-time personnel are more likely to find a way to devote time to a project if they feel fully involved in The Project. Make sure that you include them in project communications, invite them to Project Meetings, etc.
- As much as managers would like to think that they control what their employees work on, employees have significant influence on what they work on, especially if they are over-committed with work tasks. You want to try and make your project one of the things they want to work on.

RELATED QUESTIONS

8. Who would like this project to fail?

20. Does The Business really support this project?

36. HOW ARE OFFSHORE/OFFSITE RESOURCES BEING MANAGED?

"I've traveled around the world, and what's so revealing is that, despite the differences in culture, politics, language, how people dress, there is a universal feeling that we all want the same thing. We deeply want to be respected and appreciated for our differences."- Howard Schultz

WHY IS THIS QUESTION IMPORTANT?

When your Project Team is in a single location, it is relatively easy to coordinate with project resources. You can walk by and talk with them, get the team together in physical meetings, etc.

When your team is physically dispersed, team management becomes more difficult. If your team is global, this becomes infinitely more difficult given time zone, language, and cultural considerations. If I had my choice, I would always opt to have the entire Project Team in one physical location. However in today's global business and technology landscape, that is rarely attainable.

It is possible to have a very effective project with a geographically dispersed Project Team. In fact, some of my most effective projects have been with business and development teams spread around the globe. However, to be effective in these situations, you need to understand the challenges this presents and perhaps slightly alter your approach to project/resource management.

Here are some things to consider.

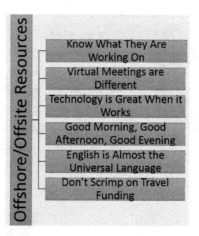

Always know who is on Your Remote Team and what they Doing- One valid complaint that I hear about the use of offshore/offsite teams is the loss of visibility over who is on the team and what are they working on today. I often share this concern. However, I try and address this through what I think of as enhanced status reporting and accountability.

If you have not worked with the remote team before, I would suggest you meet with their Management to establish ground rules for how the relationship will operate.

You should ask to see resume's from all personnel assigned to The Project and ask that you be notified before anyone is added to or removed from The Project. If you are going to be billed for these personnel, you have the right to understand who they are by name and what their qualifications are.

It is appropriate to get weekly reports showing generally what each of the resources is working on and any issues encountered. This will help you understand the work going on and make an evaluation as to the reasonableness of the staffing level.

This should follow through to billing where you should receive the number of hours by name of each resource being billed to you. A pervasive and annoying practice of some of the offshore development firms is to not disclose the names of those working on your project and billing you for time in aggregates such as 300 hours of Java Development, rather than showing you how many hours each resource is working.

You want to set the tone at the beginning of The Project that you expect individual accountability of people working on The Project remotely just as you do for people working onsite.

Virtual Meetings Must Operate Differently Than In Person Meetings- When you have a meeting where some people are in the room and others are participating remotely, the fundamental meeting dynamics change regardless of the technology that you have available. It is often difficult to follow complex conversations over a conference bridge line, especially when multiple people in the room are talking at once.

Also while electronic presentations can be shared, unless you have truly advanced technology, notes written on flip charts, whiteboards, etc. will not be visible to those participating remotely until after the meeting at best.. Here are some practices I have developed from years of running virtual meetings with widely distributed Project Teams.

1. Virtual meetings need a good facilitator that can control the room, the people and the conference line.

2. Only one person should talk at a time and the facilitator is the one who gets to decide who is going to talk if multiple people try to talk at the same time.
3. Make sure that you allow people on the phone to speak and keep them engaged in the meeting by directly asking them questions and/or soliciting.
4. We can listen to wind whispers on moons orbiting Jupiter, but cannot produce conference phone microphones that consistently work very well. Make sure that anyone speaking gets close to a microphone and periodically ask if those on the phone can hear the conversation.
5. Always have a slide deck with at least the agenda put together to share during the meeting. This will help keep the meeting on track. Email the draft deck to all meeting attendees prior to the meeting. Then if they are unable to get the desktop sharing software you are using to work, they can at least follow along with the conversation with the emailed copy.
6. Instead of making notes on a whiteboard or flip chart in the room, I prefer to have the presenter type them into the slide deck live during the meeting. In that way the people participating remotely will be able to see the same notes as the people in the room see.

Technology Is Great When It Works- When you have a mixed team of on-site and off-site personnel, currently available inexpensive technology can significantly help improve team collaboration. Cloud technology and SharePoint sites are good for file sharing. Commercial applications such as WebEx, Lync, etc. are good for computer desktop sharing during meetings, etc.

However, early in The Project, you need to ensure that the chosen collaboration tools work for all project participants. If all of The Project Team work for your Company, this is usually easy to arrange.

Q36: How Are Offshore/Offsite Resources Being Managed?

However, if it involves personnel from multiple companies, it becomes much more difficult due to differing technologies, security policies, etc..

There are a variety of technologies available for use (and honestly none is clearly the best) so often you will have to find the best common ground on The Project Team. There will potentially be browser issues, firewall issues at your and the vendor sites, security concerns, etc. You will want to ensure early in The Project that everyone regardless of location will be able to access the information they need to do their work and that there is a place to share/store the results.

Good Morning, Good Afternoon, Good Evening- If your off-site resources are located in a building across town, it is relatively easy to schedule discussions as they are in the same time zone as you are. However, if The Project Team is spread across the country or across the world, basic communications has to be planned better.

Many software development vendors current use offshore teams in locations such as India, China, and Korea. Time in these locations is offset approximately half a day from U.S. time. During much of what is the regular workday in the U.S., personnel in those areas are not at work. This requires compromise in setting meeting times. I was on one project where we had a conference call with our India team at 11:00PM every night to discuss issues with them at the start of their work day and again at 7:00AM each morning to get progress for the day from the team at the end of the work day. This does not leave much time for necessary sleep.

I have heard of some organizations that attempt to have their offshore teams work during U.S. daytime hours. This may work for short periods of time, but creates other problems due to the disruption it causes in the life of the offshore team. The best solution that I have found is to have some meetings when they inconvenience people in the U.S. and other time when it inconveniences remote resources.

When you have personnel on The Project from multiple regions, it compounds this problem as it is hard to find a single conference call time that works for the U.S., Germany, and Korea. Sometimes you have to have meetings at different times with different geographical regions just to best accommodate work schedules.

Daylight savings time which is used in many but not all parts of the world complicates this further since each country/region has their on schedule for the daylight savings time change dates. The same issue arises with National Holidays and vacation practices which vary widely between countries. The bottom line is that scheduling meetings and conversations can be challenging and will consume more time that you might expect. Ensure that Project Leadership understands these issues and has a plan to mitigate the impact.

English Is Almost the Universal Language- When you are working with remote teams in various areas of the world; you need to be cognizant of the impact of language and culture on communications. I have found that nearly all business and technology people around the global have at least a rudimentary understanding of American English and some speak better English than some people in the U.S. do.

Therefore, I always conduct global meetings in English with English language slide decks and have found little trouble in doing so. However, you need to keep in mind that different areas of the world speak slightly different versions of English flavored by the accents of their natural language.

I have found that I can understand virtually all versions of English at this point, but often find people in one part of the world have difficulties understanding those in another part of the world. For example team members in Brazil speaking a slightly Portuguese tinged version of English may have a problem understanding personnel from India speaking an often British tinged version of English spoken at a faster pace that some people find harder to understand.

Your meeting facilitator must be aware of these challenges and make sure everyone is following the conversation. Sometimes this requires you to ask people to speak a little slower or louder. And for key points, I like to have the listener restate what they understand the discussion, issue, decision, etc. to be to ensure that they were able to follow the conversation.

Don't Scrimp on Travel Funding- The usual reason for using an offshore/offsite team is to save money on labor by moving the work to areas where labor is less expensive. However, you should invest some of that savings into travel funding. Some activities such as requirements gathering, architecture design sessions, testing, etc. are best done face to face in front of a whiteboard or computer screen.

I have found it very effective to have key members of the remote team travel to your location periodically and for key members of The Project Team to travel to the remote location. This facilitates better communications, lets your team get to know each other better, and is an effective way to bridge the distance, language, cultural barriers. You want to use travel prudently, because extensive travel is expensive and depending on where your remote team is can require significant time away from the home location.

REAL WORLD EXAMPLE

I was leading a large ERP implementation project with tight timelines and some requirements that were company unique and somewhat complex. The vendor that we engage to lead the development work had a team of about 40 developers in Bangalore India developing system extensions and complex configurations. The offshore team initially struggled to fully understand our requirements even though they were some of the most intelligent and hardest working developers I have encountered.

To resolve this I went to Bangalore with one of the company Technical Leads to provide background about our company and our requirements. We also allowed a couple of days to meet with the various sub-teams to get to know the people working on our project and they got to know us.

Upon returning to the U.S., we implemented a strategy where, on a rotating basis, every few weeks we flew one of the 4 remote Technical Leads to the Corporate Offices for a week to review progress, meet with The Business to understand our requirements, and meet with the Technical Team to discuss technical issues and review code quality.

In this way, we usually had someone in the local project workspace from the India team and they usually had someone at the India location that had recently been at the Corporate Office. This greatly increased understanding and productivity. The travel was not especially cheap, but at our overall labor burn rate of $250K per week, was less than even a one week delay due to lack of understanding.

BEST PRACTICES
- If you cannot have the entire Project Team in one location, take steps to keep the team running effectively spanning the distance using technology and good communications.
- Get to know all the people on your team including those working offshore/offsite. This includes reviewing their

credentials, prudently using travel to meet your team, and understanding what they are working on at all times.

- Early in The Project establish a cadence of meetings supported by appropriate technology at timing that work for all regardless of locations. Then actively facilitate these meetings to ensure information is being effectively communicated.

ADDRESSING THE QUESTION WITH THE PROJECT TEAM

Project Manager- As with all resource issues, The Project Manager should take the lead in managing offshore/offsite resources. This should include managing resource levels, communication, personnel qualification, etc. Set the expectation that they are to raise any concerns they have over these resources just as they would any local project resources.

Business Team- In discussions with The Business Team, you should ask if they are having any issues with the offshore/offsite team including problems with language and communications. Emphasize that they should escalate these issue to The Project Manager and if unresolved bring them to your attention.

Information Technology Team- Discuss with the Technical Lead the need to monitor the technical work of everyone on The Project including the offshore/offsite team. All resources should adhere to the same coding standards, peer review process, testing, regardless of location. Also remind the Technical Lead to raise any concerns over skill level, communications ability, etc. to The Project Manager for resolution.

LESSONS LEARNED FROM PAST PROJECTS

- It does not matter if part of The Project Team is across town in a different building or half-way around the world. As soon as you have a situation where the entire Project Team cannot be co-located in one place, active steps must be taken to keep the team functioning as a single unit.

The tendency will be for the various teams to work independently with much less coordination than would take place if everyone was located in one place. The Project Manager needs to actively monitor this and take appropriate actions if there begins to be a lock of teamwork.

- Even though I had two years of high school French, I would be lost trying to follow project conversations in French and/or interact with Business Units that only speak French. Likewise when you engage an offshore team, very rarely you will encounter people with extreme difficulty communicating in English.

  Assuming that English is the de facto Project standard, people that cannot read, write or speak English will have trouble being effective on The Project. This is a personnel issue not a personal issue. Personnel on The Project that do not have acceptable fluency in the language used on The Project should be replaced on The Project.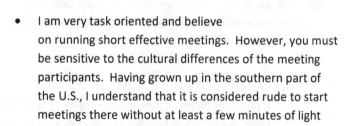

- I am very task oriented and believe on running short effective meetings. However, you must be sensitive to the cultural differences of the meeting participants. Having grown up in the southern part of the U.S., I understand that it is considered rude to start meetings there without at least a few minutes of light conversation whereas in some areas of the North East U.S., you are expected to jump right into the work. I also was taught never to contradict my elders, but some parts of the U.S. have a more confrontational approach regardless of the status of the people they are interacting with.

When you start expanding the team to people in other parts of the world, you will find that there are cultural norms in other locations that are very important to their core beliefs and way they view the world.

For example, some cultures are very reluctant to speak up in group meetings, some cultures are not comfortable challenging even what they know is incorrect information, and some cultures are reluctant to provide firm status and time estimates especially if their part of The Project is behind schedule.

On one of my projects, after nearly every meeting, I would get an email from one of the offshore Managers saying things that their culture made it virtually impossible for them to say in front of a group of people. While I would have preferred that they provide the information in the meeting for all to hear and discuss that was not a realistic possibility with this individual.

This is not to imply in any way that their cultural norms were inferior to mine, just that they are different. If you are going to have extensive contact with an offshore team, it is useful (and often fascinating) to spend some time understanding their culture and behavioral norms. Doing so will make it much easier to understand and deal with the diverse ways that people act.

RELATED QUESTIONS

5. Is there sufficient Executive oversight?

7. What are key roles for project success?

32. Are contracts structured to ensure performance?

37. How is project morale?

37. HOW IS PROJECT MORALE?

"The best morale exists when you never hear the word mentioned. When you hear a lot of talk about it, it's usually lousy."- Dwight D. Eisenhower

WHY IS THIS QUESTION IMPORTANT?

One of the most valuable lessons I learned in the US Army was the importance of morale to a team of people. You can be crawling through cold mud in the rain and still be an effective team if morale is high. Conversely, you can be sitting in the nicest office overlooking the ocean and not get anything done if morale is low.

To maintain the productivity required to have a successful project you should closely monitor morale and proactively deal with any related issues as they arise. Morale can seem like a complex thing to understand, but fundamentally involves a few key factors.

Sense of Purpose- Everyone on The Project Team from the Executive Sponsor to the college intern making copies needs to

understand The Project objectives and why The Project is important.

We are not just creating a web screen showing some data from a database, we are creating a place where people can come to see what roads are iced over in the winter so that they can drive safely. Plus, the screen showing road conditions is part of an overall system designed to reduce traffic fatalities by 30%. Understanding how your contribution and that of your peers combine to create something important helps give you a sense of purpose that is a key influencer of morale.

Sense of A Plan- It is nearly impossible to get people to work long hours on a project if they think The Project is unorganized and that they are wasting their time. There not only needs to be a plan, but it needs to be well communicated so that everyone understands exactly what they are individually expected to accomplish and how it fits into the overall schedule.

There have been many times I have had to required people to work on a holiday or weekend to accomplish some key project goal. However, I would never do so without ensuring that everyone understood why this was necessary, exactly what we were planning to accomplish, and how the work would be organized so that it could be completed as quickly as possible.

Sense of Leadership- One of my biggest pet peeves in Project Management is when people talk about Project Administration as being interchangeable with Project Management. While there are always important administrative tasks to do on a project, I believe that being a Project Manager is primarily a leadership function.

I am known for saying that "Project Management is not a spectator sport". You must lead a project not just go through the motions of completing a series of checkmarks on a project methodology.

This is especially true when it comes to morale. People want to be led not ordered around. I would never consider having my Project Team work late at night, weekends, holidays, etc. without being there myself even if there was little I could personally contribute to the work being done. Just being the first one there and one of the last people to leave significantly improves morale.

Sense of Individual Value To the Team and Company- While it is important for a Project Team to pull together and work to a common goal, it is also important for people to believe that the company cares about them and values their individual contribution. Having Senior Leadership of the company periodically recognize the contribution of individual Project Team members is important in maintaining project morale. It is disheartening to me to see ceremonies where key project leaders are publically acknowledged for their contributions but not the rest of The Project Team that did the bulk of the work.

This is not to imply that rewarding The Project leaders is wrong as they too need to be acknowledged for their hard work. However, make sure you recognize in some way each of The Project participants at the same time. This can take the form of something as simple as a certificate of appreciation, letter in their personnel file, small gift card, etc.

It is the sense of inclusion that is important. Just having a Senior Executive walk through periodically and shake everyone's hand or come to a Project Team meeting can greatly improve morale.

There was a late 2014 news report that Pope Francis showed up at the Vatican Worker's Cafeteria unannounced, went through the food line with his tray like everyone else, sat and ate at a table with a group of pharmacy stock

clerks. After he completed his meal and discussion with the shocked workers, he cleared his tray from the table like everyone else. I would imagine that this had a profound impact on morale showing that everyone is equally important in the organization.

The Power of Food- Do not underestimate the power of feeding your Project Team well in keeping morale high. One of the frequent battles that I have had with companies where I have led projects is over free food for The Project Team. Most Executives do not have any idea how much "free" labor they get on a project.

On many Technology Projects, a substantial portion of the after-hours, weekend, holiday work done on The Project is uncompensated or at best only partially compensated. This is true for employees of your organization and external consultants, both of which normally are capped at 40 hours of paid work a week. Paid overtime on projects I have been involved in is very rare.

As a result, your organization is likely to receive hundreds if not thousands of hours of unpaid work over the course of a project. I strongly believe that the least an organization can do when there is a requirement to work non-traditional hours is to feed the team.

Any amount of money that you spend feeding the team is likely

An army marches on its stomach.-

Napoleon Bonaparte

far less than what you would spend if you had to pay them for all of the hours worked. Therefore, I always feed The Project Team and feed them well when work is required. When the food arrives, we temporarily stop work, get together and have a brief Project Meeting and then just enjoy a few minutes relaxing before resuming work. This not only is a great morale boost, but also keeps your team from leaving to get food. When you make The Project Team leave to get food, sometimes they don't come back for hours.

REAL WORLD EXAMPLE

Payroll systems basically have to be deployed on January 1st. If that is not the case, significant effort is added to The Project relating to transferring year to date information, tax calculations, tax reporting, etc.

One large project that I led included implementation of a new payroll system replacing an internally developed and maintained system that had been in place for some time. The Project began to run slightly behind schedule due to issues encountered in integrating the company's rather unorthodox and highly complex profit sharing process into the off the shelf payroll system.

We worked very hard and smart on getting this part of The Project back on track but as mid-December approached, it was obvious that the timeline would be close especially with the holidays and long-planned trips during school breaks.

I assembled the team and clearly laid out the two options which were pretty basic- work some of the holidays or push off the deployment until April 1st due to the quarterly bonus structure. Even though we had been working long hours for a couple of months, morale was high and we agreed to push for the January 1st deployment which meant among

other things, everyone would be required to work until early evening on Christmas Eve.

The way our project was financially and contractually structured, not a single person was paid for working Christmas Eve, yet I had a full team of employees and consultants show up early in the morning and we worked hard on testing and defect remediation all day finally sending everyone home around 7 PM.

Throughout the day, I had various Corporate Executives including the Senior Vice President, CIO, Director of HR/Payroll, etc. come by to lend support and of course fed the team well throughout the day. Morale was extremely high that day with nearly miraculous progress being made in all areas because The Project Team understood the importance of what was being done, understood their importance in getting the work done, were presented a clear plan of what was to be accomplished and how it would be accomplished, and had the on-site support of Senior Executives a times throughout the day.

In the end, we deployed successfully on January 1st. From a financial perspective, the investment of about $600 in food that day, saved about $500K+ that it would have required to keep this portion of The Project Team funded for another 3 months had the deployment been delayed. Even the stingiest CFOs would have to reluctantly agree that was a good investment.

BEST PRACTICES
- When you are evaluating Project/Program Management candidates, focus not just on their knowledge and experience, but also on their ability to motivate and lead Project Teams. This becomes even more important and project size, complexity and duration increases.
- Ensure that you spend sufficient time with The Project Team to have a sense of their morale both as a group and

individually. If you sense morale issues, try to understand why they occur and be proactive in addressing.

- Be vigilant for warning signs of poor morale which include, absenteeism, poor participation in Project Meetings, excessive grumbling about work/people/etc.
- One of the key roles of The Project/Program Manager is to motivate the team and keep an eye on project morale.

ADDRESSING THE QUESTION WITH THE PROJECT TEAM

Project Manager - The Project Manager should take the lead in team motivation, and monitoring/improving team morale. Set the expectation with The Project Manager that you expect them to closely monitor the team for morale issues and if necessary escalate issues as needed.

Business Team- While The Project Manager is responsible for the morale of The Project Team as a whole, The Business Lead is likewise responsible for the morale of the members of The Business Team.

Information Technology Team- As with The Business Team, the Technical Lead is responsible for motivating their Technical Team and escalating issues as needed.

Steering Committee- Ensure that the Steering Committee understands their role in motivating the team. Help them understand the morale implication of team members coming to them with problems/complaints. Make sure the Steering Committee understands their need to support team morale both personally through periodically showing up for team events and financially through supporting team outings and food during off-hour work.

LESSONS LEARNED FROM PAST PROJECTS

- The Military teaches its leaders the importance of a concept called force multipliers. Force multipliers are factors that can make a smaller group as effective as a larger group. Or it can be factors which allow something that should take a week be done in a few days.

  Morale is one of the most important force multipliers. If you have a small Project Team of motivated trained people with good leadership and high morale, nearly anything can be accomplished.

- There is a tee shirt popular in Key West showing a pirate skull and crossbones symbol with the saying "The beatings will continue until morale improves". While this is funny on a tee shirt (which I actually own and sometimes wear during off-hour work), it has no place in motivating a skilled Project Team.

  Keep in mind that much of project work is mental and creative versus physically doing things. The culture in some organizations is to call in The Project Manager/ Project Team every few days to administer a verbal beating and admonishment to work faster. Nothing kills morale on a project faster than this.

- If a Project Team does not see the importance of the work being done or feels that The Project is being poorly led and/or organized, productivity will be low and quality suffer.
- It is not unusual for project to have some late tasks somewhere during the duration of The Project. However, if you sense that the team does not care that the tasks are late or have given up trying to meet deadlines, there is likely a morale problem that needs to be addressed.

- It is the role of The Project Manager to closely monitor team morale and provide motivation as needed. However, it is the role of The Project Sponsor/Executive to monitor the morale of The Project Manager and provide motivation in a similar way. If morale of The Project Manager is low, it is highly unlikely that The Project Team morale will be any better.

RELATED QUESTIONS

1. Are The Project objectives clear to all?

5. Is there sufficient Executive oversight?

9. Am I sufficiently engaged in The Project?

38. DO WE HAVE THE RIGHT PROJECT TEAM COMPOSITION?

 "Adding manpower to a late software project, makes it later."- Frederick P. Brooks Jr.(Mythical Man Month),

WHY IS THIS QUESTION IMPORTANT?

In my early years as a Project Manager, I would fight for every person I could find to work on my projects thinking that the more people I had to work on a project the faster I could get the work done. If I could not find the experienced database administrator I needed, I would settle for two entry-level database administrators instead.

What I came to understand however, is that having the right people on a project was far more important than just having a large Project Team. In fact, I came to understand the advantages of having s small experienced team over having a much larger team with less experience.

Additionally, I quickly came to understand that a Project Team should be dynamic with a core of people involved throughout the course of The Project with additional resources joining and leaving The Project Team as needed over the course of The Project. Maintaining the right Project Team composition at each stage of

38. Do We Have The Right Project Team Composition?

The Project is one of the keys to project success. Here are some things to consider.

High Level Schedule First- Before you can identify needed project resources, have to have at least a high level Project Schedule. Develop a project task/milestone schedule in as much detail as is possible given the current project stage.

You should make the best possible estimate of task duration and dependencies between the tasks. By putting this information into a scheduling tool such as MS Project or Primavera, you will get a high level view of when the various project activities will occur. This in turn will help you identify when various resources will be needed on The Project.

Resource Demand Second- For each task on the schedule you will have identify the type of resources necessary to accomplish the task and their required skill/experience levels. One efficient way to do this is to enter the resource types into your Project Schedule and then export that data into a spreadsheet. This will let you sort the data so that you can see when you need database administrators, programmers, etc. and get a sense of how many you will required.

Section3: Project Management Questions

Resource Supply Last- This is where you match the personnel that you believe are available to work on The Project to the tasks that need to be performed. I intentionally put this step last, but many projects start with this step. It is not uncommon for a Project Manager to look at the resources they have available first and then begin to distribute them across the tasks to be done. This approach however, does not take into account the skills that are needed to successfully complete the individual tasks.

For example, Bill a very junior developer is available during the month of May so you assign him to develop a complex interface that needs to be completed in May. However, if you had looked at the task first, you might have identified that you need a very experienced developer to accomplish this task with specific experience in developing real-time interfaces.

These are skills that Bill clearly does not have, so he should not have been assigned to the task just because he was available. Instead, you should consider trying to move the task in the schedule to a time when a more experienced developer is available and assign Bill to another task.

Eight women and one man cannot make a baby in one month- When there are mismatches between resource demand and resource supply or when a project begins to slip against its timeline, the tendency is to throw more people against the problem regardless of skill level. If you need a senior network engineer for 3 months, putting three junior network engineers on The Project for 2 months is usually not the answer.

Resist the tendency to just add people to a project. Instead focus on providing the right people and sequencing tasks to best use the available skills. If the required skill sets are not available within the organization, look to other parts of the organization or to outside consultants for the right skills.

38. Do We Have The Right Project Team Composition?

Sometimes the only way to win is not to play the game- This classic line from the movie War Games, is not applied often enough to projects. If you have identified the resources that you need for success and find that those resources are just not available, then you should defer The Project start until they are available.

Before you abandon a project due to lack of resources, you should do your best to adjust resources required by adjusting scope, timing, sequence, etc. Also to the extent company policy and budget allow, you should look to outside vendors for consulting help. However, in the end if there is a significant shortfall in available resources, The Project should not go forward until such resources become available.

REAL WORLD EXAMPLE

- The best example I know of the need for the correct team composition is the example told by Frederick Brooks in his classic book The Mythical Man Month first published in 1975. Brooks managed the development of the IBM mainframe OS/360 operating system in the 1960's.

The Project was well funded and well managed, but began to fall significantly behind schedule due to complexity of the task and scarcity of highly experienced resources. The response of IBM was to flood The Project with large numbers of additional resources each of which had to be indoctrinated into The Project and which increased the amount of communications necessary to sustain The Project.

Brooks concluded that his decision to add more developers to The Project was a grave mistake. He later wrote that his mistake was "adding more programmers to a project falling behind schedule, a decision that he would later conclude had, counter-intuitively, delayed The Project even further".

BEST PRACTICES

- If you have not created at least a high level project scheduling showing major tasks/activities and associated dependencies, it is not possible to create a credible Staffing Plan.
- It is a mistake to assign junior level resources to tasks whose complexity requires more senior personnel. However, it is equally a waste of expensive resources to assign senior personnel to tasks that could be completed by more junior personnel. Carefully review tasks with the appropriate Business/Technical Lead to determine the skills necessary to accomplish each task.
- A common mistake is to overload your most senior resources with more tasks than they possibly accomplish. When you have finished developing your resource plan sort it by resource name and review it to ensure that the resource will be able to accomplish all of the tasks in each time period. It may be necessary to re-sequence/retime the schedule to level the work for each resource.
- When assigning resources on your project, take into consideration any other projects/work they may have been assigned outside of your project. For critical resources, confirm with their managers how much time they will really have available to work on your project.
- The final deliverable of this effort should be a Staffing Plan showing when each person is expected to join The Project and when they are expected to leave The Project. This should become the basis for your project labor budget and should be approved by the various resources managers to confirm personnel availability.

310

ADDRESSING THE QUESTION WITH THE PROJECT TEAM

Project Manager - The Project Manager should take the lead in creating The Project Schedule and Staffing Plan based on input from the various project leads. You should spend sufficient time with The Project Manager to understand how the schedule and Staffing Plan was developed and to understand any resource shortfalls. You should support The Project Manager in efforts to validate resource availability and to address resource issues.

Business Team- The Business Lead must review The Project Schedule and Staffing Plan in sufficient detail to understand the resources requirements. Before approving the Staffing Plan, get confirmation from The Business Lead that they agree with the proposed staffing level and adequacy of the identified resources. Set the expectation with The Business Lead that you expect them to be proactive in escalating emerging resource issues so that they can be addressed before they begin to adversely impact The Project.

Information Technology Team- The discussion with the Technical Lead should be the same as with The Business Lead

Steering Committee- The Steering Committee must understand the level of required resources necessary to staff The Project and where these resources will come from. To the extent that their organization is to supply resources, the Steering Committee members must agree to supply those resources as needed. The Steering Committee also should be involved in resolving resource shortfalls either through identification of additional resources or providing necessary funding to obtain resources from external vendors.

LESSONS LEARNED FROM PAST PROJECTS

- Significant thought is usually given to resources needs at the beginning of The Project which is appropriate. However, these needs change over time, so The Project Manager should schedule periodic reviews of the Staffing Plan so that adjustments can be made as The Project unfolds.

- It is not unusual for people to like being on a Project Team so much that they do not look forward to returning to their normal job at the end of their assigned part of The Project.

  This is where having a spreadsheet with defined dates when each resource is expected to join The Project and leave The Project is very helpful. Especially on large projects, you will often find Project Team members that are still working on The Project and incurring costs well after their assigned tasks have been completed. This can have a significant impact on project budget.

- In addition to staffing levels, you also review personnel skills and performance periodically. If you have people that are not being effective on The Project you should attempt to help them to become more successful through mentoring, training, etc. However, if they still are not performing adequately, then you need to take steps to move them to other tasks or replace them on The Project. This should equally apply to internal and external resources.

RELATED QUESTIONS

25. How well are project costs being tracked?

37. How is project morale?

39. ARE PROJECT ISSUES BEING ADEQUATELY MANAGED?

"We cannot solve our problems with the same thinking we used when we created them."- Albert Einstein

WHY IS THIS QUESTION IMPORTANT?

Project Schedules are critical to project success since they outline all of the planned tasks required to complete The Project. The schedule also outlines when tasks will be worked on, resources, dependencies, etc. Most projects are highly focused on Project Schedule status and use this at as a measure of project success.

This approach is a good start towards managing projects, but don't forget the impact of issues on project success. Issues are those unplanned things that impact project that may or may not be have been planned for The Project Schedule. A good example of a real project is might be finding out that the generator that need for your new data center has a 6 month backlog at the manufacture

It is important to have just as vigorous a process for identifying and managing issues on The Project as you do for managing project tasks on the schedule. There are four aspects of issues management that you should be aware of:

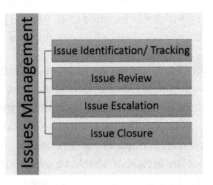

Issue Identification/Tracking- Project issues are not particularly hard to identify. People raise issues in Project Meetings, list them is status reports, share them via email, and talk about them in the hall. What is sometimes lacking is a process for tracking these issues until they are resolved.

As soon as an issue is raised, it should be entered into an Issues Log by The Project Manager. The Issues Log can be as simple as a spreadsheet describing the issue, listing a target resolution date, assigning it to someone for action, etc. The format of the Issues Log is not nearly as important as dedicated attention to managing it is. The first step towards being able to manage issues is to ensure that they are included in the Issues Log and tracked to resolution.

Issue Review- However, issues often languish on an Issues Log. Many times when I have looked at projects that have had major problems and/or failures, I find that the core issues causing the failure were long known and recorded in the Issues Log but never adequately addressed.

The items in the Issues Log need to be actively managed by The Project Team. This includes a regular review of every open item on the Issues Log. Additionally, The Project Manager should follow-up with each owner assigned to an issue to get regular status updates.

Issue Escalation- Every item in the Issues Log should have an agreed upon expected resolution date. If the issue has not be adequately resolved before the due date, then it should be escalated appropriately. The issue might be escalated to The Business or Technical Sponsor or the Steering Committee as appropriate, but the escalation should be automatic based on due date. A common mistake Project Teams make is to fail to escalate issues early enough to allow others to have time to help with a resolution.

Issue Closure- Another problem that can occur with issue management is prematurely closing issues. Sometime The Project Manager/Project Team will announce that an item in the log is no longer an issue and close it. Likewise it is not uncommon for someone to email The Project Manager that an issue is resolved and it be closed.

You want to be very careful not to close issues unless those areas affected by the issue agree that it has been resolved. Issues by their very nature are often complex or they would have been resolved before even being added to the Issues Log. Therefore, before you close an issue you want to ensure that the person who originally raised the issue and all other affected areas concur that it can be closed.

REAL WORLD EXAMPLE

A State Agency was implementing major changes to their Unemployment Compensation system. The Project had made good progress initially, but about two thirds of the way through The Project timeline, progress had fundamentally ground to a halt and the State was considering cancelling The Project even though a significant amount of money had already been spent on the changes.

I was asked to review The Project. After several interviews with The Project Team and a review of project documentation, I quickly determined that the core problem was that most remaining critical tasks on the schedule were blocked by one or more issues keeping them from being completed. Some of the issue had been recorded at various points in status reports, but there was no consolidated list of project issues.

To resolve this, we stopped all work on The Project and scheduled a half day workshop to identify and document all project issues in an Issues Log. This included items such a decisions that had not been made which impeded requirements finalization, delays in ordering hardware, policy decisions, etc.

At the end of the workshop, there was an agreed upon list of issues blocking progress on The Project. For most of the next week, the team and appropriate Executives in the Agency focused solely on resolving the open issues. By about the 6th day, most key issues were either resolved or well on the path to resolution and the regular work on The Project was resumed.

We established a culture of recording and managing issues that lasted throughout the remainder of The Project. While The Project was still slightly late in its deployment, the system was successfully and was well received by the user community. Even

though it was late, the Agency was very pleased with the results
since they had been on the verge of totally canceling The Project.

BEST PRACTICES

- The Project Manager is responsible for
  managing issues on projects. The
  primary tool to facilitate this is an Issues
  Log of all open project issues.
- Issues need to be actively managed to
  ensure that they get reviewed on a regular basis, resolved in
  a timely manner and escalated as needed,
- Issues should be closed only when there is consensus that the
  issue is no longer affecting The Project.
- You need to ensure that an environment exists where people
  are encouraged to raise issues to be added to the Issues Log
  and an environment where people feel that they are able to
  escalate issues they are unable to solve. If you punish people
  for escalating issues, they will quickly stop doing so even if
  help is desperately needed.

ADDRESSING THE QUESTION WITH THE PROJECT TEAM

Project Manager- Regularly ask to review the open items in
the Issues Log with The Project Manager. Set a strong
expectation that all issues are to be added to the log as they
are raised and then actively managed until they are resolved.
Also ensure that The Project Manager understands that they
are expected to quickly escalate issues that need help.
Emphasize that doing so will not be held against The Project
Manager or The Project Team.

Business Team- In discussions with The Business Team
encourage people to raise issues to be added to the Issues
Log emphasizing that this is a key tool in keeping The Project

on track and to bring emphasis on items that need resolution. Also set the expectation with The Business Team that they are expected to actively work on issues that are assigned to them for resolution

It is just as important if not more so to work on the open issues as it is to work on the items assigned from The Project Schedule. Make sure The Business Team understands that it not only ok to ask for help on an issue by escalating it, but timely escalation is expected.

Information Technology Team- The discussion with the Technical Team should be exactly the same as with The Business Team.

Steering Committee- Work with the Steering Committee to help them understand that one of their key roles is to assist with the resolution of issues that arise during the course of The Project. The expectation is that relatively few issues should be escalated all the way to the Steering Committee, but when one is escalated; prompt assistance is expected.

LESSONS LEARNED FROM PAST PROJECTS

- People providing oversight often find it easier to understand the concept of a late task than it is to understand the impact of issues. A tone needs to be established on The Project balancing both tasks and issues as being equally important.
- So much work is usually packed into weekly status meetings that it is not uncommon for the Issues Log to not get reviewed for several weeks in a row. This is a mistake, since items on the Issues Log could be worsening and the time to resolve them is dwindling. Having said that, it is sometimes not practical to review every issue every week. If this is the case, sort the issues to ensure that the most important ones get a regular

review along with any issue whose expected resolution date is approaching.

- Sometimes it takes the effort of several people to resolve an issue. However, you should assign a single person to be responsible for "owning" each issue. This is the person who will organize people to address the issue and report issue status to The Project Manager. You can list the other people working on the issue in a comments section, but there should be a single person with overall responsibility for working the issue until it is closed listed as the owner of each issue.

RELATED QUESTIONS

5. Is there sufficient Executive oversight?

7. What are key roles for project success?

9. Am I sufficiently engaged in The Project?

26. Are The Project risks understood?

SECTION 4: WHAT TECHNOLOGY RELATED QUESTIONS SHOULD YOU ASK?

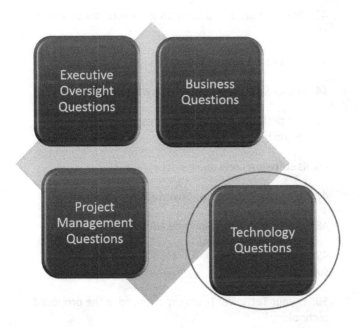

As an Executive, you will never be able to truly understand all of the nuances of the various technologies involved in projects. If they were honest with themselves and their peers, most technology professionals would admit that even they only deeply understand their relatively narrow area with only high level knowledge of other areas.

Section 4: Technology Questions

However, as an Executive with responsibilities over a Technical Project, there are a number of areas that you need to understand enough to ensure your Technical Team properly handles them.

This section focuses on the following questions you should address with the Technical Team.

40. What do you really know about the company and technology being proposed?

41. Have system interfaces been adequately planned?

42. Does the proposed technology fit into our corporate IT strategy?

43. Is there a documented technology architecture?

44. Is there a strategy for project data protection?

45. Are performance requirements being adequately addressed?

46. Is software code quality acceptable?

47. Are plans in place for post-deployment support?

48. Is data migration planning adequate?

49. Is there sufficient hardware software identified to support The Project?

50. Is your Technical Team experienced in the proposed technology?

40. WHAT DO YOU REALLY KNOW ABOUT THE COMPANY AND TECHNOLOGY BEING PROPOSED?

"Know your enemy and know yourself and you can fight a hundred battles without disaster." - Sun Tzu

WHY IS THIS QUESTION IMPORTANT?

This seems like an impolite question to ask your Project Team, but it is important to do so. Like many things in this modern consumer age, technology hardware, software, and services are marketed using slick sales pitches, professional brochures, and carefully practiced sales processes.

It is sometimes difficult to separate fact from hyperbole when it comes to technology capabilities. In your Executive oversight role, you will want to ensure that any new technology being purchased goes through a thorough Due Diligence process prior to a final purchasing decision.

This will help you understand some of the risks you are taking in dealing both with the selected vendor and the products they are offering. For example are you buying relatively immature but cutting edge technology produced by a company in business for less than a year or very mature but slightly boring technology by a company with a long track record of success.

323

Section 4: Technology Questions

Ultimately it is up to you to decide what level of risk you are willing to tolerate. You must decide if you are a Thomas Jefferson

---

With Great Risk Comes Great Reward-

Thomas Jefferson

---

type risk embracing company or an IBM type risk averse company. Either way, a competent Due Diligence process will provide information necessary to make an informed risk based decision.

Key issues that you should explore when conducting a Due Diligence evaluation of new technology include:

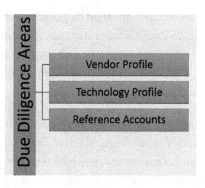

Vendor Profile- Purchasing new technology is the start of what is usually a multi-year or even multi-decade relationship between your company and the company that wants to sell you the technology. Prior to entering into such a long-term inter-company relationship, you should ensure that The Project Team has done some research on the company so that you can understand who you are potentially doing business with.

You should look at financial stability, pending litigation, major customer complaints, key personnel changes, etc. This information is fortunately easily available on the Internet. In particular, be vigilant of vendors that have been in business less than 2 years, initial product launches, and companies/products with little available information on the Internet. Small amounts of adverse information does not by themselves necessarily mean that you should avoid doing business with a vendor. Ultimately, that is your choice. However it is only by doing Due Diligence on the company that you will understand the risk you are taking.

Technology Profile - You also need to ensure that The Project Team has done sufficient research on the product that you are considering buying. This should include understanding the maturity of the product line including how long it has been sold and how many customers are using it. You should also understand the capabilities of the version you are purchasing versus what might be available in future versions.

Vendor sales teams are famous for doing demonstrations and slide shows filled with a mix of currently available features and potential future capabilities. If there are features that are critical to your purchasing decision, you should ensure that this feature  is actually available today in the version you are considering buying.

A prudent approach is to request access to a demonstration version of the software or hardware. Especially for major purchases this will give you "fingers on the keyboard" access to the technology. Keep in mind you may have to live with this technology for a decade or more, so spending a week or so reviewing the actual system even if you have to travel to a vendor site to do so, is money well spent

Reference Accounts- This is where you get convergence between your needs, the vendor's corporate profile and the vendor product. You should ask the vendor to provide you contacts at other companies of similar size and type as yours that are actually using the same version of the technology they are proposing to sell you.

If the vendor is unwilling or unable to provide reference accounts that are willing to discuss their experience with the product, you should become immediately wary and delve deeper into the technology. If the vendor does provide reference accounts, make sure that The Project Team contacts the references to get their impression of the product.

Other good sources of information about technology products include User Group Meetings and Technical Conferences. As soon as you begin to seriously consider investing in expensive new technology, you should begin to send Project Team members to these types of events. The cost of doing so is trivial compared to the value in obtaining a more balanced view of the product's capabilities directly from other users.

REAL WORLD EXAMPLE

The worst project failure I was asked to review failed in performing Due Diligence ultimately costing them their company. A large low margin wholesale technology re-seller made their profit by large volume sales at low markup.

They engaged a large national consulting firm to replace their sales order and configuration systems with an "off the shelf" cutting edge package that the vendor claimed had been installed at a number of clients. About two years into what was originally expected to be a one year project, costs continued to skyrocket with no deployment date in sight, so the Board of Directors demanded an independent project assessment.

The review discovered that the vendor did not have an "off the shelf" package, but rather a series of disjointed software modules that the vendor had been furiously trying to turn into a system without much success.

It seems that the Company had not checked the references mentioned during the sales pitch. When I followed up with these references, I very quickly discovered that **none** of the reference clients had been able to get the system to work for them and in fact two companies were in litigation with the vendor over the software with allegations of misrepresentation and fraud.

We determined that it was highly unlikely that the software could ever be made functional within any reasonable timeframe even with the expenditures of many millions of additional dollars. As a result The Project was cancelled and within 6 months the company stopped operations and sold their remains to a large Fortune 50 company due to inability to recover from the tremendous amount of money and time wasted with the vendor.

This was compounded by the ever escalating shortcomings of the legacy system they were now stuck with for the foreseeable future.

Eventually this project was the subject of multi-year litigation which resulted in a massive financial victory, but which was too late to save The Business from failure.

Section 4: Technology Questions

BEST PRACTICES

- Many large companies have personnel in the Purchasing Function that perform Due Diligence on supplier companies. They would be a good source to perform and objective company profile evaluation. If not, then assign someone who has sufficient financial background to understand the financial information the review turns up.
- The technology profile evaluation on the other hand must be done by the Technical Team as they understand the questions that need to be asked. However, ensure that there is a structured approach to the technical Due Diligence that leads to an unemotional objective evaluation.
- Ensure that the results of the Due Diligence evaluation are documented and reviewed by The Project Team and Steering Committee. Creating a written record of the evaluation will likely result in a more complete assessment.
- Reference checks with companies similar to yours that are using the product currently are best done by a small group including both Business and Technical Team members. In this way, both the technical and functional aspects of the technology can be evaluated at the same time so as to minimize the amount of time you will need the reference account to spend with you.
- Similar Due Diligence should be conducted on Companies that propose to sell you services such as development, testing, etc.

ADDRESSING THE QUESTION WITH THE PROJECT TEAM

Project Manager- Ask The Project Manager to show you where the tasks supporting Due Diligence are located in The Project Schedule. Emphasize that you expect these to be performed prior to a purchase order being issued to the vendor.

Q40: What Do You Really Know About the Company and Technology Being Proposed?

Business Team- Challenge The Business Team to ensure that they have a clear vision of the functionality that is in the **current** version of the software versus features that may be available in some future version of the product. Emphasize to The Business Lead your expectation that they actively participate in the Reference Account discussions during which they should question their counterparts in the reference company on key system features.

Information Technology Team- The Technical Team will have prime responsibility for doing the Technology Profile evaluation. Challenge them to move past the vendor marketing material to try and understand the real system characteristics by talking with their peers in other companies, challenging vendor technical personnel with detailed questions, talking to people in user groups, etc.

Steering Committee- Once you have collected objective information from the Vendor, Technology, and Reference Account investigations, you want to summarize the information and present it to the decisions makers for review. It is important to understand how much risk your organization is willing to tolerate on this project. If you chose to do business with a financial shaky company selling relatively immature technology, you should only do so with open eyes.

LESSONS LEARNED FROM PAST PROJECTS

- Do not assume that just because a company is large or has been around for a long period of time, it must be financially stable and risk free. That is what people assumed about Enron right up until the time it collapsed.
- Due Diligence should be performed by someone who is not so emotionally invested in the product review process that they

lack objectivity. It is human nature to give the benefit of doubt if you really want to buy something.

- Only organizations that are willing to tolerate considerable risk should purchase and install the 1.0 version of any software or hardware. This product is still probably being completed as they are selling it to you, it often is plagued by performance and reliability issues, and most importantly, if they are not able to sell enough copies of the product, the vendor may abandon it leaving you with no future support or upgrade path.

- If the technology you are considering is mature enough to have user groups/ yearly conferences, this can be a great way to get an unbiased view of the technology and is well worth the cost and time investment.

- If you have large company with thousands of employees and the vendor can only provide reference accounts for very small companies, you should question scalability and performance of the solution and proceed carefully.

- It is impossible to avoid all risk in making a technology product purchase. I have worked on several project where taking these risks yielded great results for the organization. However, I have also performed reviews where the opposite was the case. Understanding the risks and actively monitoring them throughout The Project will help reduce the chances of failure.

RELATED QUESTIONS

1. Are The Project objectives clear to all?

7. What are key roles for project success?

12. When should I ask for an outside review of The Project?

42. Does the proposed technology fit into our corporate IT strategy?

43. Is there a documented technology architecture?

50. Is your Technical Team experienced in the proposed technology?

41. HAVE SYSTEM INTERFACES BEEN ADEQUATELY PLANNED?

"In God we trust, all others must bring data"- W. Edwards Deming

WHY IS THIS QUESTION IMPORTANT?

One of the most deceptive things on a technical architecture drawing is a simple line connecting two systems. It is just a simple indicator that data will be passed from one system to another through something called an interface. However, this surface simplicity can quickly become highly complex when you examine the details. They share certain characteristics and complexities that you will want to ensure have been considered.

Exactly What Data Is to be Exchanged- Early in The Project the team needs to define exactly what data elements are to be

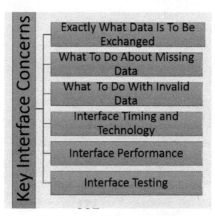

Key Interface Concerns

- Exactly What Data Is To Be Exchanged
- What To Do About Missing Data
- What To Do With Invalid Data
- Interface Timing and Technology
- Interface Performance
- Interface Testing

exchanged between the two systems. This need for precise definition must include details such as the format of each field, lists of valid values, data field lengths and required data translations. These details should be agreed to between the two Project Teams and then formalized in a document. Technical Teams sometimes balk at spending time on formal interface documentation considering it a waste of time. However, it is not enough to be able to make the two systems "talk" to each other, they must be able to "communicate".

One example showing the importance of this was a situation I encountered once with a simple field to record the sex of the customer. Both systems used a one character field to contain the value representing the customer's sex.
However, one system had two valid values "M" for male and "F" for female and you left the field blank if the sex was unknown. The other systems however used a "1" for male, "2" for female and for some reason "9" If the sex was not known. Luckily, I have never had to create an interface with Facebook that now has 51 options for gender.

So something as simple as exchanging gender identification can have significant complexity. Multiply this times the often dozens or hundreds of fields in a typical interface and you quickly come to understand why data definitions need to be formally documented and agreed to.

What To Do About Missing Data - Sometimes when an interface is being built between two systems there is data that one system declares as mandatory which the other system is not able to provide. For example, your system may require a salutation (Mr/Mrs/MS) be entered for every customer name but the other system providing data on new customers may not capture that data and thus will not be able to supply it to you for new customers.

In cases such as this, The Project Team will have to develop a strategy to deal with missing data and/or you might have to negotiate with the other system to begin requiring that data. In extreme cases, you may decide to reject the entire record if key data is missing. In any case, there needs to be formal decision endorsed by both The Business and Technical Team covering how to deal with missing and incomplete data.

What to Do With Invalid Data - This is similar to missing data, but even more complex. The other system may supply data that passes all of their edits, but does not pass your edits. A common example of might be getting an order passed to you through a third party interface. The customer may be an established customer in their system  but not in your system. So they may pass you an order from John Doe. They know who John Doe is, but you do not.

You will need to decide whether to reject the order, establish a dummy account for the customer for this order only, create an additional interface to get customer data to establish the customer in your system, or any number of other possible solutions. This will need to be recorded in the Interface Agreement and endorsed by both The Business and Technical Team for feasibility. These type of situations are sometimes difficult to predict and complex to remedy.

Interface Timing and Technology- You will need to reach agreement as to how often the interface will exchange data and how it will occur. This could run the gamut from a near real time interface that exchanges data as soon as it is entered into the system all the way to monthly data exchanges.

Q41: Have System Interfaces Been Adequately Planned?

The answer to the timing question will impact the technology used to create the interface and its cost. These technical aspects of the interface need to be agreed upon in concept early in The Project and tested with a Proof of Concept as early as possible to validate it is a good solution.

Interface Performance- Interfaces are notorious for having performance issues when systems are being deployed. This is especially true if you batch the data into a big group and exchange it daily, weekly, monthly, etc. On one big bank data warehouse project I was asked to review, the daily exchange of information between the mortgage system and the data warehouse took nearly 26 hours to complete. This meant that the system was constantly loading data and getting farther and farther behind until the weekends arrived reducing the transaction volumes allowing the system to catch up. Obviously this was an interface that needed to be tuned for efficiency.

Interface Testing- Testing an interface is at least twice as complex and time consuming as other testing on The Project since it usually involves coordination of testing activities between two different organizations. Data to be used, testing timing, defect reporting, etc. will need to be coordinated between two organizations.

This is especially problematic if one of the systems belongs to an organization that has little or no interest in the changes you are making. It can be difficult to get organizations to agree to cooperate with activities such as off-hour testing if they are not anticipating benefit from the change. The key to successful systems interfaces really comes down to understating that they need to be planned in detail early in The Project, need to be formally documented, and sufficient time and budget needs to be allocated to creation and testing.

REAL WORLD EXAMPLE

- On a critical US Navy systems project there was interface mandated by Upper Management to exchange complex technical data relating to submarine parts reliability. Our system captured data for Trident Submarines (the nuclear missile boats) and the other system captured very similar data for Fast Attack Submarines (sub killers). The Project mandate was to be able to look at reliability across both programs.

Although similar data was collected in each system, its format and structure was fundamentally different. It took at least 10 long meetings over a period of months to reach agreement on the formal Interface Agreement and then nearly two months of testing to refine the interface to successfully exchange data. Luckily, this complexity was identified early and was accounted for in The Project Schedule and budget.

BEST PRACTICES

- Interface design, construction, and testing has evolved into somewhat of a niche skill within IT teams. If you have significant interface work on The Project, consider having a dedicated team for interfaces, led by a technical resource that has experience in this area.
- A formal Interface Agreement needs to be developed and agreed to by all involved parties early in The Project covering at least the points listed above. This is true even if the interface is between two systems within the same organizational unit.
- Planning for interfaces needs to begin early in The Project with timing and resources allocated when needed.

ADDRESSING THE QUESTION WITH THE PROJECT TEAM

Project Manager- **Work with The Project Manager to ensure that detailed Interface Agreements are created early in The Project and that sufficient time and money has been included in The Project Schedule/budget to define, create and test each interface.**

Business Team- **Ensure that The Business Team has been involved in all decisions relating to missing data and data that does not meet specifications. Set expectations with The Business Lead that they are responsible for understanding the impact of subpar information provided through the interface and to make informed business decisions on how to deal with this on a case by case basis.**

Information Technology Team- **Discuss the number and variety of interfaces with the Technical Lead and ensure that there is a technology strategy envisioned for each type of interface. Ask the Technical Lead how much interaction they have had with their counterparts in the organization on the other side of the interface and to what extent The Business is involved in interface discussions.**

LESSONS LEARNED FROM PAST PROJECTS
- Interfaces nearly always take longer to construct and test than anticipated. Do not forget to factor in time to deal with inter-organization political dynamics.
- Interfaces are long lead time items. Make sure that you get status on a regular basis from the organization creating the other half of the interface. You don't want to discover when interface testing is approaching that the other side has not made sufficient progress on creating their required parts of the interface.

On one project I was involved in, we had negotiated an Interface Agreement with another part of the Company to create an interface that benefited our organization and the company as a whole. However, the interface did not really provide any benefit to the other organization.

Shortly after the Interface Agreement was signed, key management changed in the other organization and they declared the interface low priority and diverted resources away from it without informing our Project Team. This resorted in significant delays in implementing key project capabilities.

- **Always** insist that interfaces be tested with "live" data not "test" data. Test data is made up by the Technical Team and/or The Business and usually conforms well to how the team would like the data to look. However, this is often not how the real data in the systems looks with missing data, data inconsistencies, etc.
- It is not uncommon for an interface to pass testing with test data, but to fail when real data is passed through the interface. This is one of those rare must do items on a project.
- When testing interfaces, make sure that you also conduct performance testing with at least the quantity of data expected when the interface is deployed. Observe interface timing and be prepared to do performance tuning as required prior to deployment.
- Changing the frequency of an interface can be complex and may require significant technology changes. If you want to change from exchanging data once a day to twice a day, there may be little impact. However if you want to change from a weekly file update to real-time transaction updates, the impact can be significant.

Q41: Have System Interfaces Been Adequately Planned?

- Because of interface complexity and data deficiencies, it is not unusually to have to refine interfaces even after they go into production. Ensure that you retain personnel that can accomplish this for a period of time after deployment

RELATED QUESTIONS

22. Are customer and Supplier impacts of The Project understood?

23. Are project business requirements well documented?

24. Are external access requirements understood?

43. Is there a documented technology architecture?

42. DOES THE PROPOSED TECHNOLOGY FIT INTO OUR CORPORATE TECHNOLOGY STRATEGY?

"The advance of technology is based on making it fit in so that you don't really even notice it, so it's part of everyday life"- Bill Gates

WHY IS THIS QUESTION IMPORTANT?

Technology does not exist in a vacuum. Any new technology that you bring into the organization has to coexist with the technology that is already there. Your organization will have to be trained in how to operate, maintain, and expand the use of the technology. The new technology will have to interface with existing technology, etc. This is often much more complicated than might have been expected.

Let's look at a practical real world example. You are old movie aficionado with an extensive collection of classic movies on DVD. Your family decides to move totally to streaming video since "that is what all the cool people do". You can play any movie anytime you want to with just the click of a mouse is the stated value proposition.

Q42: Does the Proposed Technology Fit Into Our Corporate Technology Strategy?

In reality, you find that streamed movies do not come with the extra features like deleted scenes that are you favorite part of watching movies. Also, only the most popular movies are streamed at any given  time so you are not able to watch some movies when you want.

The final indignity is that your internet connection has never been that fast, but when everyone in the family streams video at the same time, your speed grinds to a halt and not only are movies unwatchable due to the starts and stops of buffering data, but you are not able to get your real work done on the internet any more.

This is an example of where the new technology did not fit into the current realities of your environment and did not meet your requirements. There are 4 areas that you should examine before approving major changes in technology at your organization

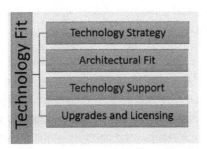

Technology Strategy- Every company should have a corporate Technology Strategy covering among other things which technologies the company supports currently and its desired future technology direction. If your company does not have A Technology Strategy, then you should start an effort to create one immediately. The Corporate Technology Strategy should be the guidebook to IT staffing, training, priorities, architecture, and future direction. Without such a strategy, it is likely that over time you will end up with a jumble of expensive to support disconnected technologies.

Architectural Fit - Assuming that you do have a corporate Technology Strategy, before you approve each Technology Project/purchase, you should understand how the solution fits into this Technology Strategy. If the technology proposed in The Project does not support the  Technology Strategy, then the solution should be closely examined before being approved to ensure there are not better alternatives that align with the strategy.

Sometimes project and Business Teams propose non-standard technologies with an argument that this solution is "cheaper" than one based on the corporate standard. The rebuttal to the cheaper argument is to look not just at the purchase price, but the total cost of ownership of using non-standard technology. Here are some particular areas to consider when looking at total cost of ownership of a non-standard technology.

Technology Support - Once a particular technology is deployed in an organization, it must be supported for the entirety of ifs lifecycle. If your organization has established a corporate direction of supporting Windows 8, it undoubtedly provides training to technical support personnel, staffs the help desk with Windows 8 personnel, develops deployment process, etc. If a new project were to bring Apple PCs into one office in your organization, then either existing personnel would have to be trained to support them or additional personnel hired just to support that one office. Without this support, personnel calling the help desk with problems will likely be turned away. Only add new technology when you are prepared to completely support it upon deployment.

Upgrades and Licensing- Beyond making personnel support more efficient, another key benefit of technology standardization is to consolidate buying power when negotiating licensing agreements. Buying licenses for a single technology for 1,000 users is generally much more cost effective than buying 100 licenses for each of 10 technologies. Likewise when it comes time to install the inevitable systems upgrades, having fewer different technologies involved will significantly reduce upgrade time and cost and lead to a more reliable upgrade.

Overall, there is only one real justification for buying technology that does not follow the corporate standard and that is absolute necessity. When you look at total cost of ownership including lifetime support and licensing considerations, non-standard technology is nearly always more expensive.

However, sometimes you do not have a viable alternative. The new non-standard technology may be a system that is critical to business operations and may just not be available on the corporate standard platform. I am not suggesting that you should never approve a technology that does not conform to the corporate Technology Strategy. Rather, you need to make an informed decision understanding the costs and impacts.

REAL WORLD EXAMPLE

A number of years ago, I worked with a large bank that had a set of well-established IT standards embodied in a formally adopted Technology Strategy. The chosen database solution was Oracle

343

and the corporation had over time had acquired significant levels of highly trained and skilled Oracle database administrators, had negotiated very favorable enterprise licensing agreements, and had a computer facility filled with hardware optimized to support high performance/high reliability Oracle databases.

One newer and less profitable division of the bank decided to create a new system to support internal data analysis needs. Because of limited funding, they chose to by less expensive hardware from a company called Prime (defunct since about 1992), that came bundled with a proprietary database management tool. This required much less investment of funds up front than installing the system on the corporate standard infrastructure would have required. As a result, strong-willed Executives insisted the solution be approved regardless of the corporate standards.

However, the fallacy in that decision was discovered less than half way into the development process. Even though the bank had a large development staff, no one knew how to develop software for the Prime database. Attempts were made to hire personnel to support The Project which were unsuccessful since it was a niche technology that few people supported.

As parts of the system were approaching completion, it also became obvious that the hardware purchased did not have sufficient capacity to process the data required in the required timeframes and no one in the organization had the knowledge and experience to tune the system for performance purposes.

The bottom line is that the system was never completed or deployed and all money spent on hardware and development was written off as having no value. This is a great example of why you should understand how the technology will be integrated into the organizational Technology Strategy.

BEST PRACTICES

- Exceptions to the corporate Technology Strategy should only be approved after carefully consideration of impact and then only when business necessity justifies.
- In all cases where non-standard technology is approved, a plan outlining how that technology will be supported over its life cycle should be developed including cost and staffing estimates.
- There should be sufficient internal controls within the corporate purchasing to ensure that all technology purchases are reviewed for adherence to the Technology Strategy prior to being approved.

ADDRESSING THE QUESTION WITH THE PROJECT TEAM

Project Manager- Discuss with The Project Manager the need to ensure that all technology components being considered for The Project are reviewed for compliance with the approved corporate Technology Strategy. There should be tasks in The Project Schedule to plan the timing of these reviews. Ask to see them as part of your schedule review process.

Business Team - The Business Team should only be involved in this issue if they are the one's pushing for the acquisition of non-standard technology. If that is the case, a discussion of the real costs of using non-standard technology should take place. Often, IT does not take the time to explain the costs associated with some of The Business requests.

Information Technology Team- Set an expectation with the Technical Lead that you expect them to be responsible for ensuring that all proposed technical solutions are in accordance with the established corporate Technology

Strategy. Any deviations from the standard must be fully justified and reviewed far in advance of deployment.

LESSONS LEARNED FROM PAST PROJECTS

- Most companies with a formal Technology Strategy have some type of a governance process to ensure proposed solutions adhere to the standards such as an Architectural Review Board. Ensure that this group is engaged very early in the process so that any potential architectural issues are discovered as early as possible

- The most common "offenders" when it comes to purchasing non-standard technologies tends to be remote locations, plants, branch office, joint ventures and other parts of the organizations outside of the central office. It is not a bad rule of thumb that the farther a Business Unit is from the central office, the more likely it is to want to deviate from the standards. The best way to prevent this is through mandating an IT review of all technology purchases.
- In cases where business necessity mandates adoption of non-standard technology, you should amend the Technology Strategy to include the new technology and develop a formal process to support it going forward.

RELATED QUESTIONS

40. What do you really know about the company and technology being proposed?

43. Is there a documented technology architecture?

50. Is your Technical Team experienced in the proposed technology?

43. IS THERE A DOCUMENTED TECHNOLOGY ARCHITECTURE?

"Architecture starts when you carefully put two bricks together. There it begins."- Ludwig Mies van der Rohe

WHY IS THIS QUESTION IMPORTANT?

Consider a scenario where you hire a company to build you a house. They show up on the first day and start digging a big hole in the ground, others are going off to buy things that they think might be needed at the hardware store, and others start cutting up lumber because that is what carpenters do.

You arrive on the scene and ask the general contractor what the house is going to look like and they reply that everyone on The Project knows their job and how it looks will take shape as the construction progresses. They tell you not to worry everything will be fine. Hopefully, you would never build a house this way and you shouldn't allow your Project Team to build your system that way either.

Prior to any significant work occurring on a Technology Project, an architectural drawing outlining how the various technology components are going to be integrated should be developed. This

347

pictorial depiction of the technology components should include major hardware and software components, Internal and external systems interfaces, and data storage locations at a minimum. All major purchased and/or custom built hardware and software components should also be represented on the drawing.

This is a crucial project deliverable because it communicates to The Business Team, Technical Team, Project Manager, Purchasing Department, Executive approvers, etc. what the major system components are and how they will be integrated. Once this architectural depiction is completed and approved by all involved groups, then it will serve as the system roadmap. You should be able to tie any purchase of hardware/ software back to the Architecture Drawing when The Project Team asks for Purchase Order approval.

REAL WORLD EXAMPLE

I have a friend who was working on a large Federal systems project a few years ago. Purchasing of the various technology components of The Project was decentralized across several regions of the Agency. Work was well underway and there was a flood of hardware purchase orders to acquire all of the needed hardware components. Everything seemed to be progressing until a chance comment in weekly coordination meeting triggered a discussion. It was discovered that one of the regions had their own ideas about what should be purchased and ended purchasing a technology infrastructure that  was incompatible with that being purchased on the rest of The Project.

Root cause analysis of the issue revealed that The Project had never developed an overall architecture drawing showing the technology components and how they would be interconnected. Thus, significant effort and funding were wasted and The Project was faced with two uncomfortable alternatives- purchasing the correct hardware and disposing of that originally purchased or finding a way to make the systems work together.

The Project eventually chose the second alternative and ended up with a clunky inefficient interface that performed poorly, was prone to failure, and required significant effort to keep it operational. It was an easily avoidable situation that could have been remedied with a simple architectural drawing driving a complex purchasing process.

BEST PRACTICES

- All projects should have a detailed architectural drawing showing all of the significant hardware and software components and which shows the interfaces with external systems. The architectural drawing should be as large and detailed as necessary to show the detailed needed to understand the technology being purchased.
- There also needs to be a one page high level view of the architecture. This depiction may need to contain less detail in order to fit on a normal sheet of paper, but such a depiction

It is not the beauty of a building you should look at; it is the construction of the foundation that will stand the test of time.

David Allan Coe

is very useful in communication the high level concept to business personnel, other technical personnel, vendors, Executives, etc. The one page drawing should contain an annotation of how to find the more detailed drawing.

ADDRESSING THE QUESTION WITH THE PROJECT TEAM

Project Manager- Ensure with The Project Manager that there are tasks early in the timeline of The Project Schedule to create and gain approval for a high level systems architecture (hardware/software). There should also be follow-on tasks as The Project progresses to refine and create this architecture.

Business Team- The Business Team does not have much involvement in this area. However, you should ensure that The Business Lead has reviewed the Architecture Document and is in agreement.

Information Technology Team- The Technical Lead should be able to identify who is responsible for project architecture in general and for creation of the Architecture Document. Set the expectation that a high level architecture that is aligned with the corporate architectural Strategy must be created, reviewed with all key technical and business personnel, and approved prior to any major technology purchases.

LESSONS LEARNED FROM PAST PROJECTS

- If the organization is large with one or more decentralized IT groups, the Architecture Document should be reviewed and approved by all affected groups.
- Once the initial architecture is agreed upon, it should be placed under Change Control and thereafter only modified after a cost and time impact has been completed and the change has been formally approved.
- Architectural changes must be well communicated to all involved groups upon approval.
- Periodically, the approved architecture should be reviewed with both the Technical and Business Teams to ensure that it is still valid and that it is being implemented as approved.

Q43: Is There a Documented Technology Architecture?

- On several projects I have been involved in, the development and infrastructure teams failed to follow the approved architecture basically ignoring established standards. **This is unacceptable**. If The Project Team discovers requirements and/or system capabilities that indicate a change is needed, the approved architecture needs to be formally modified though Change Request. This is OK as long as the impact of that change on cost and schedule is understood and approved.

- Corporate direction changes from time to time when it comes to technologies. If there is a shift in corporate direction in the middle of a longer project, you will have to decide whether to continue to develop the system based on the approved architecture or stop and update the architecture to the new standard. It is often best to "grandfather" The Project so that it can be completed and deployed as initially planned and then updated as needed after deployment as part of a new project.

RELATED QUESTIONS

23. Are project business requirements well documented?
24. Are external access requirements understood?
42. Does the proposed technology fit into our corporate IT strategy?
47. Are plans in place for post-deployment support?

44. IS THERE A STRATEGY FOR PROJECT DATA PROTECTION?

"Social security, bank account, and credit card numbers aren't just data. In the wrong hands they can wipe out someone's life savings, wreck their credit and cause financial ruin."- Melissa Bean

WHY IS THIS QUESTION IMPORTANT?

The era where you have to sit down in an office at a computer connected to your corporate system in order to access corporate information is over. The modern trend is wireless connection in the office, access to corporate systems over the internet, and even accessing corporate data from your smart phone while watching your kids play soccer.

While arguably adversely impacting family and personal activities, being able to access data when needed regardless of where you are is a significant productivity tool. However, the more ubiquitous our ability to access company information anywhere becomes, the more casual people seem to have become about safeguarding sensitive corporate data.

Any Technology Project that changes existing external access to data and/or creates new access mechanisms needs to also ensure that sufficient safeguards are in place to prevent corporate data from falling into the wrong hands. This should include both safeguards during The Project and permanent safeguards as the system is being used.

When examining data security outside of your organizational walls, you not only have to worry about electronic access to data from outside the building, but also data that walks out of the front door on phones, laptops and USB data drives. Here are some general areas that should be considered when examining data security outside of the organization.

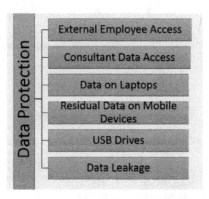

External Employee Access- If this project will make changes to how employees will be able to access data from outside the walls of the company, then you should ensure that a security analysis has been conducted to identify the risks of this access and to ensure The Project puts sufficient protection in place to mitigate these risks.

Consultant Data Access- If this project involves the use of external consultants; you should give careful consideration to what data the consultants will be able to access and what they can do with it. It is not uncommon for consultants to ask for and receive huge amounts of sensitive company data during the course of a project.

Section 4: Technology Questions

You should ensure that any data provided to consultants is absolutely needed and that it will be effectively secured. I have repeated seen consultants that have sensitive data from a number of clients on their laptop well after The Project has been concluded.

One common puzzle for the security-minded is how to work with confidential data on the road. Sometimes you can't bring your laptop, or don't want to. But working on somebody else's machine exposes you to malware and leaves behind all kinds of electronic trails.

Barton Gellman

Data on Laptop Computers- Not to be overly paranoid, but you should assume that any laptop (employee or consultant) that walks out the front door of your offices could well be stolen by someone. You should ensure that all data storage devices that could be removed from the office are encrypted to levels making it very difficult for someone to extract data.

Do not assume that all of the consulting companies that you might engage on The Project automatically encrypt the information on their laptops or that they will delete the data at the end of The Project. All organizational data that leaves the protection of the internal company network should be encrypted.

Residual Data on Mobile Devices- With the proliferation of mobile devices like smart phones and iPads, accessing company information has gotten much more convenient. However, if your project results in changes to mobile access, you want to ensure that this does not create a new data security issue.

As with laptops, you should assume that sooner or later one or more of the mobile devices that access your system will be lost or stolen. You will want to ensure that any passwords stored on the mobile devices, data downloaded to the devices, and even bits of data called "cookies" that are left during data access are sufficiently protected if the device falls into the wrong hands.

USB Data Drives- These are exceptionally convenient to move documentation, data, and other project information between groups and computers. It is very common in a Project Meeting for someone to copy a file to a USB drive and then hand it to someone else on The Project to copy to their machine. These are rarely encrypted and very easily lost. If the data on your project is considered sensitive, you should have a policy in place concerning data on USB drives.

Data Leakage- This is a polite term for unintentionally sending data to someone that you should not have received it. A very common cause of this on Technology Projects is through email. Projects often create multiple mailing lists for different groupings of people on The Project. If someone on The Project sends sensitive business data to a mailing list that includes customers you plan on testing with, a data leakage occurs.

Likewise if in the rush to send an email, someone attaches the wrong attachment or forwards an email with an attachment that shouldn't be distributed, a data leakage occurs. These can also occur in the day to day non-project environment, but tend to be more frequent during projects due to the fast pace, stress, and flood of new names that generally accompany a project.

REAL WORLD EXAMPLE

When I wonder if I am too paranoid about data exposure on projects, I just have to recall what I call the Tippy's Taco House incident on one of my projects to remind me why I am so paranoid about data. I was on a military project where all data was classified at the top secret or above level.

I was pushing the team hard to meet a deployment deadline including some night and weekend work. One afternoon, I found my office filled with a very serious looking security detail with a stack of papers in their hand and knew we were not going to have a pleasant discussion.

It seems that a group of my young smart eager developers with decidedly poor decision-making skills had decided to work through lunch at a local establishment called Tippy's Taco house which was near our facility. It seems that my team had taken a stack of printouts with them to work on during
lunch and at the end of the lunch mistakenly left them on the table.

Someone (I assume it was Tippy himself perhaps) found the printouts and noticed that there was a security warning on the bottom of each page with a phone number to call if you found the documents which is exactly what Tippy did.

He quickly got a visit from base security quickly leading to the meeting in my office and a discussion of how this highly classified data came to be in the possession of the owner of Tippy's Taco House. The only thing that kept us all from being in jail for the rest of our lives or wishing that was the worst they could do to us, is that I had insisted all test data we used be cleansed so that locations were amusement parks, individuals were cartoon characters, etc.

It was clear from looking at the data that it was not sensitive notwithstanding the notation we printed on every page of every report. Because of this, we escaped with only a stern warning and a contrite visit to the Colonel's office. Disclosure of live data would have been a whole different matter.

BEST PRACTICES

- Organizations are rarely paranoid enough about data security until they have had a data breach of some type.
- Unless you are sure that there are absolutely no possible data security issues related to a project, you should assign someone on the team to have responsibility for managing the data security aspects of The Project. This person should be the gatekeeper for all project data requests.
- You should always discuss data security with The Project Team during kickoff meetings and periodically in team meetings. If data is especially sensitive, you should have one-on-one meetings with key team members to reinforce their roles.
- All requests to provide bulk data to anyone who does not normally have access to that data should be approved by The Business Owner of that data. This includes other employees, developers, testers, etc. Since The Business owns the data, they should be aware of who is accessing that data and be able to control that access.
- As data sensitivity dictates, it should be addressed in vendor contracts and someone at each vendor should be responsible for security of data after it is delivered to the vendor.

ADDRESSING THE QUESTION WITH THE PROJECT TEAM

Project Manager- Work with The Project Manager to identify who on The Project Team will be responsible for managing data security. The Project Manager should include tasks in The Project Schedule to address data security as appropriate.

Section 4: Technology Questions

Business Team- In discussions with The Business Team, you should set the expectation that they own The Business data and that they have a responsibility to safeguard it appropriately. Encourage them to consider the possible impact if information were to be disclosed to competitors, vendors, etc.

Information Technology Team- You should set the expectation with the Technical Team that they are not to provide any data to consultants, vendors, etc. without approval from the person responsible for data security on The Project and/or The Business Team lead.

If some of The Project data is especially sensitive, discuss with the Technical Team strategies for cleansing the data to remove its sensitivity prior to providing it to The Project Team. This can often be done with simply developed programs.

LESSONS LEARNED FROM PAST PROJECTS

- Given my background on government projects with significant security requirements, I am always puzzled by the willingness of organizations to give outside consultants they first met last week large files of data on a USB drive or CD that they would not let long time trusted employees have.
- Ensure that data you allow to leave your network is somehow "cleansed" to render it less sensitive. This can include changing customer information to random names, changing inventory/order quantities to random numbers, etc.
- Ensure that data is permanently removed from any hard drives leaving the company after equipment replacement. Unless there is a compelling reason not to,

the best option is to remove all hard drives from machines being recycled and physically destroying the drives. There are always over-stressed people on a project that will jump at the opportunity to batter hardware with a sledge hammer at no cost to you.

- Once data is provided to someone, you lose all control over where else it can end up. Often consultants that you have given the appropriate data security instructions and who have been vetted by their companies, pass that information on to others in the company and outside of their company as examples of their work.
- At the end of The Project ask that each consultant individually sign a document indicating that they have removed all project data from their systems. This should be coordinated with the Vendor Delivery Manager and should be included as a requirement in the contract.
- Concern over data security should also extend to consultant access to workspaces. It is not uncommon to allow consultant teams 24 X 7 unfettered access to The Project area. This is usually necessary due to off-hour testing, weekend work, etc. and often results in consultants being in your company workspaces by themselves.

You should give some consideration to what else in the building that gives people access to and whether that is an issue. On one project I was given 24X7 access to an 8 story building housing thousands of employees spread across multiple departments of the company. At night, I could wander out of The Project area into purchasing areas, engineering design areas, Executive offices, etc. if I so desired.

- If you are deploying new web or mobile device applications as part of The Project, ensure that you have personnel on The Project with experience in managing

security on these types of applications. This is one area
that you want to ensure you have state of the art
practices and technology in place.

RELATED QUESTIONS

23. Are project business requirements well documented?

24. Are external access requirements understood?

29. Are intellectual property rights contractually protected?

43. Is there a documented technology architecture?

45 ARE PERFORMANCE REQUIREMENTS BEING ADEQUATELY ADDRESSED?

 "When you play the 12-string guitar, you spend half your life tuning the instrument and the other half playing it out of tune." - Pete Seeger

WHY IS THIS QUESTION IMPORTANT?

When a new system is deployed or a major change is made to an existing system, one frequent complaint from users is that it is too slow. The Project Team should address performance prior to deployment and be prepared to quickly address residual performance issues after deployment. Resolving performance issues often requires tweaking multiple aspects of the system and can be difficult to diagnose and address. There are several different aspects of system performance that you should be aware of.

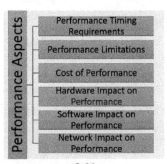

Section 4: Technology Questions

Performance Timing Requirements- System performance is a subjective and even emotional issue with users. To address this concern, performance expectations should be documented as the system is being defined. This can be in the form of general performance requirements such as "all screens must return search results within 5 seconds after proper search criteria is entered" or it can be on a screen by screen basis.

Regardless of how your Project Team records the requirements, you want to ensure that there are written, achievable performance measures for key systems functions. This will create a standard that can be tested against and which can be used to evaluate the validity of user performance concerns.

Performance Limitations- While everyone would like to have quick system response, it is important that all involved in The Project understand that there are limits on how fast most systems can perform without extraordinary and expensive effort. Usually the basic system architecture to a large extent establishes maximum system performance levels.

If you want a system that can be used on mobile devices, you are at the mercy of the wireless providers that service your devices. If you need complex graphics/video, it is likely that performance will not be awe inspiring. Likewise, if you want extensive data validation requiring comparison to data already in a database, you are likely to experience at least some slowness.

The Business and Technical Teams need to have frank discussions on how The Business and system requirements potentially affect performance so that performance expectations are set early.

Cost of Performance- Performance is not free and in fact can be very expensive. I have often heard users say they want their system to be as fast as Google searches. This is a perfect example of the cost of performance. There are many estimates of the investment Google makes in their hardware to achieve the performance everyone expects.

One estimate is that Google has "an investment pattern of 200,000 servers per quarter, 800,000 per year. With an average lifetime of 3 years, this puts the ballpark estimate of the size of Google's server farm at 2.4 million servers. There are entire countries that do not have that many servers. There are entire countries that do not have that many PCs."

Few companies are willing to make this type of investment to make their website run faster. If users are adamant in the need for faster performance, you should examine how much you are willing to pay for a faster system.

Hardware Impact on Performance- Of the actions you can take to improve performance, hardware upgrades are often the easiest improvement. Adding more servers, faster processors, more memory, etc. can have a profound effect on system performance.

However, this is not always the case. It is easy to blame performance issues on the computer hardware. Before you agree to throw expensive hardware at the performance problem issue, you want an objective analysis showing that the hardware is a constraint and that additional hardware is likely to have a positive impact on performance. Challenge the Technical Team to produce evidence such as server and memory utilization logs documenting performance bottlenecks before you authorize the purchase of additional hardware to address performance issues.

Software Impact on Performance- Custom built software and packaged software that has been extensively modified usually benefits from performance "tuning" after deployment. Tuning the software is usually the first step you should take if you believe you are having performance problems.

This can include optimizing queries, re-organizing database design, changing how the software is spread across your servers, etc. Most IT organizations are well versed in performance tuning software. If you organization does not have expertise in this area, you should engage outside resources to help with performance tuning. This generally has more impact on performance than even adding more hardware to support the system. It also is usually far less expensive than adding new hardware to a system.

Network/Internet Impact on Performance- When all systems were used within the walls of the organization, it was easier to provide consistent system performance. Now with highly decentralized access to applications including on mobile devices, this is much more difficult.

When you access sales data while watching your kids soccer game in a remote field somewhere while simultaneously streaming the World Cup play by play commentary, there is little The Project Team can do to improve performance other than provide training on how certain things impact performance such as number of other apps you have running on your phone, amount of phone memory, speed of your wireless network etc. You should hold your Project Team responsible for maximizing performance up to the line of demarcation leading outside of your company, but they cannot be held responsible for end to end timing.

REAL WORLD EXAMPLE

A manufacturing company implementing a major Enterprise Resource Planning (ERP) system experienced significant performance issues upon deployment. After a significant concentrated effort the problems were determined to be, speed of data connections, poor database tuning, number of network connection points to reach some plants, server memory, and network load balancing.

This was determined and fixed over the period of about 4 months requiring the involvement of vendor personnel, database experts, phone company personnel, and developers. During this period of time, the user community was very disappointed because of the impact of productivity during this period of time.

I believe the root cause of the problem was not these technical items which as discovered were resolved. The root cause was the lack of performance testing prior to deployment. If adequate performance testing on sufficiently sized hardware had been carried out, the performance issues would have been identified and substantially addressed prior to deployment.

BEST PRACTICES

- Performance expectations must be achievable, well defined, and measurable and should be clearly documented and agreed to during system construction. This will be the objective standard that performance is measured against.
- You should have a documented Performance Testing Plan that as closely as possible tests the system using production level data volumes and expected user load prior to deployment. There are software tools that simulate having hundreds of users on a systems. This is often a cost effective way to doing performance testing.
- Upon deployment there should be an identified team involving both Business and Technical Team members to address performance concerns.

ADDRESSING THE QUESTION WITH THE PROJECT TEAM

Project Manager- Ask The Project Manager to share the Performance Testing Plan with you and to show you the tasks in The Project Schedule related to performance testing. Also discuss with The Project Manager the need to ensure that performance requirements are included in the documented system requirements.

Business Team- Set the expectation with The Business Team that they own setting performance requirements, but that they have to be reasonable in their expectations. Ensure that they understand how some of the features they request adversely impact performance and that they should work with the Technical Team to understand the impact of decisions that are made on future performance.

Information Technology Team- In discussions with the Technical Lead, clearly establish the expectation that you hold them responsible for identifying potential performance issues well before deployment. They should be proactive in identifying to The Business Team and Stakeholders any requirements/design decisions that are likely to adversely impact performance. This will allow an evaluation of the need for these potentially impactful requirements prior to significant effort being spent on development.

Additionally set the expectation that the Technical Team is expected to design and execute performance testing that as accurately as possible mimics the conditions expected after the system is placed into production. The Technical Team should use the results of the performance testing to tune the application prior to deployment.

LESSONS LEARNED FROM PAST PROJECTS

- Performance problems are rarely a complete surprise. It is common after the fact to have business users complain that they first noticed the slowness during testing or even system demonstrations. Also, it is not uncommon to have Technical Team members report that they knew there we going to have performance problems when the user asked for a certain system feature. **You need to establish an environment where it is expected that performance concerns be openly discussed throughout the life of The Project.**

- Project Team leaders often ignore performance concerns until after deployment in the belief that the rush to get the system deployed is more important than system performance at the point of deployment. This is a decision that should only be made with the concurrence of The Business Team.

- If you are contracting with an outside vendor to create software, ensure that sufficient protections are included in the contract to ensure the vendor addresses performance issues. Many development contracts that I have reviewed have absolutely no incentive to ensure a vendor delivers a system that performs to expectations.

Including formal performance times in the system requirements is a good way to address performance concerns. It is frustrating to have to go back to the Steering Committee and ask for money to give a vendor to improve performance on software that you paid them to create in the first place. You may have to do just that however, if you do not structure the contract adequately..

Surprisingly, many people dramatically overstate how long it takes systems to respond. Unless you pay attention to it, it is hard for most people to judge how long 10 seconds is. When you are testing performance, use a stopwatch to add objectivity to the testing.

Section 4: Technology Questions

- Database tuning is often key to addressing system performance issues. Do not hesitate to bring in outside assistance with this since it is a highly specialized skillset.
- If you are implementing a third party system with performance issues, you can often get some amount of free assistance with performance problem identification from the Vendor. Work with the vendor Deliver Manager or Sales Executive to request such assistance.

RELATED QUESTIONS

23. Are project business requirements well documented?

49. Is there sufficient hardware software identified to support The Project?

50. Is your Technical Team experienced in the proposed technology?

46. IS THE SOFTWARE CODE QUALITY ACCEPTABLE?

"Quality is not an act, it is a habit."- Aristotle

WHY IS THIS QUESTION IMPORTANT?

I used to love the game called mousetrap. In that game you strung together a Rube Goldberg type device that had a ball rolling through a series of falls and turns triggering other things that happened eventually if it all worked resulted in a trap falling hopefully catching the mouse.

You could argue that the machine worked since the mouse sometimes was caught. However, the machine usually failed as often as it worked and as I recall occasionally fell apart entirely. If your goal is to catch the mouse in the most efficient and repeatable way possible, you would use a modern spring loaded mousetrap probably to greatly improved results.

You may ask what this has to do with writing computer software and the answer is everything. It is possible to string a system together consisting of disjointed segments of code that are fundamentally incompatible, not well conceived or written, and which are impossible to maintain. The root of system performance issues is often at least in part because of poorly written code. It is not enough that you catch the mouse, you want to catch it efficiently with a trap that is not prone to breaking

Projects that involve writing considerable amounts of software must take steps to ensure code quality and sustainability. This is not only true for software that is written by employees of your company, but also true of any code written by vendors you bring in to help on The Project. The key to code quality essentially comes down to a few simple activities.

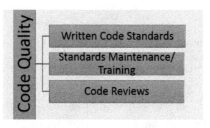

Written Coding Standards- Your organization should have written coding standards that are applicable to all developed systems. If this does not exist, then they should be created to support the current project. Coding Standards cover such things as naming conventions, error handling, design standards, screen standards, standardized database access methods, etc.

Having a good and enforced coding standard helps ensure consistency across systems and makes systems more reliable and easier to maintain and enhance.

Coding Standard Training/Mentoring- It is not enough to merely have coding standards; you need to ensure that your developers understand and use them. I have seen projects that email a coding standards document to new developers expecting them to read and follow the document. To be effective, you should have a process to ensure your developers understand the standards including providing mentoring on the standards for a period of time for all new developers. This is an area where a formal classroom training session that allows discussion among the developers can be very helpful in obtaining standards compliance

Code Reviews- Sometimes also called Peer Reviews, there should be a process where all code written on The Project is reviewed by other developers on The Project. It is like grade school where you grade homework by exchanging papers among your classmates so that someone other than you reviews your work. It does not have to be a large formal gathering of all of the developers on a project, but conducting a peer review of all software is a very cost effective way of finding errors and creating software that is more efficient, reliable, and sustainable.

Additionally, the mere understanding that they will have to show their work to other developers encourages developers to create better code.

REAL WORLD EXAMPLE

A military system was being developed by a team of developers assembled from a number of different organizational units and multiple external contractors. After some false starts and allocation of responsibility issues were resolved, the software came together, passed testing and was deployed.

Problems emerged immediately upon deployment relating to coding standards. One critical example was related to handling of data errors. One organization wrote all data errors to an error file, another group sent emails out with the errors, and a third just rejected incorrectly formatted data with no errors being reported.

As a result depending on which part of the system you were in, the way users learned of data errors was very different which was extremely confusing and inefficient. If The Project had agreed on formal coding standards which would include how errors are handled, the software would have been much easier to understand, operate, and maintain.

BEST PRACTICES

- Every organization that develops software should have a written set of coding standards that all developers must follow.
- If you are using outside vendors to develop all or part of the software on your project, you likely want to insist that they adhere to your coding standards rather than their own. This should be part of the vendor contract.
- It is best practice to withhold at least some payment from outside vendors for software development until the software has passed your internal code review. This helps ensure you get software that meets your standards.
- Provide classroom training to all developers at the start of The Project on coding standards and make allowances for additional training as people are added to The Project.

ADDRESSING THE QUESTION WITH THE PROJECT TEAM

Project Manager- Ask The Project Manager where code reviews are specifically called out in The Project Schedule. This helps ensure that time is allocated for the reviews and that review completion is tracked as part of The Project status reporting.

Business Team - The Business Team should have little to no involvement in code quality. However, it is sometimes

372

helpful to invite more technologically savvy Business Team member to the meeting to address any questions of functionality that might occur.

Information Technology Team- Ask the Technical Lead to see the coding standards and discuss how they intend to ensure the standards are followed. Set the expectation that code quality is a high priority and a process should be in place for both internal and external developers.

Discuss how and when code reviews will be handled to ensure that the Technical Lead has a concept of how they will be accomplished within the framework of The Project work.

LESSONS LEARNED FROM PAST PROJECTS

- In the rush to deliver a project, code reviews are often sacrificed to get something deployed. This is a mistake that often haunts systems for the life of the system. Remember that you will have to pay to maintain and enhance software well after The Project is closed. Poorly written software makes this more expensive.
- Do not wait until the end of The Projects and try to do a large number of code reviews right before deployment. This leaves little time to bring code up to standards. Have some reviews very early in the development process so that all developers understand the importance of good code and so that you can make use of the lessons learned from the reviews to improve the remaining development activities.
- Development groups often try to establish a policy where the development lead must personally review all software prior to deployment. This can create a bottleneck especially if there are a number of developers that can lead to cursory reviews.

Having a true peer review process involving small groups of programs reviewing each other's code can be more efficient. The Development Lead can then spot check the results of the peer reviews and focus their time on review of critical software components. This is usually a better option especially on larger project.

- If your organization does not have formal coding standards, it is fairly easy to find examples on the internet that you can use as a pattern and modify as

---

Quality is never an accident. It is always the result of intelligent effort.

John Ruskin

---

needed. This greatly speeds up the standards creation process.

- You should review your coding standards at the beginning of each project for relevance especially if The Project is deploying new technology or is using a software language not previously used. You made need to extend your existing standards to support The Project.
- Surprising, I have found that the developers that cause the greatest code quality issues are sometimes your most senior developers. Over their careers they may have developed coding habits that may or may not adhere to your standards. Some senior developers see coding standards as interfering with their "artistic freedom" to design code the way they see fit. When you have several senior developers each following their own concept of good code, the result is sometimes not pretty.

- You should take particular care to get the senior developers invested in your coding standards as it will trickle down from them to more junior developers that come to them for help and advice.

- Monitor code quality/peer reviews to ensure that they are being effectively conducted and that developers come to the meeting prepared. It is not enough to just have the meeting, it must also add value to the development process. As part of the reviews, there should be a process to record the review findings and follow-up to ensure comments are addressed.

- I have seen code reviews denigrate into sessions where everyone offers their opinion of more clever ways code could have been written. Keep in mind that there are usually multiple ways to create quality software.

- The reviews should look at whether the approach taken was reasonable and whether the developer adhered to the formal coding standards. Do not allow code reviews to become competitions focusing on who is the cleverest coder or they will become a waste of time.

RELATED QUESTIONS

7. What are key roles for project success?

32. Are contracts structured to ensure performance?

47. ARE PLANS IN PLACE FOR POST-DEPLOYMENT SUPPORT?

"Maintaining a consistent platform also helps improve product support - a significant problem in the software industry."- Bill Gates

WHY IS THIS QUESTION IMPORTANT?

Technology Projects are exactly like getting a new puppy for your family. It starts with the eager anticipation of all the fun you are going to have and the joy of people remarking how cute the new puppy is. Then everyone goes to bed the first night and the puppy starts barking and eats your running shoes and you begin to understand that you will have to deal with this new puppy for years to come and it might be unpleasant and expensive to do so.

All technology needs care and feeding at a certain level and your organization must be prepared to provide that support. You need to plan for post-deployment support during the course of The Project in order to be prepared to provide the support when needed. Here are some traditional areas where project support will be required.

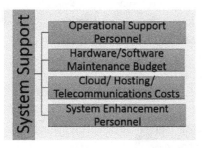

Operations Support Personnel- Provision must be made to have skilled personnel available to support the technology after deployment. You may have engaged outside support to install hardware, create software, etc., but in the long term, you will need expertise to keep this running. This is an area where you usually will want to develop internal resources to support this long-term commitment. Support personnel must be sufficiently trained in the technology being implemented to keep it operational and deal with problems that might arise. Alternatively you may choose to out-source operational support.

Hardware/Software Maintenance Budget- Major computer hardware and purchased software usually comes with a yearly maintenance fee that covers upgrades, hardware repairs, firmware upgrades, etc. Even if the vendor does not offer a yearly maintenance plan, there will over time be costs to repair/replace the components. You need to ensure that the cost of these have been included in you yearly budget going forward.

Cloud/Hosting/Telecommunications Yearly Costs- Some companies chose to reduce the upfront costs of deploying new systems by selecting operations models that do not require support of systems hardware in your environment. In these cases, you pay a fee to a vendor to host and operate the system for you.

377

There are variations of this outsourced support model with the new vogue being called "The Cloud". In the cloud concept, you do not need to know or care where your system is physically located. You can access it from anywhere.

Other vendors operate your system on dedicated hardware in their data center. Regardless of The Business model, If you chose to outsource some or all of the hardware for your project, you will need to ensure that the cost of doing so are included in your post-support budget. Ensure you have realistic estimates of the cost of these options before you make a decision since the can be substantial.

System Enhancement Personnel- It is an unusual project where the users get all desired/required features in the initial release of a system. Usually, there are what seems like a never ending stream of minor or not so minor enhancements that the users will request over the life of a system. It is a reality that most large software systems will require a permanent cadre of support and enhancement personnel until it is retired. You need to understand this and take it into account in future staffing/budget discussions.

REAL WORLD EXAMPLE

A Government Agency was installing its first non-mainframe system. They hired a vendor to install the hardware, configure the system, and operate the environments during the course of The Project and for approximately one month thereafter.

They intended to operate the system without any changes for a period of time so training of operational personnel was made a low priority with only basic instruction provided during The Project. Even though no changes were made to The Business system, the servers were configured to automatically download service updates and security patches.

One of these downloads was incompatible with some web server components and the Agency website abruptly crashed. With only cursory training and no experience in the new technology, the overwhelmed personnel were unable to restore service. This led to an expensive emergency support contract and bad publicity for the Agency.

The lesson here is that your organization must have personnel capable of fully supporting the new technology. If this is not possible or desirable, then you need to engage outside help to support the system. This must be in place prior to deployment.

BEST PRACTICES

- Create a post-deployment support plan to cover how the system will be supported after The Project has been disbanded.
- Include the cost of post-deployment support in you overall organization budget going forward.
- When completing a cost-benefit analysis prior to The Project being approved, be sure and include a good-faith estimate of post-deployment support costs.
- The best way to train personnel to support the technology after the conclusion of The Project is for them to be actively engaged during The Project. If vendor personnel are used on a project, the internal personnel that will eventually support the systems going forward should be working side by side with them as much as possible.

ADDRESSING THE QUESTION WITH THE PROJECT TEAM

Project Manager- Work with The Project Manager to ensure that a post-deployment support plan is developed by The

Project Team and that tasks are included in The Project Schedule to support creation of this plan.

Business Team- Post-deployment support is primarily a technical consideration, but you should discuss with The Business Leader how The Business plans to support their portion of The Project Scope going forward. In particular, you want to identify any recurring needs for training, additional personnel, etc and ensure that they have been included in department plans.

Information Technology Team- Your IT organization should give considerable thought as to how the technology will be supported post-deployment. This should occur early in The Project so that resources selected for post-deployment support are given an opportunity to work with the Technical Team. Early in The Project, you should discuss post-deployment support with your IT Manager and set the expectation that a written plan to provide support be agreed upon and integrated into The Project budget and schedule.

LESSONS LEARNED FROM PAST PROJECTS

- Sometimes the Technical Team working on The Project becomes disconnected from the day to day operations of the IT Department. In cases like this, the IT Department is sometimes relegated to keeping the existing system's operational while The Project Team is developing the new technology.

  You want to be very careful that this disconnect does not become too pronounced. Usually after The Project Team is disbanded, it is left to the regular IT Department to keep the systems operational and provide enhancements over the life of the system. It is hard for them to do so without adequate training and documentation.

- Consider adding provisions to software/ hardware vendor contracts that include knowledge transfer and training of internal personnel in the new technology. Without this, sometimes vendors are reluctant to spend any time preparing your personnel to operate the new technology. Many vendors that provide project support also provide post-deployment support services. Human nature is that they would prefer to sell you these support services rather than train your personnel to support them internally.

- If the technology is especially cutting edge or complex, you may want to consider retaining some level of outside support post- 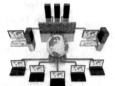 deployment to train and mentor internal personnel in system operations and maintenance for a period of time.

- Usually, you should give existing company personnel an opportunity to get training/experience in the new technology rather than bringing in new people to support it. The worst case I have seen is where an organization hired a number of new people to support the new technology and laid off many of the people supporting the decommissioned legacy technology. This is not good for morale.

- Ensure that at the conclusion of The Project, all external vendors are contractually obligated to deliver all life cycle documentation created as part of The Project. Then at the end of The Project ensure that this delivery occurs as it is often needed to support the system going forward.

- Some organizations justify new systems based on reducing the number of developers, database personnel, etc. need to support the current system. In my experience, it is rare that a new system will require fewer personnel to support than the system it is replacing. That is not to say that it does not happen in some cases, but treat any estimate that justifies a system by claiming dramatic IT personnel reductions with some skepticism. In these cases, insist on details of exactly how the personnel reductions will take place.

- If you expect your internal personnel to support the system post-deployment, it is a good idea to begin to transition system support to them gradually prior to deployment especially in the hardware operations area.

RELATED QUESTIONS

1. Are The Project objectives clear to all?

11. What will the post-deployment organization look like?

50. Is your Technical Team experienced in the proposed technology?

48. IS DATA MIGRATION PLANNING ADEQUATE?

"We're entering a new world in which data may be more important than software."- Tim O'Reilly

WHY IS THIS QUESTION IMPORTANT?

Existing data contained in your organization's information systems is a valuable asset that needs to be adequately managed. This is especially true if The Project involves transformation of data from one format or database to another. Data migration is time consuming, expensive, and often not addressed until well into The Project after schedules and budgets have already been finalized.

REAL WORLD EXAMPLE

A company is implementing a new sales order system to improve productivity. As you start to plan The Project, you discover the need to move currently open sales orders into the new system at the time of deployment.

Additionally, you may want to move some or all closed orders to be able to access the data for customer inquiries or historic reporting. This seems simple enough until you realize that the data fields in the new sales order system are not the same as the old system so some data that is mandatory in the new system may not be available in the old system.

Then you discover that to enter a sales order in your new system you have to also convert the information about the customer the orders pertain to and that is also in a different format with missing or incomplete data. Your business experts then remind you that the data in existing system is not very reliable and that is why you are implementing a new system in the first place. Often this all is discovered only when you are trying to load test data into the new system which more often than not will delay deployment and increase costs.

Planning for data migration is complex and nearly always underestimated by even experienced Project Teams. It is a messy process that few people are enthusiastic about taking responsibility for. In my experience, it does not often cause a project to fail outright, but often delays deployments and leads to cost over-runs. Unfortunately, this does not end at deployment, since data conversion issues can cause causes business issues and inefficiencies well after deployment.

BEST PRACTICES

- Data migration is not an IT only function or a business only function, it is a joint function. It must identify what kinds of data will be needed in the new system and then work with The Business to identify where that data will originate.
- Unless The Project involves no data migration, a detailed Data Migration Strategy Document needs to be created and agreed to by both The Business and IT early in The Project. The strategy should include what can be migrated programmatically and what will require manual migration. If the migration strategy requires modification as The Project moves forward it should only be altered through

a formal change process that includes an assessment of time/cost impact.

- Data migration must be included in The Project Schedule and budget explicitly from the very beginning including identification of the personnel by name that will be responsible for implementing it. Often the same users that are identified for testing at the end of a project are also expected to do data migration which both tend to occur during the same time period leading to delays.

ADDRESSING THE QUESTION WITH THE PROJECT TEAM

Project Manager- Prior to the finalization of The Project Schedule/budget, you should ask The Project Manager to see the approved Data Migration Strategy Document. If the document has not been created or not formally approved, you should request a prompt IT/Business Team meeting chaired by The Project Manager to address the item.

If the Data Migration Strategy has been created and approved, then you ask to see the specific tasks with assigned resources in The Project Schedule that address data migration.

Business Team- In discussions with The Business Team, you should ask if they agree with the Data Migration Strategy Document. You should also ask if they are comfortable with the time and resource data migration estimates in the schedule.

A particular area to focus on with The Business Team is whether they are comfortable that they can accomplish the required manual data migration in the estimated timeframes. If you do not get positive answers to these questions, you should direct that an issue be entered in The Project Log to reach agreement on data migration and that issue should be tracked to closure.

Technical Team- As with The Business Team, you should ask the Technical Team if they have reviewed and are in agreement with the time and resource estimates. Additionally, you should gain understanding of how much of the migration with be done with automated tools and how much will have to be migrated manually by users.

LESSONS LEARNED FROM PAST PROJECTS

- Data quality is often not fully understood causing cost/time estimates to be inaccurate. Consult with knowledgeable business users to help understand the quality of existing data.
- Automated data migrations are traditionally done with tools called ETL Tools (extract, transform, and load). Some of these tools are fairly complex with considerable lead time to master and all can be rather costly. You should ask IT if your company already owns the tools or not and if not, ensure they are in the budget and that sufficient time has been provided to master the tools.
- If a new automated data migration tool is being introduced for the first time, complexity and time to master is nearly always underestimated. Consider retaining one or more senior developers with experience in the tool for The Project. This is not a good "learn as you go" activity. However, if you use outside consultants, make sure you concurrently develop the internal expertise necessary to sustain the tool post-project.

386

- If there is any significant amount of data migration needed for The Project, there should be a dedicated data migration team. If data migration is just another job of one of the teams, it is likely to not get the attention it needs to be successful. This is true of both business and technical resources
- The data migration process needs to be substantially complete prior the start of testing so that real world test data is available to support the testing process. Testing with real migrated data greatly improves the quality of the testing process and results in a significantly better system at the point of initial deployment since the data you test with will be the data you use live after deployment.
- Waiting until deployment to have a working data migration process is too late. Since the testing process should also be a test of the data migration process.
- If data in the existing system is of very low quality, you should consider only converting the actively open transactional records and basically starting from scratch in the new system.

Data is a precious thing and will last longer than the systems themselves.

Tim Berners-Lee

Then you can use the old system for historic reference and the new system going forward. When this is first considered, this approach is often violently opposed by The Business as being inefficient and unworkable. However, the alternative may be to pollute your new system with incomplete and/or inaccurate data or spend massive amounts of time manually repairing old data record by record.

- Surprisingly perhaps, the larger The Project/system being implemented, the more likely you are to convert only minimal data.
- Data migrations need a full scale practice run prior to the point of deployment. Data migration processes often run for extremely long periods of time especially if a large amount of data is being migrated. Since it is likely that The Business Team will have to suspend some operations while data is migrated to the new system at the time of deployment, there needs to be a good understanding of how long this will take to complete. This can only be determined by real world testing of the migration process.
- Make sure that all migration processes have restart potential. I have seen too many migrations that were stopped by a data, network, or other type problem that had to be re-started at the very beginning after flushing data from the new system. There needs to be capability to resume migration at the point that it encountered the problem. This can save many hours/days during deployments.

RELATED QUESTIONS

23. Are project business requirements well documented?

43. Is there a documented technology architecture?

49. IS THERE SUFFICIENT HARDWARE/ SOFTWARE IDENTIFIED TO SUPPORT THE PROJECT?

"Don't Rob Peter, and pay Paul"- Robert Burton
16th Century English Scholar

WHY IS THIS QUESTION IMPORTANT?

Many Executives that have not been involved in Technology Projects do not understand how much computer hardware and associated software is required to support `Technology Projects. Computer hardware/software is necessary not only to complete The Project, but also to support system deployment and to sustain the system in production. You want to ensure that hardware/software is available when needed and that the required hardware/software has been included in The Project budget since these items can represent a significant portion of the budget. Here are some of the areas that you want to ensure The Project Team has taken into account in planning for hardware/software.

Development Environments- The team of people developing your new system will need a hardware/software environment in which to work that mimics the environment that will used in production. This includes all servers, workstations, databases, and attendant software necessary to create and operate the application. The hardware in the development environment is usually not as powerful as in the production environment, as that would be cost prohibitive. However, it needs to match the intended production environment as closely as possible to reduce the likelihood of problems during testing/deployments

Some companies initially attempt to use their existing development environment to also handle development of the new system/system changes. If your Project Team is proposing this, you need to ensure that they have thought through the implications of doing so.

During the time you are working on the new system which could be a number of months or more, you will likely still have to perform maintenance on your existing system. If you are making changes to the existing system in the same environment that you are using to build the new system, it is easy to imagine issues arising. This is especially true if the new environment is somewhat different from the existing environment. Make sure the Technical Team can explain how you will support both the new and old systems.

Testing Environments- As the Development Team completes software components they must be independently testing. A dedicated testing environment is required that  very closely mimics the eventual production environment. If The Project Team proposes using your existing testing environment for this purpose, then the same issues discussed in the development environment will apply as you will have to support testing both the current and new system in the same environment.

Performance Testing Environment- One of the most common problems encountered when you deploy a new system is slow performance. The system works, but the screens come up so slow or the data is exchanged so slow that the system is considered not fully usable. In some cases, this can be quickly diagnosed and fixed through network and/or database tuning. In other cases, it this can take considerable effort to resolve over a period of time. The best way to avoid unpleasant performance testing surprises is to conduct performance testing prior to deployment.

To accomplish this, you will need a testing environment that can be dedicated to performance testing for a period of time that exactly mimics the production environment. It can be very expensive to mimic the production environment, so often Project Teams will propose testing on less powerful hardware/software and extrapolating the result to what will be encountered in production. This sounds good when you are trying to find ways to save money on projects, but in my experience rarely gives you a good indication of actual performance in production.

If you are not able to stand up a true performance testing environment, then you should be prepared to spend some time resolving performance issues at deployment.

Production Environment- This is the environment where the system will be used on an everyday basis with all of your data loaded. This is the area where you want high performance, high availability, and high reliability. In an attempt to save money on a project, Project Teams routinely underestimate the total cost of the production environment so you should challenge the estimates and prepare yourself for the possibility more will need to be spent here after deployment.

Failover/Disaster Recover Environment- From time to time despite the inherent reliability of modern computer hardware/software, components are going to fail bringing down your production system. Sometimes, the problem is even more serious like a fire or natural disaster destroying your data center.

To mitigate the impact of this, most companies will establish a mirror production environment that would take over if the primary system were to fail either temporarily or for a longer period of time. Your Project Team should document this capability in their hardware and software architecture. While expensive, such failover environments at least for business critical systems are necessary for Business Continuity in case of a disaster of some form.

Mobile Devices- With The Business world increasing moving to mobile computing on phones, tablet computers and now even watches, there is an ever increasing need to develop systems that will correctly operate on a number of different mobile platforms. If your Technology Project includes such requirements, then you need to ensure that provision has been made in the budget/schedule to acquire the variety of target devices and configure them for use.

This includes sufficient numbers of the various devices to support, development, test, and eventual support/help desk. This seems like a small thing, but easily can become complicated if you decide to deploy on multiple mobile platforms of which there are usually different versions commonly used. It becomes even more complicated in the case of phones which will need to be active phones with phone plans, contracts, data plans, etc. There is the question of what you do with these devices at the end of The Project and how to keep control of these easily stolen items.

REAL WORLD EXAMPLE

- A very large system being developed by a foreign government was plagued by a number of problems prior to deployment. In this three year project, end user workstations and servers were purchased and deployed at the very beginning of The Project even before system requirements were fully comprehended. As The Project progressed, it became obvious that the end user PCs which accounted for about $30M of The Project budget were dramatically undersized for the system being developed. This was primarily discovered when all of the developer and tester workstations had to be replaced in order to support the development effort.

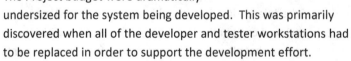

Additionally, the server configurations purchased were not appropriate for the architecture of the software and also had to be replaced. The net effect was a significant budget overrun and waste of money that could have been avoided by staging hardware/software purchases as the hardware/software was really needed.

BEST PRACTICES

- All projects should have a Hardware/Software Plan that outlines what system environments are required for The Project (Development, Test, Performance, etc) and identify what of the hardware/software is re-use of existing hardware/software and what is new hardware/software to be purchased.
- The Hardware/software Plan should also include identification of when each of the environments is required along with the acquisition lead time. This helps ensure that you purchase hardware/software as it is needed. This also helps avoid buying the wrong hardware/software if the specifications change as The Project progresses.
- All necessary system environments should be estimated in The Project budget including the cost of the hardware/software, cost to install/configure, operations personnel, computer facility changes if needed, etc. This should represent the total cost of ownership of the environments not just the cost of the hardware/software itself.

ADDRESSING THE QUESTION WITH THE PROJECT TEAM

Project Manager- Prior to the finalization of The Project Schedule/budget, you should ask The Project Manager to review a copy of the Hardware/software Plan with you to ensure that all necessary hardware/software components have been identified and that all costs relating to establishing the needed hardware/software environment have been accounted for in The Project budget. Also ensure that The

Project Schedule indicate when each environment is to be established.

Business Team - The Business Team will have little direct involvement in this issue, but the final Hardware/software Plan should be discussed with The Business Stakeholders so that they understand the hardware/software investment being made for The Project.

Information Technology Team- Work with the Technical Lead to ensure that the issue of Hardware/Software environments has been adequately considered by the Technical Team. Encourage them to identify needed hardware/software on an environment by environment basis.

The Plan should include all of the technical components needed to support each environment including items such as servers, PCs, database software, development tools, network equipment, etc. Also work with the team to understand when these environments are required so that a timing plan can be developed.

Steering Committee- Since Computer Hardware/Software often represents a significant part of The Project budget, you want to ensure that the Steering Committee understand at a high level what equipment is going to be required during the various project stages. Then as The Project Team begins to acquire the items, you will be able to show were items on each Purchase Order fit into the plan.

LESSONS LEARNED FROM PAST PROJECTS

- There are emulators that will approximate how the system will look on various mobile devices and internet browsers. It can be a cost effective way to quickly test systems on a number of different platforms very quickly.

However, if you have a graphics intense application or one where having the application look "exactly" a certain way is a critical requirement, these emulators are no substitute from testing the application on each of the devices you intend to support.

- It is worth re-iterating that you want to wait as late as possible to buy each hardware/software component. This helps ensure that you are buying the correct hardware if the development effort changes from the originally approved specification.

It also helps the company financially by deferring purchases until needed and ensures that you are buying the most currently available versions of the various components. Executives are justifiably irked if they find that the hardware they purchased several months ago is still sitting in a box in the hallway.

- Be careful not to underestimate the amount of time it takes to build a hardware/software environment for a project. The hardware has to be specified and a vendor selected through your purchasing process and the order  has to be placed and fulfilled by the vendor. Then the hardware must be shipped to you, unpacked and installed. Only after this can the necessary databases/tools be installed and configured along with the tasks necessary to make the hardware communicate with your network.

Overall, this can easily take 3-4 months and even longer if the configuration is complex and/or if your corporate purchasing process is rigid. Ensure that tasks are included in The Project Schedule for the major tasks required to stand up each of the required environments.

- It is not uncommon for Executives to have "sticker shock" over the cost of the required hardware/software environments which can be very substantial. It is often suggested that you "double up" the environments to save money such as using one environment for both development and testing. Unless your project is very small, this is nearly always a major mistake. You usually need to do development and testing concurrently and having to share the environments makes this difficult since the two groups generally use different data for their function.

   While hardware and software is expensive, the cost savings on combining environments is often overshadowed by the cost of having a team of developers, testers and business people sitting idle while their environments are being used by other groups.

   I was on one project where our labor burn rate was in excess of $250K per week. The company initially balked at buying about $50K of hardware/software for testing until I explained that even one day lost due to environment sharing paid for the purchase.

- If your project involves working with complex off the shelf software like Enterprise Resource Planning (ERP) systems or simultaneous work on multiple release of a system, you need to consider the need to additional environment such as multiple development environments to accommodate the various activities that are progressing at the same time.
- If your project involves decommissioning of existing hardware, it is prudent to remove the hard drives and

any static memory devices from the equipment and physically destroy them prior to recycling the hardware. It is easy to get Project Team member to volunteer to smash hard drives with a sledge hammer and it buys a lot of peace of mind that you are not inadvertently exposing company information. Merely erasing the hard drives is not nearly enough to really get rid of all company information.

- Regardless of how thorough the Hardware Plan and estimating processes are, at least half of all of The Projects I have been involved with require purchase of additional hardware/software beyond that originally planned due to performance issues, changing requirements, etc.

   You should consider adding contingency into The Project budget to accommodate unexpected events. This could even be in the form of a contingency that the Executive agree to but is not made available to The Project Team unless needed.

- Do not underestimate the physical space needed to support The Project's computer hardware. You will have to ensure that power is sufficient, air conditioning is adequate, network cabling is in place, etc. Space is often a concern since you usually will have to continue to support hardware for the existing system while you ramp up the hardware for the new system.

- It is not uncommon to need computer facility alterations to support a larger project. Ensure that such changes are recognized and represented in The Project budget/schedule.

- A final lesson learned the wrong way is to not underestimate the physical logistics of installing computer equipment, especially if you are deploying new end user computers as part of The Projects. Computer hardware often comes in large heavy crated boxes that must be unloaded from trucks and moved to where they are needed. Then after unpacking and installing the systems, there is often a considerable amount of bulky trash to be disposed of along with old equipment that needs to be disposed of correctly. You should ensure that the physical logistics of the hardware changes has been planned for and consider using vendors experienced in hardware logistics/disposal to accomplish the work if there is any significant amount of hardware involved.

In what I consider one of my largest ever planning failures, I ordered 300 PCs with large screen monitors for a State agency. They arrived one Friday afternoon at our building in a Tractor Trailer Truck full of boxes. The building did not have a ramped loading dock, so I had to enlist practically every abled bodied person in the Agency to help get boxes off of the truck.

Thankfully the union foreman saw the humor in the situation and allowed the union employees to participate as long as I bought pizza and beer for everyone. It took about 4 hours to get the boxes off the truck and up the elevators to where they were needed.

Then over the next 3 days we unpacked and installed each PC creating a huge mountain of un-crushable boxes full of Styrofoam behind the building. Of course, we had a thunderstorm in the middle of this and ended up with a mountain of wet smelly boxes by the end of the installation process and a significant bill to pay a company to haul off the boxes.

RELATED QUESTIONS

43. Is there a documented technology architecture?

45. Are performance requirements being adequately addressed?

50. IS YOUR TECHNICAL TEAM EXPERIENCED IN THE PROPOSED TECHNOLOGY?

"Experience is simply the name we give our mistakes."- Oscar Wilde

WHY IS THIS QUESTION IMPORTANT?

I write this with all the respect in the world as I consider myself a geek at heart, but geeks love to droll over the newest technology. They read about it in blogs and hear about it at conferences and during chance meetings with their fellow geeks and just have to have it.

That new network load balancer or new database tool becomes just what your company needs to solve problems you may not have even known you had. Setting aside the issue of whether the new technology has the potential to solve a real business problem (which is discussed elsewhere in this book), you need to make sure that your Technical Team has the ability to successfully implement the new product.

Don't assume that just because your team can recite every specification and marketing claim of the new technology that they actual know how to use it.

Section 4: Technology Questions

As part of the purchasing decision for the new technology, there needs to be an honest assessment of the ability of the Technical Team to have a successful implementation. Just as in flying an airplane or playing chess, there is a considerable difference in reading about something and being a master of it.

sLack of expertise in a new technology usually does not imply that you shouldn't purchase a new technology. However, it does mean that you will need to consider providing your Technical Team assistance to implement it. Assuming you do not have sufficient experts on staff to support the new technology, there are a couple of things you should consider doing.

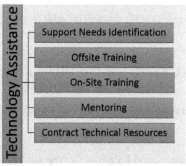

Support Needs Identification- You will need to determine who in your organization will support the new technology and what level of expertise they will need to attain. Discussions with the technology vendor and/or other companies that use the product can be very helpful in determining the optimal support level.

Once you understand the number and mix of personnel that will be needed to support the new technology, then you can determine whether existing personnel will provide this support or new staffing will be required.

Q50: Is Your Technical Team Experienced In The Proposed Technology?

Offsite Training- Most vendors offer formal training in their products. If you only have a small number of personnel that need to be trained, sending your staff to vendor classes is usually the easiest way to begin the training process. This is usually expert training in the latest product version and generally includes classes ranging from basic introductory classes to advanced classes.

If you negotiate training credits at the same time that you are negotiating the technology purchase, you can usually get a significant price discount. If the technology is mature, you should be able to find third party vendors that offer technology training, often a better price than the vendor.

Onsite Training- If you have a number of people that need to be trained in a new technology, it is often more cost effective to do on-site training at your facility. This has several advantages including having all of your personnel hear the same message at the same time and having the ability to customize the training to your situation.

Onsite training also reduces travel costs to send your personnel to non-local training. Surprisingly, the breakeven point for sending personnel out to training vs bringing a trainer on-site to deliver customized training can be as few as 5-6 people in some cases.

Mentoring/On Job Training- It the new technology is especially complex and/or you are using it in perhaps a non-standard way, then you should consider bringing an expert in the technology onto The Project for a period of time to provide mentoring and guidance to your technical personnel as they learn how to use the new technology. This has the additional advantage of having expert assistance in completing The Project while at the same time helping prepare your personnel to operate the system going forward.

Contract Technical Resources- This is different from the mentoring option mentioned above. Here, you are bringing in one or more people to actually configure and deploy the technology. The primary purpose would be to actually perform the work rather than the mentoring option which involves showing your personnel how to do things. Sometimes technology is difficult to initially deploy and then much simpler to operate thereafter.

If that is the case, the fastest path to getting the technology up and running is usually to bring in one or more consultants specifically to configure and deploy the technology while your personnel go to training on how to operate the technology post-deployment.

REAL WORLD EXAMPLE

You cannot create experience.
You must undergo it.

Albert Camus

A large regional financial company with significant expertise in the management of Oracle databases, embarked on a project to implement an off the shelf risk management system. Unfortunately, the new system only operated on a database system called SQL Server from Microsoft. The company had no expertise in the installation, operation, tuning and management of SQL Server database.

Q50: Is Your Technical Team Experienced In The Proposed Technology?

Due to extremely tight timeframes to get the system operational, I recommended that they bring in an outside expert in SQL Server. Initially, this expert conducted a 2 day boot camp on the technology to the database team. Then they performed the initial database setup activities in the development and test environments so that The Project could progress quickly.

As The Project progressed, they assumed more and more of a mentoring role allowing company personnel to perform the work while providing their assistance as needed. By the time the expert left approximately 1 month after deployment, company personnel were well able to support the databases going forward.

BEST PRACTICES

- Establish a strategy to provide training/mentoring in the new technology to ensure personnel are able to support the system post-deployment.
- If lack of real world expertise in the new technology is going to delay The Project start or extend the timeframe, it is usually best to bring in outside help to jumpstart The Project. It is better to pay for an expert for a few months than it is to have a whole team of developers, business experts, etc., wasting time until the new technology is ready for their use.

Section 4: Technology Questions

The only source of knowledge is experience.

Albert Einstein

- Having a trainer customize training and deliver it at your location is usually the best possible classroom training and is surprisingly cost effective.
- When considering the number of people needed to support the technology post-deployment, take into consideration, vacations, off-hour support, system complexity, etc. If you are running an operation that needs 24X7 technical support, you could need 5-7 people just to ensure constant coverage.

ADDRESSING THE QUESTION WITH THE PROJECT TEAM

Project Manager- Work with The Project Manager to ensure that there are tasks in The Project Schedule and dollars in the budget to support technical training as needed to support both project needs and post-deployment support.

Business Team - The Business Team is not usually involved in these discussions However, there may be a need for The Business Team to provide training in system functionality to their user base.

Information Technology Team - The Technical Team needs to identify the quantity of personnel and required skillsets to support the new technology. Work with the team to identify who needs training and the best method to deliver that training.

LESSONS LEARNED FROM PAST PROJECTS

- IT attracts many bright people that can learn new things quickly. The tendency on at least half of The Projects I have been involved with that involved new technology is to let the team learn the new technology by reading the manual and learning how to use it by trial and error. What you miss in doing this is advanced knowledge of the technology that only an expert brings to the table.

  Unless the technology that you are implementing is relatively simple with straightforward deployment, this approach can lead to costly missteps and  project delays. Consider the game of Chess where the basic moves can be learned in a few hours, but true mastery of the nuances can take the rest of your life.

- If you expect outside experts on a project to also train and mentor your personnel, make sure you include that expectation in the vendor contract. Most vendors are reluctant to give away knowledge and techniques unless you specifically pay for that knowledge transfer.

RELATED QUESTIONS

40. What do you really know about the company and technology being proposed?

42. Does the proposed technology fit into our corporate IT strategy?

47. Are plans in place for post-deployment support?

FINAL THOUGHTS

"If you're trying to achieve, there will be roadblocks. I've had them; everybody has had them. But obstacles don't have to stop you. If you run into a wall, don't turn around and give up. Figure out how to climb it, go through it, or work around it."- Michael Jordan

Based on the material in this book, you might have the impression that I believe all Technology Projects are a total mess that are so unlikely to achieve their business benefits that they should be avoided at all costs. This is absolutely not how I feel about Technical Projects.

I have had the honor of being involved in a number of highly successful projects. Projects that were delivered on time and on

Experience is not what happens to you; it's what you do with what happens to you.

Aldous Huxley

budget and which exceeded user expectations There is nothing more personally satisfying than seeing a team of dedicated people come together in a complex endeavor to create a system that works as planned. When you see the new website come up on your iPad, see thousands of users working on-line, see checks coming off printers for the first time, or see coils of steel moving through a plant, then you understand how well technology projects can support The Business.

What frustrates me to no end however, is seeing projects that were massive failures that did not have to turn out that way. Some projects fail because of legitimate reasons like costing more than the company is willing to invest, changing business priorities, and even requirements that are beyond the current capabilities of technology to accomplish. However, if you were to do a root cause analysis of project failures, you would find that most fail for reasons that if recognized early enough could have been prevented from affecting The Project.

 One of the roles of an Executive is to recognize these potential issues and bring resources and attention to them. Hopefully this book will help you understand some of the areas that deserve your attention and provide insight in how to address these areas of concern.

GARY DEARING TOP TEN LIST

David Letterman is famous for his top ten lists on a variety of tops so I thought I would leave you with my top ten list of the things Executives should do to help ensure project success.

10. Scope- Do not allow a project to start until you have well defined scope and business objectives supported by all Stakeholders

9. People- Invest time in carefully selecting The Business, technical, and project personnel that will lead your project making sure that they have the skill and experience to run a project of this size and complexity

8. Morale- Constantly monitor morale of The Project Team and its leadership. Deal with morale issues quickly as morale is a key to project success. Showing up unannounced at Project Meetings and in The Project workspace is a great way to understand project morale.

7. Schedule and Issues- While there are many project management deliverables that are important for different purposes, insist that a Project Schedule and issues/risk list be created and actively updated. Then invest your time on a recurring basis in understanding what they can tell you about project health.

6. Vendors- Pay careful attention to vendor contracts to ensure that you get good value for your money and so that your data and intellectual property rights are protected. Then after contracts are signed ensure that they are monitored for compliance.

5. Honest Reporting- Establish an environment where honesty in status reporting is not punished and set an expectation that you want to always hear the truth about The Project.

4. Personnel Performance- Take emotion out of personnel decisions.

Being entirely honest with oneself is a good exercise.

Sigmund Freud

If you do not have anyone internal that has the required skills and experience, look for it externally. Also if someone is not performing as needed do not hesitate to make a personnel change. This is in the best interest of the company, The Project and the individual.

3. Budget and Timeline- Pay very close attention to The Project budget and timeline. Ensure adequate steps are taken to correctly capture and report all project costs. Always know your "burn rate" for personnel costs. It is often very helpful in making decisions on project to understand the general cost of a delay.

2. Don't Micro-Manage- Keep a close eye on The Project, but also give your team the space to organize work and make most decisions. Once you start to micro-manage a project, you likely will adversely impact morale and commit yourself to having to continue to micro-manage it going forward.

1. Find a leader. The Project Manager position is key to project success. While business knowledge, technical knowledge, bureaucratic skills etc. are certainly of some value in a Project Manager, leadership skills are the most important trait. Find someone  who can motivate the team, organize the work, lead the group through making decisions, interact at all levels from the shop floor maintenance crew to the CEO, and who has a passionate desire to be successful.

This is the general who is going to lead your troops through the series of battles that make up a Technology Project. While a good leader cannot guarantee project success, it greatly increases the odds. However, it is a very rare project that can be successful if The Project Manager is ineffective.

ABOUT THE AUTHOR

Mr. Dearing has over 35 years of experience in managing Technology Projects starting with his first job where he attained the rank of Captain in the US Army while managing computer projects and systems in Washington DC. After leaving the military, he worked in various management capacities on several large military Technology Projects including projects for the US Navy Pay and Personnel System, The US Navy Trident Submarine Program, and the Air Force Command and Control System.

For the last nearly 20 years, Mr. Dearing has been an independent consultant specializing in helping large organizations deal with complex Technology Projects. Major clients have include, General Motors, Honda, Worthington Industries, Xerox, Federal Government of Canada, various US Government Agencies, the States of West Virginia and Ohio, National City Bank, Pemco Financial, and Union Carbide.

His resume defines him as an: "Exceptionally well-qualified senior level IT Program/Project Manager with a successful track record of driving on-time on-budget delivery of large global multi-million dollar programs in the supply chain, manufacturing, financial services, Military, and Federal/State Government domains. An experienced expert in large project risk assessment/ remediation, implementation of Project Management Offices (PMO) methodologies, portfolio management and the remote management of large multi-location global Programs. Results oriented success driven professional acknowledged for integrity, high professional standards, and "grace under fire" with a strong customer-service orientation, "big-picture" vision, and strong sensitivity to the bottom-line."

Since this section is also supposed to include some interesting facts, Mr. Dearing is proud to be an Eagle Scout, has actually been on a

Trident Missile Submarine, has been involved in Technology Projects on every continent except Antarctica, and for two years taught Computer Science at night in the Maximum Security Unit of the DC State Prison. His website is www.thetechnologyguild.com and he can be reached by email at gdearing@thetechnologyguild.com.